CW00536396

GLORY, GLORY MAN UTD

GLORY, GLORY MAN UTD

A CELEBRATORY HISTORY

NEVILLE MOIR

POLARIS
PUBLISHING

This edition first published in 2022 by

POLARIS PUBLISHING LTD
c/o Aberdein Considine
2nd Floor, Elder House
Multrees Walk
Edinburgh, EH1 3DX

Distributed by
Birlinn Limited

www.polarispublishing.com

Text copyright © Neville Moir, 2022

ISBN: 9781913538644
eBook ISBN: 9781913538651

THIS IS AN UNOFFICIAL PRODUCT

British Library Cataloguing-in-Publication Data
A catalogue record for this book is available on request from the British Library.

Designed and typeset by Polaris Publishing, Edinburgh
Printed in Great Britain by CPI Group (UK) Ltd, Croydon, CR0 4YY

CONTENTS

United will always be United. To me, they are still the best, and whatever disappointments they're having at the moment, don't worry – they'll bounce back. They always do.
Roy Keane

PREFACE

Growing up in Belfast in the sixties, many of my schoolmates were supporters of Manchester United, the team that our local hero, George Best, played for. My grandfather, a player in his day, was also a fan. I had no specific allegiance back in the sixties and seventies; I just loved English football, brimming with brilliant teams battling each other for league and FA Cup glory. But then I moved to Scotland to escape the Troubles and to study. The local broadcasters limited coverage of English football to a five-minute slot at the end of their programmes, so if I wanted my football fix, I would have to become acquainted with the likes of Rangers, Celtic, Hibs and, er, Morton.

Scottish football induced a culture shock: the sport was a game played at 100mph in a country whose media was obsessed by the Old Firm duopoly, until along came a cocky young manager determined to shake things up. Alex Ferguson's Aberdeen piqued my interest. He was a managerial genius, rubbing the Old Firm's noses in the dirt while winning trophies both at home and in Europe. When, in November 1986, Fergie moved south to Old Trafford, we all wondered what he might go on to achieve. From that point on, I became a devoted United supporter.

It needed a fair amount of patience in the early Ferguson years; there was precious little to cheer. Then Fergie's side began to click into gear. First, there was the 1990 FA Cup win; that was quickly followed by a thrilling victory in the Cup Winners' Cup final. Of course, in the classic story arc, our heroes have to suffer a setback before they can finally triumph. On New Year's Day, 1992 – a new year that was meant to bring the long-awaited league title – United were beaten 4–1 at home by Queens Park Rangers. That wasn't supposed to happen. Nor were Leeds supposed to snatch the title in a disastrous end to the season.

Adversity puts iron in the soul, though. How can you fully appreciate the good times if you haven't tasted the bad? The collapse at the end of the 1991/92 season continued into the autumn, until, with the stroke of a pen, everything changed.

Eric Cantona signed.

The following two decades were glorious as United swept all before them. Fergie's teams rose to every challenge: Arsenal's Invincibles, Chelski, the nouveau riche Manchester City, all were brushed aside and the Champions League was won. It was doubles and trebles all round. In the post-Ferguson era, we have had to view games from behind the couch as often as on it, but it's all but impossible to avert the eyes (the latter half of the 2021/22 season was an extremely difficult watch).

In the spring of 2020, as lockdown was imposed, I took early retirement. Looking for something to do in confinement, I decided to write a book. I was going to write a celebratory book about the Red Devils. One, I hope, that is affectionate without being so adulatory as to bore the pants off readers. There are a few conceits, a few literary references (I did work in the publishing business for many decades) and digressions into the lighter side of the football circus. Mostly, I wanted to pick out the key moments, the big players, the great managers, the owners and the crunch games that have forged United's unique identity.

In the course of researching this book I have become increasingly fascinated by the history of the club. It's hard to believe how humble its beginnings were and, apart from a flourish in the early part of the 20th century, how it struggled to achieve its benefactor John Henry Davies' grand ambitions until after the Second World War. Indeed, at times it was a battle for survival; bankruptcy was a real danger in the Depression years. Thereafter, as I learned more about the Busby era, my admiration grew. The Busby Babes were a phenomenon; the Munich air disaster was traumatic; and the reconstruction of the team to win two Division One titles and the European Cup was heroic. The following quarter of a century lacked the glory of Busby's reign but was rarely dull. Busby's ethos of playing entertaining, attacking football – the 'United Way' – had taken root and was now in the club's DNA, and it has carried on right through to the current era when the 'cultural reboot' was made under Ole Gunnar Solskjær's watch.

Regrettably, due to the constraints of book production, there has to be a limit to the length of this book. There are omissions of which I am only too aware: the likes of George Mutch, Charlie Mitten, Eddie Colman and many cup finals, and I would have liked to have written more about the present-day side – Bruno and de Gea et al. But I wanted to weave my book around the main historical events, and it is hard to write about the immediate past without the help of historical perspective.

The United story is an inspiring one. In 2022, 144 years after its foundation, the club is at another crossroads, but thanks to the constant devotion and vigilance of its supporters, the traditions set by Busby and Ferguson will be honoured – the gold standard for future managers to match.

Neville Moir
August 2022

IN THE BEGINNING
Newton Heath

In 1878, the dining room committee of the Lancashire and Yorkshire Railway decided something had to be done about the moral and physical well-being of their employees. The august group – which listed amongst its vice-presidents a future editor of the *Manchester Guardian*, C.P. Scott and a future prime minister in A.J. Balfour – decided to form football and cricket teams as a way of distracting the men from the sin of alcohol. The two recreations were considered to be more gentlemanly than rugby, the more popular game of the time.

The cricket team has faded into obscurity, but the football team proved more enduring. The club was based at the Carriage & Works Department depot at Newton Heath, and took the name Newton Heath L&YR Football Club. Early opponents included another railway team made up of employees from the department known as Newton Heath Locomotive.

The team, affectionately known as the Heathens, played on a pitch at North Road in Monsall, in a pit of Victorian industrial pollution between railway tracks on one side and the steel and chemical works on the other. The changing rooms were half a mile away at the Three Crowns pub in Oldham Road.

To begin with, the Heathens made do with local competition in friendlies and in the Lancashire Cup and Manchester and

District Challenge Cups, winning on four occasions in the 1880s. Their first venture into national competition came in the 1886 FA Cup when they were unceremoniously dumped out after a 7–2 thrashing by Blackburn Olympic.

In their non-league days, the team wore the colours of the railway company – green and gold halves – a strip revived as the third-choice kit for the 1992/93 centenary season. Although as often as not, Newton Heath played in colours nearer to the present-day Tottenham Hotspur side – white shirts with dark blue knickerbockers – the iconic green and gold was worn for a total of six seasons.

The club was ambitious. Although the Football Association's ban on professionalism was not lifted until 1885, the club was able to attract talent by offering players employment at the railway works. Newton Heath were able to recruit from far and wide, from Scotland and, in particular, a crop of Welsh internationals including Jack Powell and the Doughty brothers.

Association football was fast becoming a major spectator sport, drawing increasingly large crowds, and the bigger clubs agreed, in 1888, to set up a league of teams with a scheduled fixture list of home and away games. The Heathens were keen to be part of the action, but it took until 1892 – after a couple of years in the Football Combination and the short-lived Football Alliance – before the Football League expanded to form a Second Division to which Newton Heath were admitted.

In their efforts to win admission, Newton Heath built two new stands at North Road, which in turn led to a falling-out with the Lancashire and Yorkshire Railway Company; they refused to pay for the building costs and the club were then evicted from the site. Ties were cut, and the club left Newton Heath to strike out on its own, setting up as a limited company and moving to a new ground at Bank Street, some three miles away in Clayton, in 1893.

The Bank Street pitch was notorious; it was a blasted heath. In March 1895, when Walsall Town Swifts turned up at the ground they were greeted by what they regarded as a 'toxic waste dump'. Only taking the field after lodging a formal complaint about the pitch to the referee, they were beaten 14–0. However, the Football League ruled in favour of Walsall, and the match was ordered to be replayed, though the result was not much better for the visitors second time round; this time they lost 9–0.

Newton Heath's first season in the Football League was pretty inauspicious. Despite being given a place in the top division, the Heathens faced immediate relegation after finishing second from bottom. They only survived the drop by winning a 'test match' or play-off against the Second Division champions, Small Heath. The following year, there was to be no reprieve and Newton Heath suffered their first relegation.

The initial share flotation of the new limited company hadn't been a great success, and throughout the 1890s the club were dogged by financial problems. The cost of the new ground and the wages of the playing staff were heavy burdens to bear. The team languished in the Second Division for the remainder of the century. What was needed was a bit of good fortune – and that came in the early years of the new century through the unlikely agency of a St Bernard called Major.

MAJOR AND THE CAPTAIN
The Creation of Manchester United

There are differing accounts of how Harry Stafford, Newton Heath's captain, and the brewing magnate John Henry Davies (better known as J.H. Davies) met, but their encounter was crucial to the survival and future success of the club.

Harold 'Harry' Stafford joined Newton Heath from Crewe Alexandra in 1896, quickly becoming a regular in the first team and making the right-back berth his own. Following the departure of Caesar Jenkyns to Walsall, he was made captain, a position he held for the following six seasons in one of the most taxing periods in the club's history (not that they would have paid much to the Inland Revenue). The move from North Road to Bank Street had proved costly, and the expense of paying professional wages placed a strain on Newton Heath's meagre funds. They had become a selling club in a vain attempt at balancing the books.

Davies was a wealthy Manchester businessman with interests in brewing, pubs and off-licences. From relatively humble stock, Davies' fortune was due in some degree to his own efforts and in no small part to marrying into money; his wife Amy was the ward and niece of Sir Henry Tate, the sugar baron. Tate had been generous with his wealth, supporting a number of good causes and sports in the Manchester area.

So parlous were the finances of Newton Heath at the beginning of the new century that the club had been served with a winding-up order. As well as captaining the team, Stafford was an energetic fundraiser for the club. He and his pet St Bernard, 'Major' (the definite article is sometimes used to preface the dog's rank but is anything but definite; most histories list him as just plain 'Major'), toured the local pubs seeking donations. Major even appears in a team photograph with a collecting box under his chin where you might normally expect to see a brandy barrel; either way, first aid was urgently needed.

Following a predictably unsuccessful four-day bazaar to raise funds at St James' Hall in February 1901 – the event was actually loss-making – Major went missing. The timeline of events that followed is difficult to plot as there are so many varying accounts. One version has it that Major wandered into a pub just off Oxford Street leased from Davies. Once Davies saw the dog, he thought he had the ideal birthday present for his 12-year-old daughter, Elsie. However, shortly afterwards, Davies spotted an advertisement placed by Stafford in the lost and found section of the *Manchester Evening News* and the Heathens' captain was duly reunited with his beloved pet.

Davies offered to buy Major, and although Stafford initially refused to sell, after much negotiation he eventually relented. Shrewd businessman that he was, and impressed by Stafford's enthusiasm, Davies could see that the Heathens' skipper was a popular character in north Manchester, and in July 1901 Stafford became landlord of one of Davies' establishments, the Bridge Inn, in Ancoats. The men became firm friends.

Meanwhile, at Bank Street, the club's finances continued to dwindle. In January 1902, Newton Heath was served with another winding up-order. Despite the best efforts of Stafford, his team-mates and supporters, with debts in excess of £2,600, the club seemed doomed. The situation was so parlous that Stafford had to go door-to-door raising a collection of £80 to cover the cost of the team's travel to Bristol to fulfil a league fixture. But Stafford had been working hard behind the scenes; the captain was on manoeuvres.

In March 1902, Stafford took to the stage at the New Islington Hall during a supporters' meeting to announce that he and four local businessmen, including Davies, were each investing £200 (some reports put the figure at £500) – sufficient funds to save the club. A new committee was formed with Davies as president, and Stafford and secretary James West in charge of football affairs. This made Stafford de facto club captain, co-manager and a director. As a board member he had no option but to revert to amateur status.

On 26 April 1902, the club announced the change of name to Manchester United Football Club. On the same day, Stafford captained Newton Heath in their last ever game, a 2–1 win in the Manchester Senior Cup final against Manchester City at Hyde Road. It was his only winners' medal in his time at Bank Street. Both on and off the field, the captain had won the day.

A BRIEF HISTORY OF CLUB MASCOTS

Michael the Bank Street Canary

During the 1890s, readers of Newton Heath FC's matchday programmes may have seen advertisements to hear 'Michael the Bank Street Canary sing' for a nominal fee. However, Michael was neither able to sing, nor was he a canary. In truth, Michael was a goose and an unwitting participant in the money-making schemes that the club were using during their early financial difficulties.

Major the Dog (1902–06)

Major was the prized St Bernard of Newton Heath's club captain, Harry Stafford, and was well known to Mancunian pub-goers for accompanying his owner with a collection box on his collar looking to raise much-needed funds for the cash-strapped club. Then, famously, the dog became the unlikely broker of football's deal of the century as he was traded to brewing magnate J.H. Davies, who wanted to gift him to his daughter as a birthday present in return for investment in the club.

Davies rang the changes when he took charge: a new name, a new kit and a new mascot in the shape of Major.

Billy the Goat (1906–09)

Following the retirement of Major, the club decided to adopt a new mascot. Half-back Charlie Roberts had recently been given a goat by The Bensons, a theatre company. Like Major before him, Billy was also paraded around the ground before home matches.

However, it was Billy's taste for alcohol that would be his undoing. No party was complete without Billy, and the bearded ruminant would often accompany the players to a local hostelry for post-match refreshments. After the 1909 FA Cup final, Billy took part in the celebrations with the players, but, unfortunately, he consumed too much champagne and died of alcohol poisoning soon after. It would be nice to think he died happy.

Billy's preserved head may be seen on display in the Manchester United Museum.

'Hoppy' Thorne the One-legged Wonder (late 1930s to late 1940s)

William 'Hoppy' Thorne was a British soldier during the First World War. He lost a leg in combat and was marked as an invalid on his return to Britain. He managed to find work at Old Trafford, sweeping up after home matches and operating the scoreboard at reserve team matches. It was Hoppy's pre-match entertainments that made him a local celebrity. Before home matches, he would strip off his clothes, down to his running gear, and hop or run around the pitch, depending on whether he'd attached his false leg or not.

However, Hoppy's tenure as club mascot came to an end towards the end of the 1940s after a rift formed between him and the club when they failed to give him tickets for the Reds' 1948 visit to Wembley.

Jack Irons

John Thomas 'Jack' Irons was the mascot from the late 1940s for around 15 years. He would parade around the pitch in a red-and-white dinner suit before kick-off, holding a red-and-white umbrella while signing autographs and greeting the fans, and even tossing the coin for the kick-off on occasion.

Irons retired in 1963 but made a one-match comeback for the 1968 European Cup final. While others had occasional spells under the umbrella, the practice of the friendly mascot had to be abandoned due to the rise of football hooliganism.

Fred the Red

Since the early 1990s, the Manchester United mascot has been Fred the Red, in the form of a Red Devil as a tribute to the team's nickname. Wearing the number 55 on his replica shirt, Fred was voted the most popular mascot by *Match* magazine in 2011 and achieved internet notoriety after taunting Leeds United fans in a pre-season (un)friendly in 2019 – after abuse and beer were thrown at him by opposing fans.

MANGNALL AND MEREDITH
The Making of Manchester United
LEAGUE CHAMPIONS 1907/08

April 1902 was a new dawn in Manchester, a fresh start for the struggling football club rescued by local brewing magnate J.H. Davies, who, with three other investors, had bailed out the near-bankrupt Newton Heath. The club was rebranded as Manchester United and given a new look, the old colours of white and blue (the cheapest money could buy) making way for bold red shirts and white shorts.

The 1902/03 season was eagerly anticipated with 15,000 fans turning up to Bank Street to see the opening game of the season – an improvement of 750% on Newton Heath's last game. But, as the old saying goes, Rome wasn't built in a day. Taking United from the Second Division to championship winners would take time, money, the recruitment of talent and a bit of luck.

Team management had been left in the hands of the Heathen old boys, secretary James West and club captain Harry Stafford, until poor results led to West's resignation at the end of the season and, piling Pelion upon Ossa, both he and Stafford were investigated by the FA for financial irregularities in the affairs of Newton Heath, resulting in their both being banned from involvement in the game.

Davies lost no time in acting on a tip from the president of the Football League and appointed Ernest Mangnall, someone with proven administrative experience gained in his time at Burnley. Although given the title of club secretary, Mangnall became United's first de facto manager. Davies trusted him with a £3,000 war chest to strengthen the playing staff. He combined this acuity with a shrewd understanding of football tactics and a fierce competitiveness.

Mangnall laid the foundations for the new side with a formidable defence featuring Harry Moger in goal and a back line of Duckworth, Roberts and Bell aka 'Ducrobel'. After narrowly missing out on two occasions, United finally won promotion to the First Division in 1906. What they now needed was a sharper cutting edge up front.

The answer came from somewhat fortuitous circumstances although Mangnall's quick thinking also played its part. In 1905, neighbours Manchester City had become embroiled in financial scandal. Several players and officials were banned for up to five years and, needing to raise funds, City planned to auction off their best players at the Queen's Hotel. But before the event took place, Mangnall swooped in and signed contracts with four lots and, in so doing, acquired a new forward line and a left-back free of charge. Their bans expiring at the end of 1906, Jimmy Bannister, Sandy Turnbull, Herbert Burgess and Billy Meredith were able to take their places in the United line-up for the first time on New Year's Day. The capacity crowd of 40,000 that packed into Bank Street cheered as Sandy Turnbull scored the decisive goal on debut.

Good though Turnbull was, Meredith was the real prize. His two nicknames, the 'Welsh Wizard' and 'Old Skinny' reveal some clues to the personality of this remarkable individual. Growing up in north Wales, he was sent to work down the pit aged 12 before a career in football saved him from a life of hard labour. He joined United at the age of 32 as a skilful right-winger. The first superstar in professional football, he was the Edwardian equivalent of David Beckham. Skilful, and possessing great control and balance, Meredith was capable of beating players and delivering crosses with pinpoint accuracy from the right wing into his strike partners. All that he lacked was a yard of pace – *pace* Becks.

United now went through the gears, winning 12 of their remaining 17 league fixtures that season, moving from fifteenth to eighth in the process. Carrying on their form into the new season, United had a blistering start, winning 13 of their first 14 league games – 1907 had been a spectacular year for Mangnall's team. While they couldn't maintain those performance levels, they held on to win their first league title by a comfortable nine-point margin. The City refugees had bagged 44 goals between them.

It had taken just six years for the new ownership to take the club from the brink of bankruptcy to the pinnacle of English football. Cynics complained that the nouveau riche Bank Street outfit – or 'Moneybags United' as they were sometimes labelled – had bought the title. Such criticism unfairly belittled the parts played by Mangnall and Meredith in producing a winning formula. No matter how they had achieved their success, no one could deny that Manchester United were now a force to be reckoned with.

RUNNING RIOT IN BUDAPEST
Ferencváros 0 Manchester United 7
24 MAY 1908

J.H. Davies' ambition for the club he helped to save six years previously bore fruit with United's first league title in 1908, thanks to the combination of a strong defence, the drive of manager Ernest Mangnall and the arrival of the mercurial Billy Meredith.

United went on to win the FA Charity Shield in a replay against Queens Park Rangers on 24 April, but there was no thought of heading for the beach (that would have been a bit chilly in the Blackpool spring); instead, by way of celebration, Davies paid for the team to go on a four-week tour of central Europe, playing friendlies in the Austro-Hungarian Empire.

On May Day, the party left Manchester's Piccadilly station for London, stopping over at the Imperial Hotel where complimentary fish suppers were served. Then it was onward via the boat train to Paris the following day, then to Prague via Switzerland to take on Slavia Prague, followed by three games in Vienna and finally to Budapest to play Ferencváros.

Little expense was spared: the expedition involved staying in some of the finest hotels with sight-seeing trips around Paris, Lake Lucerne and Vienna, and even a cruise down the 'Blue Danube'.

The tour was not without incident. On his return to England, Mangnall vowed never to play against Slavia Prague again. The exact cause of his displeasure was unclear, but sporting cultural differences were almost certainly to blame. The rules of the game were interpreted differently by European referees from home officials – in Mangnall's view, 'It was a rare thing that they knew the rules.' And while the British game, then as now, was characterised by a greater degree of physical contact, Mangnall told the press that foreign players were dirty: 'All they have to do is kick, push and hack.'

But these gripes were minor; leading up to their final game against Ferencvárosi, the aggregate score of the previous six tour matches was a favourable 23–2. It was only to be expected; at the beginning of the 20th century the British game was more advanced than its European counterparts, having been established earlier and on a more professional footing.

It was the final game of the tour against Ferencvárosi that drew the most notoriety. The Green Eagles had won the Hungarian championship three times in the previous five seasons, and the side picked to play United included their legendary striker, Imre Schlosser.

The game was reportedly full of controversies: a disputed penalty – a United forward 'cleverly rolled into the penalty area' after being fouled – and, according to Hungarian sources, the referee only gave the award after succumbing to pressure by the Manchester United players, an all-too-familiar feature of the modern game but unheard of in this Austro-Hungarian capital.

Ferencvárosi lost two players to injury, and insult was added as United's goalkeeper, Harry Moger, scored the penalty to make it a humiliating 7–0 hammering. A sizeable crowd of 16,000 had turned up to see the 'friendly', but, incensed by the score line, the refereeing and the aggressive demeanour of the visiting team, they turned ugly. They rioted, and the police were forced to draw sabres. The United players were spat on and pelted with stones as they left the ground under police escort, fortunately suffering only a minor injury to Ernest Thompson. In hindsight, travelling back to the hotel in an open-top bus probably wasn't the greatest idea.

As for Mangnall, the last game of the tour had left a sour taste and rather than an early bath he advocated an early Brexit. United wouldn't return to play in Europe for a further 19 years.

UP FOR THE CUP
Manchester United 1 Bristol City 0
24 APRIL 1909, CRYSTAL PALACE

Winning the league title in 1908 was an immense achievement for Manchester United, but the trophy that the club and its supporters prized above all was the FA Cup, and the final at London's Crystal Palace was considered the showpiece event of the football calendar.

Before then, United had never progressed beyond the fourth round of the competition. Having seen off Brighton, 1906 winners Everton and Blackburn Rovers, they once again advanced to the quarter-finals for a tie against Burnley. With 18 minutes left to play, and Burnley leading 1–0, it looked like the same old story until the weather, never that great in Burnley at the best of times, came to United's rescue. In blizzard conditions, the referee had little option but to abandon the game; the official, possibly suffering hypothermia, was so cold he was incapable of blowing his whistle, and it was left to United's captain, Charlie Roberts, to sound the end of play. Five days later, United returned to Turf Moor and won the tie 3–2.

The mighty Newcastle United awaited United in the semi-final. Unlike the present-day team, in the early years of the 20th century, the Magpies were serial over-achievers: twice league champions and twice FA Cup finalists in the previous four years and now clear leaders in the 1908/09 title race. In a hard-fought contest at Bramall Lane, a goal from Harold Halse in the 73rd minute was enough for United to make it through to the final. Despite being denied a historic 'double', the entire Newcastle team sportingly waited for 15 minutes in torrential rain aboard an open coach so they could applaud the United players after the game. The past really is a different country.

Their opponents in the final were Bristol City. The West Country boys were no mugs, finishing runners-up to league champions Newcastle two years previously. In the 1908/09 league season, Bristol had had the better of United, winning one and drawing the other. The final was billed as a battle between Charlie Roberts and Bristol's captain and rival for the England centre-half position, Billy Wedlock.

But you couldn't keep Billy Meredith out of the spotlight. Because of a colour clash of shirts, both teams chose to wear away strips. Instead of the usual change kit of all-white shirts, Meredith produced a new variation. The enterprising Welshman owned a sports equipment shop – started with the financial help of the ubiquitous J.H. Davies – trading under the name of Pilling, Briggs & Meredith. The outfitters supplied a new strip for the final: a white shirt with a red chevron. Perhaps it was a subliminal V for victory; either that or it was a job lot of St Helens rugby league shirts. For an extra bit of showbiz glamour, the music hall star George Robey made the formal presentation of the new kit to the United players.

On the day of the final, having stayed overnight in Chingford, the United players made their way to the Crystal Palace venue by train and bus. Crystal Palace Park, now the National Sports Centre, was packed with 71,000 spectators eagerly anticipating a close match as the first kick of the game was ceremoniously made by the Home Secretary's mother, Jennie, Lady Randolph Churchill. United had injury concerns; Sandy Turnbull, their main goal threat was a doubt before the game, but Roberts thought he was worth the risk, telling Mangnall, '[Turnbull] might get a goal and if he does we can afford to carry him.'

But they also had the Welsh Wizard in their starting line-up. Meredith was football's poster-boy or, more accurately, the mustachioed face on a collectible cigarette card. At the time he was arguably the GOAT – the greatest of all time. It surprised few at Crystal Palace that Billy Meredith was the man of the match. Twenty-two minutes in, he laid on the pass for Harold Halse whose shot hit the woodwork before Sandy Turnbull put home the rebound. A history of the early FA Cup, *Fifty Years of FA Cup Finals*, records that 'Meredith in particular played beautiful football: his clever footwork, rare control of the ball, sure passes and long shots into goal gave the deadliness to his side's attack.' At the other end of the field, the threat of Wedlock was nullified by United's resolute back line. Despite full-back Vince Hayes suffering a broken rib that forced him to leave the field, United reorganised and held on to win the game 1–0. Adding the FA Cup to their league title the year before underlined their top-table status – United were now a footballing powerhouse.

For Meredith, Roberts and the rest of the team, their return to Manchester was greeted by cheering crowds lining the streets in their thousands as the victory parade in a horse-drawn carriage took them from Central station back to the town hall.

What was now needed was a home fit for these conquering heroes. The foundation stone of the United Stadium in Old Trafford had already been laid, and in less than a year's time there would be a brand-new 60,000-capacity stadium to fill and more history to make.

STRONGER UNITED

Charlie Roberts, Winning Captain
and Co-founder of the Players' Union

In April 1904, 21-year-old Charlie Roberts joined Manchester United from Grimsby Town for a fee of £600. Flush with the new money that chairman J.H. Davies had injected into the club, United manager Ernest Mangnall embarked on a spending spree. He viewed Roberts' arrival at United as a building block for future success; a strong, skilful, fast centre-half with a good range of passing, together with Alex Bell and Dick Duckworth, he formed a key part of United's formidable defensive line. His leadership qualities saw him made captain in only his second season, a role he held until he left the club in 1913.

Charlie's form soon earned him recognition at international level. He became the first United player to play for England, winning the first of his three caps in 1905 against Ireland, and would probably have won many more had he not fallen foul of the FA.

In April 1907, the Scottish defender Tommy Blackstock, 25, collapsed and died on the pitch after heading a ball during a United reserve match against St Helens. His death spurred Roberts and his teammate Billy Meredith into action.

On 2 December 1907, at a meeting at the Imperial Hotel, Roberts and Meredith were instrumental in setting up the Players'

Union, or the Association Football Players' and Trainers' Union to give it its full name. The union was not recognised by the FA but it did attract considerable support from fellow league clubs. Professional footballers were aggrieved at the maximum wage cap, then £4, which they felt unjust; many players had to supplement their wages with other employment to make ends meet.

Things came to a head in August 1909 when the FA threatened to suspend any player who admitted to being a member of the union, following which Roberts and his Manchester United teammates were summoned to a meeting with the United management. The players refused to relinquish their membership, choosing to train alone. In the face of the FA's threat of suspension, union membership fell away, but the United players, who called themselves 'The Outcasts FC' held firm. Suspended by the club, some of the players broke into the old ground at Bank Street looking to take what they could, including even the FA Cup, before cooler heads prevailed.

The dispute was resolved when the FA recognised the Players' Union and allowed players to earn bonuses in addition to the capped wage. In return, the union agreed not to affiliate to the General Federation of Trade Unions, thereby forgoing the right to strike.

Roberts had a glittering career at United, captaining the side to two league titles in 1908 and 1911 and its first FA Cup in 1909 before being sold to Oldham Athletic in 1913 after making 299 appearances and scoring 23 goals for the club. He was not above exploiting his celebrity; he promoted the branded Ducrobel cigars – a portmanteau word derived from the famous back line of Duckworth, Roberts and Bell – which he sold in his tobacconist's shop in Manchester.

More than a century after his playing days at United, Roberts was inducted into the National Football Museum's Hall of Fame in 2017 as recognition for his work in setting up the Players' Union and serving as its chairman between 1919 and 1921. The union was the longest-established sportspersons' organisation of its kind in the world, and the forerunner of the PFA. The award was accepted by Charlie's grandson, Ted, who recalled the tragic incident that sparked the creation of the union: 'There was nothing available for Blackstock's family, and my grandfather was horrified that nothing was available. So they decided to do something about it.'

OLD TRAFFORD
A New Hope

We can thank Sir Bobby Charlton, a man known more for his ball skills than his *bons mots*, for coining the epithet 'the Theatre of Dreams' to describe the Old Trafford stadium, a description that first appeared in John Riley's book, *Soccer*, published in 1987. For a stadium that had witnessed so much entertainment, artistry and drama, it seemed more than appropriate – it was poetic genius.

The modern stadium is the largest club ground in England, capable of seating 74,140 spectators, and complete with museum, restaurants, gymnasia and a megastore. But Manchester United have not always enjoyed such grand surroundings. Old Trafford is United's third home: their first games, as Newton Heath L&YR FC, were played at North Road in Moston near the Newton Heath railway yards, a ground that lacked even the basic amenity of a changing room and suffered a pitch beset by drainage problems, being described as 'little better than a clay pit'. Parting company with their railway company owners and being incorporated as a limited company, the 'Heathens' were then unceremoniously evicted by their pious landlords, the Manchester Deans and Canons, finding new accommodation three miles away at Bank Street in Clayton.

The Bank Street stadium, situated in what is now the Manchester Velodrome car park, was notorious for the industrial smog and miasma that came from the nearby chemical works;

opponents claimed it gave the home side an unfair advantage. It was only following the takeover and rescue from bankruptcy in 1902 that the ground received some much-needed investment. The new chairman, J.H. Davies, built stands to cover all four sides of the Bank Street stadium, enough to hold 50,000 fans, and it was thought good enough to host a representative match between a Football League XI against a Scottish League side in 1904.

But Davies had yet more ambitious plans to have a stadium that reflected the growing status of the club. He commissioned Archibald Leitch, pioneer of football stadium design and the architect who had overseen the redevelopment of Ibrox Stadium in Glasgow, Bramall Lane in Sheffield and the central stand at Anfield. His brief was to build a stadium grand enough to hold 100,000 spectators who would bear witness to the scale of Davies' ambition; United's home attendances in the first decade of the century averaged less than 20,000.

Unlike the Bank Street ground, which was surrounded by terraced houses and so run down that parts of the roof would blow off during high winds, the new arena was set in 16 acres of industrial Trafford Park. Cost overruns meant that Leitch had to rein in expenditure and the capacity was reduced to 80,000.

The first league match at Old Trafford took place on 19 February 1910, attracting 45,000 spectators to watch Liverpool rain on their parade, the visitors winning by the odd goal in seven. If fans weren't enjoying the action on the pitch, they could marvel at the vast terraces sprinkled with hundreds of steel crush barriers, a trademark of Leitch's stadia, or the massive, covered grandstand. The *Umpire* was impressed that the fans' experience was taken into account: 'The grandstand with its 60 rows of seats, is considerably larger than any stand in a football ground in the kingdom, and yet the ground is so compact, unlike the Crystal

Palace and other grounds, you always seem reasonably near the playing pitch.'

The *Manchester Guardian* marvelled at the imposing grandstand as 'a new luxury, unknown until then'. The ground also made a big impression on the reporter from the *Sporting Chronicle*, who described the new stadium as 'the most handsomest, the most spacious and the most remarkable arena I have ever seen. As a football ground it is unrivalled in the world, it is an honour to Manchester and the home of a team who can do wonders when they are so disposed.'

They were so disposed the following season when United pipped Aston Villa to become league champions once again and added insult to injury to the Brummies by dumping Villa out of the FA Cup at the second-round stage in front of a huge Old Trafford crowd of 65,000, easily a record for a home game. For Davies the brewing magnate, it must have been an intoxicating sight.

The stage was set for dreams to be played out in the new theatre. But the intervention and upheaval of war, a match-fixing scandal and the hangover from the crippling cost of construction turned the dream into a nightmare. The years following the peace were a desert for a struggling United side. The bright new future at Old Trafford turned out to be a mirage, albeit a mirage made in heaven.

THE NEAREST RUN THING
Relegation Decider, 5 May 1928

By the mid-1920s Britain had gone from post-war boom to bust, but for the followers of Manchester United the period was distinctly more bust than boom. The pre-war success was a distant memory, and by the middle of the decade fans had to live off the meagre rations of Second Division football. The club was also suffering financial problems; the long illness and death in 1927 of their chairman and benefactor J.H. Davies bequeathed the unhappy prospect of an uncertain future.

Different managers were tried – Jack Robson gave way to John Chapman, lured from Airdrieonians, before Herbert Bamlett took over in 1927. They even changed the first team shirts in superstitious attempts to improve their fortunes. Chapman revived the 1909 cup-winning white shirt with red chevron, coincidentally the same design as Airdrie's, which probably made him feel more at home; and at one point they even tried maroon and white hoops.

United, whose style was as dour as their Presbyterian manager, eventually won promotion to the First Division in 1924/25 thanks to a parsimonious defence marshalled by the frankly scary Frank Barson – a tough guy who reportedly once pulled a gun on one of his former managers. Up front, the team grew increasingly dependent on the goals from their main striker, Joe Spence. The long-suffering fans in the Pop Side (which later became the Sir Alex Ferguson stand) held up banners imploring the team to 'Give it to Joe' (at least it made a change from picket line placards).

Joe Spence, aka the 'Scotswood Whippet', was sent down the pit aged 13 and served as a machine-gunner in the Great War before joining United in 1919 – no soft YTS schemes or academies for aspiring footballers in those days. Spence, the club's leading scorer on six occasions, was enjoying a purple patch under new manager Herbert Bamlett, and, as the 1927/28 campaign reached a climax, he remained United's best hope of avoiding relegation back to Division Two. For as the table below shows, United were in deep trouble going into the last game of the season. To stay up, they would have to beat, of all teams, Liverpool and hope that other results went their way. They needed Joe Spence.

Pos		Pl	W	D	L	GA	Pts
17	Portsmouth	41	16	7	18	0.756	39
18	Tottenham H	42	15	8	19	0.86	38
19	Sheff Weds	41	12	13	16	1.013	37
20	Middlesbrough	41	11	15	15	0.953	37
21	Sunderland	41	14	9	18	0.934	37
22	Man United	41	15	7	19	0.835	37

Astonishingly, a spread of only two points separated the teams in the bottom half of the table from Liverpool in 12th and United in 22nd and last place. Relegation was a real and terrifying prospect that carried grim implications for the finances of the cash-strapped club.

A bigger than average crowd of 30,625 turned up to Old Trafford to watch the crunch game. Liverpool were but a shadow of the great 'Untouchables' side of the early 1920s and were certainly not unbeatable. The home support was repaid with an emphatic performance from United and, especially, their star man;

Joe Spence fired a hat-trick as the home side thrashed Liverpool 6–1. It remains United's biggest ever win against their arch-rivals.

Fans around the country anxiously consulted their pink papers that Saturday tea-time for the final reckoning to learn their team's fate.

Pos		Pl	W	D	L	GA	Pts
17	West Ham U	42	14	11	17	0.92	39
18	Man United	42	16	7	19	0.900	39
19	Burnley	42	16	7	19	0.837	39
20	Portsmouth	42	16	7	19	0.733	39
21	Tottenham H	42	15	8	19	0.860	38
22	Middlesbrough	42	11	15	16	0.920	37

Middlesbrough's home defeat to fellow strugglers Sunderland consigned the Teessiders to the drop along with Spurs. United finished level on points with Liverpool, whose marginally better goal average placed them sixteenth. In one of the most closely fought relegation battles anyone could remember, United's supporters avoided their Waterloo. They would have savoured their momentous victory over their Merseyside opponents knowing they had flirted with disaster. Like Wellington, they knew that the stakes were high and would have concurred with the Iron Duke's famous post-match comments: 'It has been a damned nice thing – the nearest run thing you ever saw in your life.'

INTO THE LIONS' DEN
Millwall 0 Manchester United 2
5 MAY 1934

The great escape against Liverpool in May 1928 had been merely a stay of execution for United. A run of six years in the top division came to a juddering halt at the end of the 1930/31 season. The campaign started badly – losing their first 12 games – and never fully recovered, the club ending nine points adrift at the foot of the table with a goal difference of minus 62. Probably the worst season in their history.

Manager Herbert Bamlett paid the price for failure as the United board chose not to renew his contract, prevailing upon secretary Walter Crickmer to take temporary charge, with Louis Rocca acting as his assistant. Understandably, fans were mutinous at the sad state of the club both on the pitch and in the boardroom. George Greenhough, elected secretary of the Manchester United Supporters' Club in 1930, demanded an FA investigation into the club's financial dealings. He also issued a five-point petition that included a demand for a shareholders' rights issue and the election of a new board. He even convened a meeting at Hulme Town Hall where his call for a match day boycott received a standing ovation.

By 1931, as the Great Depression took its grip on the nation, attendances fell. Manchester United Ltd was loss-making and still mired in debt from building works on the stadium. By the winter, the money had run out and creditors were running low on patience before James Gibson rode to the rescue when he and four others invested a total of £10,000 to pay the most pressing debts and set some aside for a transfer fund. Greenhough's complaints were finally given a hearing, and a new official supporters' club was established to give fans a voice.

If the crisis off the pitch had been averted – Gibson's management skills turned the company around to become profitable once again – the team itself showed little sign of improvement. Joe Spence, scorer of 168 goals for the club in more than 500 appearances and so often a beacon of light amidst the gloom, left the club in 1933. In new manager Scott Duncan's first two seasons United finished in the middle of the pack without ever threatening to challenge for promotion.

Mid-table mediocrity may have been dull, but it was preferable to the gut-wrenching trauma of the 1933/34 season. In a discontented winter, United went on a run of just one point in nine games and slid into the relegation places. Summer would be anything but glorious if it only held the prospect of playing in the Third Division North in the autumn.

As the final game of the season approached, they were still in the drop zone. Six years to the day since their heroics against Liverpool, they travelled to Millwall, one point above them in the table, knowing that anything less than a victory would be enough to send them down.

United were hardly nailed-on favourites; they hadn't won away since the beginning of February and their previous visit to the Den had resulted in a 2–0 defeat. The Lions' home form had picked up in April when they won all three games. In front of 24,000 fans, United eased their nerves by scoring on eight minutes through Tommy Manley, and then a goal at the start of the second half by new signing Jack Cape put the game beyond Millwall's reach.

Reports of the game suggest that United played as if their lives depended on it. Quite so. For had they not secured victory, the team and their manager would have been thrown to the lions.

HOLDING THE FORT
Walter Crickmer, Club Legend

In the pantheon of Manchester United managers, people often cite Walter Crickmer as one of the great names of the past. In truth, he never formally took on the title of manager, but that should not diminish his standing.

Crickmer joined the club as a junior clerk shortly after the First World War, rising to the position of club secretary in 1926. The years between the two wars were turbulent for the club: on the pitch, results were disappointing, United twice suffering relegation, and, off it, the finances were in a parlous state. By the beginning of the 1930s, as the country entered the Great Depression, the club was in dire straits: mounting debts of £30,000 combined with falling turnover and dwindling gate receipts were crippling the club; fewer than 4,000 spectators paid to see the final home game of the 1930/31 season.

With the departure of manager Herbert Bamlett in April 1931, Crickmer found himself fighting fires on two fronts as he took on team affairs in addition to his administrative duties, remaining in charge until the appointment of Scott Duncan the following summer. Supporters had grown restive – in the autumn of 1930 there had been a public meeting about the state of the club and calls for a boycott of the big game against Arsenal. Something had to be done.

By December the money had run out: the gas had been cut off and the club weren't able to pay players' wages. The bank informed Crickmer that it was withdrawing credit to the club. But Crickmer found a solution – a white knight in the shape of Salford-born clothing magnate James W. Gibson. It was Crickmer who called on Gibson at his home in Hale, and left with a cheque for £2,000 – enough to pay off the immediate debts, the unpaid wages and even provide each player with a turkey for Christmas. It was the start of a fruitful relationship. Gibson and Crickmer, with the help of the irrepressible Louis Rocca (see page 46), turned round the club's fortunes. Within three years the club was profitable again, and with further investment from Gibson the finances were at last placed on a sound footing.

On the pitch, results had improved under Scott Duncan, but when the Scot was lured away to manage Ipswich Town in 1938, Crickmer once again stepped in to take temporary charge – temporary, as in seven years. He and Gibson decided to invest in youth. In 1938, they established the academy, the 'Manchester United Junior Athletic Club', so that they could develop home-grown talent rather than splashing the cash in the transfer market.

The strategy would bear fruit, but not until after the war had ended. The first academy players provided the backbone of the successful side that won the FA Cup in 1948 and the 1951/52 title, and they in turn were followed by the Busby Babes. The war had not been kind to Crickmer; still de facto manager, he had to cope without Old Trafford, which had been flattened by a German air raid in 1941, until it reopened in 1949. Then he narrowly avoided death while on duty as a special constable when the police headquarters were bombed. He was buried under rubble for several hours; he survived, but many of his colleagues weren't so lucky.

Sadly, tragedy did strike when Crickmer, a servant of the club for nearly 40 years and its secretary for over 30, joined the United party on their trip to Belgrade in February 1958 for the return leg of their European Cup quarter-final against Red Star. Returning from the tie, he was among the 23 players, staff and journalists who perished in the Munich air disaster.

The flower of Manchester was cruelly crushed that day, but the culture, ethos and dream of Manchester United that Crickmer did so much to build lived on.

UNITED'S SCHOOL OF EXCELLENCE
Manchester United Junior Athletic Club

The inter-war years had been pretty dismal for United with little to show other than winning the Second Division championship in 1936 and losing an FA Cup semi-final to neighbours City ten years previously. By 1937, United were back in the second tier and the club had parted company with manager Scott Duncan, who left to join non-league Ipswich Town.

Although the financial woes of the 1920s had been put behind them once James Gibson had taken control in 1932, Duncan's policy of splashing the cash on transfers hadn't brought the immediate success the fans craved. United were now looking to the future and putting their faith in youth.

Duncan set the ball rolling that same year with the establishment of United's first 'A' team – the club's third level at the time, after the first team and the reserves – which would compete in the amateur Manchester League and serve largely as a vehicle for developing and promoting young players from the local area.

Duncan described the club's thinking in the *Manchester Evening Chronicle*: 'By running a team in the Manchester League, we shall be able to give all likely juniors a chance of showing their paces, and United hope to discover from their number more than average finds.'

After he departed Old Trafford in November 1937 to take charge of Ipswich Town, old hands Walter Crickmer, Louis Rocca and trainer Tom Curry were now in charge. True to Gibson's vision of producing an all-Manchester team, they pressed on with plans to set up an academy.

Having decided in a board meeting on 1 June 1937 to give 'special attention to the coaching of youth players', on 22 February 1938 a schoolboy football scheme was approved and its organisation left in Crickmer's capable hands. The Manchester United Junior Athletic Club was born. They worked with local schools to create a Manchester United youth team and provide training facilities and coaching for aspiring footballers.

By June 1938, Gibson had secured a 99-year lease for the MUJAC to play at the Old Broughton Rangers Rugby Club ground, known as the Cliff. Crickmer added two new youth sides to the club's system, a first XI and a second team, to provide a pathway for players to work their way up through the tiers to the first team.

In the autumn of 1938, writing in the *Manchester Evening Chronicle*, Alf Clarke was enthusiastic about the new set-up: 'History was created in Manchester United football circles today. This afternoon, there are no fewer than five United teams on duty. They are the senior side, Central League XI, 'A' team, MUJAC first team and MUJAC second XI . . . no club in the country is better served with junior players than Manchester United.'

The seeds of success had been planted. Stan Pearson made his debut in 1937, Charlie Mitten and John Aston were blooded in 1938/39, the season which saw United win promotion back to the First Division, and Allenby Chilton graduated at the beginning of the following season, a week before war was declared. These academy products would team up with the best of Duncan's signings, Johnny Carey and Jack Rowley, to form the basis of Busby's first great side that won the cup in 1948 and, in 1952, United's first league title in 40 years.

Faith in youth has been an enduring feature of United's football philosophy from the foundation of MUJAC and, astonishingly, United have fielded a player who has come through the academy's ranks in every match day squad since 30 October 1937 – more than 4,000 consecutive games and counting.

THE WHOLE KIT AND CABOODLE
United's Kits Through the Years

Everyone knows that Manchester United started off in the 19th century as Newton Heath. Correct. They also know that the Heathens played in green and gold halved shirts. Well yes, but not as a league side; they sported the dabbled strip for a six-year period in the 1880s. There is evidence for the team turning out in green shirts with a gold collar and then green and gold striped shirts in the mid-1890s, but otherwise they played in either red and white quarters or plain white with blue knickerbockers; in the very early days a blue cord would be worn diagonally over the shirt. The main reason for choosing white seems to have been purely economic – it was the cheapest option for a hard-up club that by 1902 was faced with bankruptcy.

The club's fortunes changed when J.H. Davies and his associates took over the running of the club. A new beginning required a new name and a new kit. Thenceforth, with some strange exceptions in the inter-war period, United's home kit has been the famous red shirt, white shorts and, generally, black socks. The more creative kit designs – some less-well-advised than others – featured on the away strip.

In the 1920s, John Chapman decided that United should adopt the colours of his previous club, Airdrieonians: a white shirt with a red chevron or V. Unhappily, they proceeded to play like Airdrie. Some older fans would have enjoyed the similarity to the 1909 cup-winning shirt (United and Bristol City both wore change strips due to a clash of colours) presented to the players by George Robey and sold to the club by its star player Billy Meredith's sports shop. The unfortunate experiment lasted five seasons from 1922/23 to 1926/27, and after the departure of Chapman the team reverted to their red shirts which they had been using as their change strip in the interim: waste not want not in those cash-strapped times.

There was another bizarre variation of the home kit in the early 1930s. The period was one of the least successful in United's playing history, and in 1933/34 they were in danger of sliding down into the Third Division North. Clutching at straws, the club changed their home kit midway through the season. The excellent unitedkits.com website recounts this desperate throw of the dice: 'The players began to regard the hooped change kit as "lucky", especially after they beat Burnley 4–1 at Turf Moor on February 3rd 1934. It was their first victory in 11 games. Minutes from a Board Meeting confirm the Directors decided to adopt this kit (described as "maroon and hoop") as the home kit and it was registered as such with the Football League. The "lucky kit" was first worn as the official home kit for the match against Bury on March 3rd 1934 at Old Trafford. United won 2–1.'

It may just have worked as those two wins may have been the difference in their fight for survival in League Division Two. The hoops didn't last long, though; they were demoted to become the change kit the following season and followed by the fleeting appearance of a black-and-white version before disappearing altogether before the war.

United have sported various away colours over the years with the most popular ones being white and – famously in the 1948

Cup final and the European Cup final in 1968 – royal blue. But every so often they would wear something of a different stripe. The notorious 2020/21 black-and-white rotating stripe third kit was inspired by Mangnall's title-winning side (a message woven into the collar read '110 years of stripes'). Fans likened the shirt more to a Zebra crossing or in captioned photos of Paul Pogba described the effect as 'galloping through midfield like a zebra through the Serengeti'; it was quite possibly the worst in United's history. Mangnall's men wore blue-and-white stripes, and that pattern reappeared in the 1990s for United's third kit, but it lacked class – more Sheffield Wednesday than Argentina.

A debt of gratitude is due once more to unitedkits.com for telling the story of the disputed stripes on United's mid-1970s change shirt. United were the second club to sign up with shirtmaker Admiral, who designed a much-loved white shirt with three black vertical stripes running down the left of its front. Not surprisingly, the people at Adidas took exception to the design and sued for breach of copyright. After much expensive legal wrangling, a compromise was reached whereby a fourth stripe was added for the playing team although the replicas – selling at an eye-watering £15 a pop – only had three. Eventually, Admiral agreed to pay a retainer to Adidas to allow them to produce a three-stripe version.

From the 1990s, as a result of the increasing commercialisation of the sport and the relaxation of social dress codes, the popularity of replica kits led shirt manufacturers to create designs to appeal to this growing market. For the 1995/96 season Umbro designed a grey change kit which they thought would look particularly cool worn with denims. In the four times it was worn by the players during that title-winning season United picked up precisely one point. Their biggest humiliation came at the Dell when Southampton put three past United in the first half. Players complained that they couldn't pick out their teammates against the crowd. Alex Ferguson's reaction was to make the players change into an old 1994 kit (with the wrong Premier League patches on the sleeves). They lost the game 3–1 but at least they won the second half.On the 100th anniversary of United's accession to league football, the club marked the occasion by introducing a green-and-gold third strip in honour of its founders, Newton Heath. And although it is unlikely that the Manchester United first team ever played in those colours, they have since taken on a new symbolic importance for fans. Opponents of the Glazers' takeover sported the 'Heathen' shirts and waved green-and-gold scarves in protest at the change of ownership. These fans yearned for the real United, wishing to uphold the traditions of an authentic football club and that it not be prey to big business.

They were having to swim against the tide; not just the club, but kits have become big business. The original sponsorship deal with Admiral was worth £15,000 plus bonuses; in 2021, TeamViewer agreed to pay £47 million per annum, while Kohler cough up £20 million just to be on the sleeve! Adidas pay up to £75 million a year, depending on regular Champions League participation, whereas Umbro shelled out roughly £6 million a year in the 1990s. To buy an 'authentic' replica shirt with 'cooling and comfort technologies' and a player's name and number pressed on the back a fan would have to find a cool £115 in 2022 (actually the same as an Admiral shirt, inflation-adjusted) – and that's before the 'authentic' shorts at £43.

Where once a replica kit came in plain colours and only in children's sizes in an Umbroset box, now there is a bewildering choice: home kit, change, third and European plus several variants thereof. The United online store has more kits than IKEA with more than 1,400 items for sale.

The Grammarist website has an interesting take on the word 'caboodle': 'The word *caboodle* in the phrase the *whole kit and caboodle* is an alliteration of the word *boodle*. *Boodle* appears in the United States in the 1830s to mean a crowd of people, later evolving to mean a large amount of ill-gotten money.' A description that might arguably be applied to the United superstore on matchdays . . .

THE MANAGERS
From 1892 to the Present Day

In the 130 years since the accession of Newton Heath to the Football League, the club have had 27 different managers; in fact 29 if you include Casey Stoney, who took charge of the women's team from 2018 to 2021, and her successor, Marc Skinner. Of the 29, four acted as caretakers, player managers or as consultants.

The term 'manager' didn't come into common usage until Jack Robson took the job at the end of 1914; previously, the role was part of the club secretary's job description, but due to his innovative tactics and coaching, Ernest Mangnall deserves to be called United's first manager.

Three names stand out: Ernest Mangnall, winner of United's first two top division titles, and the two Scottish knights – Matt Busby and Alex Ferguson. In fact, the hot seat was warmed by six Caledonian posteriors for more than 67 years.

Leaving aside the caretaker managers, the roll call of honour, in chronological order, is as follows:

Alfred Albut (1892 to May 1900): age on appointment and previous club unknown; 285 games in charge with a win percentage (WP) of 44.5%.
James West (1900 to 1903): aged 44(?) on appointment; ex-Lincoln City; 118 games with a WP of 40.5%.

Ernest Mangnall (October 1903 to September 1912): aged 37; ex-Burnley; 370 games with a WP of 54%. Division One champions on two occasions and FA Cup winners once.

John Bentley (October 1912 to December 1914): aged 52; ex-Turton FC; 91 games with a WP of 39.5%.

Jack Robson (December 1914 to October 1921): aged 54; ex-Brighton and Hove Albion; 121 games with a WP of 31.5%.

John Chapman (December 1921 to October 1926): aged 39; ex-Airdrieonians; 221 games with a WP of 39%.

Herbert Bamlett (April 1927 to April 1931): aged 45; 200 games with a WP of 30.5%.

Walter Crickmer (1931/32; 1937–45): aged 31; 105 games with a WP of 42%.

Scott Duncan (July 1932 to November 1937): aged 43; ex-Cowdenbeath; 235 games with a WP of 39%. Division Two champions 1935/36.

Sir Matt Busby (1945–69; 1970/71): aged 36; ex-army; 1,140 games with a WP of 50.5%. Division One champions five times; FA Cup winners twice; European Cup winners once.

Wilf McGuinness (June 1968 to December 1970): aged 31; 88 games with a WP of 36.5%.

Frank O'Farrell (June 1971 to December 1972): aged 43; ex-Leicester City; 81 games with a WP of 37%.

Tommy Docherty (December 1972 to July 1977): aged 44; ex-Scotland national team; 228 games with a WP of 47%. Second Division champions 1974/75; FA Cup winners 1977.

Dave Sexton (July 1977 to April 1981): aged 47; ex-Queens Park Rangers; 201 games with a WP of 40.5%.

Ron Atkinson (June 1981 to November 1986): aged 42; ex-West Bromwich Albion; 292 games with a WP of 50%. FA Cup winners twice.

Sir Alex Ferguson (November 1986 to May 2013): aged 45; ex-Aberdeen; 1,500 games with a WP of 59.67%. Premier League champions 13 times; FA Cup winners five times; League Cup winners four times; Champions League winners twice; European Cup Winners' Cup winners once.

David Moyes (June 2013 to April 2014): aged 40; ex-Everton; 51 games with a WP of 53%.

Louis van Gaal (May 2014 to May 2016): aged 52; ex-Netherlands national team; 103 games with a WP of 52.5%. FA Cup winners 2016.

José Mourinho (May 2016 to December 2018): aged 52; ex-Chelsea144 games with a WP of 58.33%. League Cup Winners 2017; Europa League champions 2017.

Ole Gunnar Solskjær (December 2018 to November 2021): aged 45; ex-Molde; 168 ganes with a WP of 54.17%.

Erik ten Hag (From May 2022): aged 52; ex-Ajax.

Who has been the most successful? In terms of trophies, Sir Alex wins hands down, winning, in all, 38 trophies, including 13 Premier League titles, while Busby had to be content with a baker's dozen and Mangnall with five. If one judges by win ratio percentages, then, as you might expect, Sir Alex comes out top with a mighty 59.67%, but the runner-up is more surprising: José Mourinho achieved 58.33%. It should be said that Casey Stoney's record of 71% surpasses all of these, but then she was in charge for a mere 62 games compared to Sir Alex's 1,500.

And the least successful? Discounting Jimmy Murphy's short tenure in 1958 under the most trying of circumstances after the Munich air disaster, Ralf Ragnick's was the worst record of any 'manager' in the Premier League era, his win percentage of 37.9% only fractionally better than Frank O'Farrell's.

Statistics alone are not enough to answer the question of who is the greatest United manager of all time; so many more factors have to be weighed up before passing judgement. It is the subject of endless debate which, inevitably, continues on page 318 of this book.

NAMING UNITED
Louis Rocca: United, Man and Boy

The history of Manchester United is littered with trophies, glory, great players, celebrities and success on and off the field. But the club grew from humble beginnings and the path to fame and fortune was not an easy one.

At the turn of the 20th century, the club known as Newton Heath languished in the second tier of the Football League and was virtually bankrupt thanks to the move to their new ground at Bank Street and the increasing cost of player wages. But at the beginning of the new century, things began to look up.

After owner J.H. Davies invested serious money in the club, debts were cleared, funds were available for the playing squad and plans for a new stadium could be laid. The links to Newton Heath had been severed and Davies wanted a fresh start.

At the famous supporters' meeting held on 26 April 1902 to choose a new name, fans were arguing over the dubious merits of Manchester Celtic and Manchester Central when a teenager stepped forward with the suggestion of Manchester United.

The young man, Louis Rocca, was the son of Italian immigrants/ He had been smitten by Newton Heath as a boy. He started going to matches as an 8-year-old, 'sneaking under the boards' to get into the ground. At the age of 10 he was holding up candles to provide lighting for a club meeting in 1892 after the gas company had cut off the supply. At 12, he was caught by a steward trying to get in the ground and threatened with a 'walloping', but he struck a deal, agreeing to make the players tea and coffee and clean the baths in return for free admission. 'Before Newton Heath was taken over, I was an active servant of the club, and like the little band of its workers at that time, received no pay,' said Rocca. 'We tended the ground, did running repairs to the hoardings and club quarters, and did the scouting jobs around local teams.'

So began an association with the club that spanned more than half a century.

He became a popular figure at the club: on the horse-drawn carriage parading through the city of Manchester with the FA Cup they won in 1909, players at the front sat under a huge umbrella emblazoned with the words 'Rocca's Brigade' in tribute.

In 1906, Rocca was appointed chief scout and proceeded to revolutionise the scouting system for Manchester United, building up a network of lookouts around the country, especially in the North, made up of Roman Catholic priests, schoolmasters and friends who wanted to help Manchester United in any way they could. And he, along with Walter Crickmer and chairman James Gibson, was instrumental in setting up the junior academy in 1938, which nurtured the young Johnny Carey, Stan Pearson and Charlie Mitten and always placed faith in a youth system.

Gradually, he worked his way up. He did almost every job at the club except chairman and manager – even then, he was assistant manager in the 1930s. He also acted as the club's chief fixer. Some of his methods were unorthodox: in 1927, he arranged the transfer of Hugh McLenahan from Stockport County in exchange for three freezers full of ice cream from the Rocca family business.

After the death of their benefactor J.H. Davies in 1927 and the onset of the Great Depression the club was on its uppers. Fans were even washing the players' match day kit to save on laundry bills. At one point, Rocca had to negotiate with a deputation of, in his words, 'thirty dour professionals' demanding their wages without the means to pay them. Fortunately for Rocca, a saviour was riding to the rescue in the shape of local clothing manufacturer James Gibson. Gibson, Rocca and Walter Crickmer forged a formidable business team that would lay the foundation for greatness.

Rocca's most lasting contribution was persuading Matt Busby to become United's manager after the war. Rocca knew him through the local Catholic community – both were members of the Manchester Catholic Sports Club – and admired Busby as a player for both Liverpool and Manchester City. He had even tried to bring Busby to United in 1930, but the club didn't have the necessary £250 to seal the deal. United hadn't appointed a permanent manager since the departure of Scott Duncan in 1937 – Walter Crickmer manfully took on the role in the interim – and the board were anxious to find someone who could take the club forward. Rocca told them, 'Leave it to me . . .'

HEADHUNTING BUSBY
Louis Rocca's Letter to RSM Matt Busby

In December 1944, as the Second World War drew to a close, Rocca wrote to his old friend, Matt Busby. Still on active service, Busby, who had been offered the position of assistant manager at Liverpool where he had played before the war, pitched up in Manchester, two months after Rocca's letter was sent, for a meeting with Rocca and James Gibson. He laid down his terms, United agreed, and, on 19 February 1945, Busby signed a five-year contract to become United's new manager.

This is a transcript of the letter written by Louis Rocca to Sergeant-Major Matt Busby, then serving as a coach in the Army Physical Training Corps. The letter was addressed to Busby c/o Sandhurst.

57 Craigwell Road,
Prestwich,
Manchester.

15 December 1944

Dear Matt,
No doubt you will be surprised to get this letter from your old pal Louis. Well Matt I have been trying to find you and not having your Reg. address I could not trust a letter going to Liverpool, as what I

*have to say is so important. I don't know if you have considered about
what you are going to do after the war is over, but I have a great job
for you if you are willing to take it on. Will you get in touch with me
at the above address and when you do I can explain things better,
when I know there is no danger of interception. Now Matt I hope
this is plain to you. You see I have not forgotten my old friend either
in my prayer or in your future welfare. I hope your good wife and
family are all well and please God you will soon be home to join their
happy circle.*

*Wishing you a very Happy Xmas and a lucky New Year with all
God's Blessing in you and yours.*

*Your Old Pal
Louis Rocca*

It worked. United had their man.

THE CUP THAT CHEERS
The 1948 FA Cup Run

Manchester in the immediate post-war years was weary after six years of conflict and in much need of repair. The city had been bombed in December 1940 and again in the spring the following year. Manchester United suffered collateral damage when the Luftwaffe targeted the industrial and munitions factories in Trafford Park. In March 1941, direct hits on Old Trafford destroyed the main stand, the club offices and the dressing rooms, and the training ground at the Cliff was also hit.

Newly appointed manager Matt Busby had no pitch, no ground and no training facilities. What he did have was a talented group of players, many of whom had come through the club's academy before and immediately after the war. Many of his squad had seen action during the war – Jack Rowley and Allenby Chilton took part in the D-Day landings – but they were just as likely to have played in the wartime Regional League North. United's team even fielded a 15-year-old – Arthur Rowley, younger brother of Jack, who would later become English football's all-time top goal scorer. By 1945, the boys had grown into men.

Football as a spectator sport in the late 1940s was enjoying a revival. While attendances at Old Trafford in the 1930s regularly averaged fewer than 30,000 (and well below 20,000 in the Depression years), by the 1947/48 season United were attracting in excess of 50,000. Football brought colour and excitement into the grey lives of working men (almost exclusively men) in a time of ration-book austerity.

Busby's team soon clicked into gear. The perennial pre-war under-achievers were high flyers; in the first season after the league's resumption, United narrowly missed out on the title, finishing one point behind the champions Liverpool. Their attacking style of play produced 95 goals, the second-highest in the league. The strike partnership of Rowley and Pearson scored 45 between them, many provided by the crafty wing play of Jimmy Delaney. Delaney had been a star of the pre-war Celtic side, but at the age of 31 and injury-prone he was a surprise buy. Delaney forged a productive partnership with academy graduate Johnny Morris on the right wing and on the left they had the magical skills of the dashing Charlie Mitten.

In the following season, United once again challenged in the league. Morris had been given more game time and repaid Busby's faith by contributing 18 goals and becoming an increasingly influential member of the team. Once again, the Reds were frustrated as they finished runners-up to Arsenal. The cup, however, was a different story.

United approached their third-round tie away to Aston Villa in a rich vein of form having won their five previous league fixtures. The crowd of 58,683 that attended were treated to a classic. Having fallen behind in the first minute, United blitzed the Villans with goals from Rowley, Morris (2), Pearson and Delaney to go into half-time 5–1 up. In the second half, the home team staged a fightback, reducing United's advantage to 4–5 with nine minutes to go, setting up a nail-biting finish. The tension was finally relieved as Stan Pearson scored his second and United's sixth goal in the 88th minute.

United may have had the good fortune to be drawn at home in the next three rounds but had to play the first two away from their temporary Maine Road home as their City landlords had prior engagements. Undeterred, United hit Liverpool for three without reply in front of 74,000 at Goodison before despatching Charlton at Huddersfield. In their one tie in Manchester, United fired four against Preston to set up their first FA Cup semi-final for 22 years. Stan Pearson put the Reds into a two-goal lead in the first half before their semi-final opponents, Derby County, pulled one back just before half-time. Any jitters were dispelled ten minutes into the second half when Pearson completed his hat-trick to send United on their way to a first-ever trip to Wembley.

It had been an incredible run. United had played five top-flight sides, scored 18 goals and entertained crowds well in excess of a quarter of a million. And the best was yet to come.

The final was a classic, regarded by many as one of the finest games the famous stadium has seen. United's opponents, Blackpool, carried the twin threats of the two great Stans: Mortensen and Matthews. The Seasiders took an early lead through a penalty and Rowley's equaliser was countered by a Mortensen strike which restored Blackpool's slender advantage. United trailed until the 70th minute when Pearson put two and Johnny Anderson a third past Robinson in a 15-minute onslaught to see United eventually tiumph 4–2.

It was a triumph for Busby, chairman James Gibson and the whole team – United's first FA Cup success in 39 years and their first major trophy since 1911. Two world wars had been fought in the interim. The clouds of war had lifted, and the gloom that hung over Old Trafford had given way to optimism. The old bomb-wrecked stadium was being restored now that the War Damage Commission had granted funds to clear the debris and rebuild the stands; as the nation and the city of Manchester recovered, United had restored their pride.

THE LONG CLIMB TO THE TOP
Manchester United in 1951/52

A Scotsman walks into Old Trafford to take on the manager's post, waits three years to win a cup, and after six has finished as runners-up, again, having failed to win the top prize of the league title. Sound familiar? As Matt Busby weighed up his side's prospects at the beginning of the 1951/52 season, he could be forgiven for wondering if the fates were conspiring against him; since his arrival his team had finished second on no fewer than four occasions, their lowest position fourth.

When Busby took the job in February 1945, he turned down coaching offers from a number of clubs including his pre-war employers Liverpool to join United because the ambitious 35-year-old wanted the chance to impose his vision and his methods on the game. He dictated his terms – complete control over team affairs and transfers and no interference from the club's directors – and advised his future employers that he would need five years to build a team that could win the league. The United grandees, chairman Gibson, secretary and caretaker manager Crickmer and fixer-in-chief Rocca accepted; they couldn't countenance the new post-war era without a full-time manager.

Busby performed minor miracles in those difficult years immediately after the war when he had to cope without a ground or proper training facilities. They were runners-up in the first two seasons and, gloriously, FA Cup winners in 1948. In late August 1949, they were finally able to play their first post-war fixture at Old Trafford, where a crowd of over 41,000 watched the Reds beat Bolton 3–0.

United were consistently challenging in the league but were prone to damaging runs of inconsistency. Going into their home game against Liverpool on the ides of March 1950, they led the field by four points. They then failed to win any of their next nine games, which included a 2–0 home defeat to eventual champions Portsmouth. The Reds were acquiring an unwanted reputation as nearly men who were cup specialists (they reached the semis in 1949 and quarters in 1950) but not quite good enough to win the league title.

Although United's attacking style won them many admirers, much of their success was built on defensive solidity. The two pillars of the back line were Allenby Chilton, whom Busby regarded as his best-ever centre-half, and Johnny Carey, who was club captain for eight years and voted the Football Writers' Association Footballer of the Year in 1948/49.

Back in the day, United weren't the richest club in the land. Although they had help from the War Damage Commission to rebuild the stadium, they were burdened with debt. Busby, as tight with money as any cartoon Scotsman, lost two of his star players. In March 1949, Johnny Morris left for Derby County and, in sensational fashion, Charlie Mitten defected to Independiente Santa Fe during the club's tour of the US in 1950. The Colombian club had offered Mitten, thereafter branded the 'Bogota Bandit', a signing-on fee of £5,000 and increased his wages by 250% to £40 per week.

In the 1950/51 season, it was a case of same old, same old. They finished runners-up to Arthur Rowe's famous push-and-run

Spurs side, a clear six points ahead of Blackpool in third. Close again but no cigar for the pipe-smoking Carey and his men.

Jack Rowley was smokin' at the beginning of the following season. His 14 goals in the first seven games included hat-tricks against West Bromwich, Middlesbrough and Stoke. During the summer, Busby had added Johnny Berry to his forward line. The outside-right had impressed against United while playing for Birmingham, and Busby needed to strengthen his wing-play following the departures of Mitten and Jimmy Delaney. Later that autumn, an even more significant personality made his debut, one who would play an unexpected but crucial role in the outcome of United's season.

Local boy Roger Byrne was a late developer, only joining United at the ripe old age of 20. He made his first start against Liverpool in November 1951 at left-back, a position he would make his own for both club and country over the next six years. He impressed on debut with an assured display and quickly became a regular in the first team. He had excellent game intelligence, control and a good turn of pace which allowed him to become an early exponent of overlapping full-back play.

At the business end of the season, approaching the crucial Easter fixtures, three teams were level at the top of the table: United, Portsmouth and Arsenal, who had a game in hand. Busby then made a decisive tactical change by moving Byrne to outside-left. The reluctant number 11 – Byrne would later refuse to play anywhere other than left-back – put on the afterburners, proceeding to score seven goals in the six games that remained.

By quirk of the fixture list, United's last game was at home to Arsenal. The Gunners had only the slimmest of mathematical chances of denying United their long-awaited title: they would have to win by a margin of 7–0. As it turned out, the game featured seven goals, but six of those went to the home team as Arsenal were put to the sword. The scorers were, appropriately, Rowley, who ended the season as he had begun with a hat-trick, his partner in crime Stan Pearson with two, and who else but Roger Byrne.

At last, United had cast off the tag of 'champion runners-up'. Sadly, James Gibson, the chairman who had rescued the club from oblivion and helped to build the foundations of future glory, didn't live to see United claim their first title in 41 years; he died the previous September after 20 years at the helm. Matt had achieved what he promised: maybe not quite in the five years he had envisaged, but, in the year that Hillary and Tenzing had conquered Everest, he had reached the summit of English football.

THE CLASS OF '52
Manchester United 23 Nantwich Town 0
FA YOUTH CUP, 4 NOVEMBER 1952

The Manchester United Junior Athletic Club, brainchild of James Gibson, Walter Crickmer and Louis Rocca, was founded shortly before the outbreak of the Second World War. Their belief that investment in youth was a surer and less expensive path to success than spending in the transfer market was fully embraced by the new management team of Matt Busby and Jimmy Murphy as football resumed after the war. The early products of the MUJAC academy – Stan Pearson, John Aston (senior) and Allenby Chilton – had helped United win their first league title for 40 years in 1951/52, and soon a new crop of youth players would take the football world by storm.

An early portent of great things to come was clear to all who came to see Manchester United's youth team take on the 'Dabbers' of Nantwich Town on 4 November 1952 in the second round of the inaugural FA Youth Cup. The United line-up included a Brummie by the name of Duncan Edwards, barely a month past his 16th birthday, who had signed for United in the summer, and two promising forwards destined to become future stars: David Pegg and Albert Scanlon.

It was a one-sided affair. By half-time, Nantwich were 10–0 down. One Dabber later recalled a voice chirping up at half-time saying that at least the second half couldn't be as bad as the first.

In fact, it was worse. United ended up winning 23–0, and it could have been more but for the heroics of the Nantwich keeper – reportedly, Busby thought about signing him on the strength of his performance. That may have been one of Matt's little jokes.

There is some debate about the scorers. Jim White, author of *Manchester United: The Biography*, mentions Pegg, John Doherty and Edwards scoring five apiece and Eddie Lewis four, whereas a hand-annotated match programme auctioned in 2018 suggests Pegg scored six, Lewis, Doherty and Edwards five each, and Norton and Scanlon making up the numbers. I guess it was easy to lose count.

Despite Pegg and Lewis being drafted into the senior squad before the end of the year, the United youngsters went on to lift the cup in 1953 – and 1954, 1955, 1956 and 1957. The Class of '92 is rightly heralded as one of the greatest groups of players who went on to become the mainstays of Ferguson's glory years, but a similar claim can be made for the youth side that put Nantwich to the sword. Duncan Edwards, David Pegg and Albert Scanlon were part of the Busby Babes side that won two league championships; Ronnie Cope was picked in defence more than 100 times; Eddie Lewis played 24 times and scored 11 goals for the senior side but had limited opportunities to play because of the form of the great Tommy Taylor; John Doherty made a similar number of appearances before his promising career was hobbled by injuries.

Perhaps this particular vintage may not stand out as much as the Class of '92 because the youth system was producing great teams every year; new starlets Billy Whelan, Bobby Charlton, Eddie Colman (the 1954/55 youth team captain) and Wilf McGuinness would soon step into the side. But these were big shoes to fill, and on that November evening in 1952, the old boys certainly filled their boots.

HOW GOOD WAS DUNCAN EDWARDS?

Duncan Edwards played football in an age before YouTube, MUTV and wall-to-wall satellite TV coverage, and left behind barely any video footprint. Yet many still talk about him as the greatest ever to have played the game. To construct a portrait of Edwards, eye-witness accounts from his teammates, his managers, opponents, press reports and books must provide the tools.

Capped for England Schoolboys, the young Edwards was scouted by many of the big clubs. The Schoolboys coach Joe Mercer added his voice to those urging Busby to sign up the phenomenon. With the help of a shiny new washing machine, Jimmy Murphy and coach Bert Whalley managed to convince the Edwards family that his future lay at Old Trafford in the summer of 1952. He immediately stood out, not least in his sheer physical presence. At a time when the average British male measured five foot seven and when rationing was still in force, his near six-foot height and muscular frame were imposing.

In April 1953, three days before Edwards made his first team debut aged just 16½, George Follows tipped off his readers in the *Daily Herald* about the arrival of a new star: 'Like the father of the first atom bomb, Manchester United are waiting for something tremendous to happen. This tremendous football force they have discovered is Duncan Edwards, who is exactly sixteen and a half this morning. What can you expect to see in Edwards? Well, the first important thing is that this boy Edwards is a man of 12st and 5ft 10ins in height [he was still growing]. This gives him his first great asset of power. When he heads the ball, it is not a flabby flirtation with fortune, it is bold and decisive. When he tackles, it is with a man-trap bite, and when he shoots with either foot, not even Jack Rowley – the pride of Old Trafford – is shooting harder. Though nobody can tell exactly what will happen when Edwards explodes into First Division football, one thing is certain: it will be spectacular.'

And on his Home Championship debut against Scotland in 1955, Edwards made an immediate impression. Scottish forward Lawrie Reilly turned to his teammate Tommy Docherty during the first half and exclaimed: 'Where the hell did they find him? They've built battleships on the Clyde that are smaller.' England won 7–2.

Edwards occupied the left wing-back position in the customary 2-3-5 system of the time, but far from being defensive he played a role best described as an all-action, box-to-box midfielder. He himself outlined the key points of the midfielder's job description in his book, *Tackle Soccer This Way*.

Roy Keane would approve of this:

'But before a ball is kicked or a tackle made, the keynote of this position is stamina. The wing-half is never still. Either he is foraging in his opponents' half, or else back helping his own defence withstand pressure.'

Bryan Robson could have written this:

'The wing-half needs all the defensive skill, power of recovery and hardness of tackle of the full-back, yet he must ally these to the enterprise of the inside-forward.'

And Paul Pogba or Michael Carrick would surely agree with this comment:

'Then his two-footedness is a prize asset in switching the direction

of play suddenly. The wing-half moving away to his left can suddenly pivot on his right foot and slam a long ball away to his right-winger. There is nothing like a change in direction to splinter a defence.'

Add to all that the shooting ability of Bobby Charlton, the heading ability of Steve Bruce, the big-game temperament of Ronaldo and the touch of Paul Scholes and you have the complete package.

He established himself in the United side by the autumn of that year, combining his first-team duties with the captaincy of United's all-conquering youth team. In 1955, he began his two years of National Service but still managed to get a pass to play for United as well as turning out for army matches. He played as many as 100 games in a season.

By the 1956/57 campaign, the Busby Babes were taking the First Division by storm. Edwards, still not old enough to vote, was the heartbeat of the team. Assistant manager Jimmy Murphy described him as the 'Koh-i-Noor diamond among our crown jewels'. He was soon a regular in the England team; after excelling in a friendly against West Germany, his captain Billy Wright purred, 'The name of Duncan Edwards was on the lips of everyone who saw this match; he was phenomenal. There have been few individual performances to match what he produced that day. Duncan tackled like a lion, attacked at every opportunity and topped it off with that cracker of a goal. He was still only 19, but already a world-class player.'

In total Edwards played 177 games for United, scoring 21 goals, winning two league titles; for England he won 18 caps and scored five times. The day before the Munich air disaster, United had reached their second successive European Cup semi-final. He died 15 days after the crash aged only 21. Had he survived, many seasoned observers were convinced he could have been the driving force that would have led United to European domination and England to World Cup glory before 1966. Yes, he was that good.

*

Here are just a few insights into the quality of Edwards from those best qualified to judge:

'We used to look at players in training to see if we might have to get them to concentrate more on something. We looked at Duncan, and gave up trying to spot flaws in his game' – Sir Matt Busby

'He was Roy Keane and Bryan Robson combined, but in a bigger body. He could play as an attacker, creator or defender and be the best player on the pitch . . . He was world class when United had the ball, and when the opposition had the ball he was our best defender' – Wilf McGuinness, former teammate and later United manager

'You can play him anywhere and he would slot into that position as if he'd been playing there season after season. When the going gets rough, Duncan is like a rock in a raging sea' – Sir Stanley Matthews

'When United won the league in 1956, they were losing to Blackpool and they turned to Duncan at half-time and said: "Come on, Duncan, get us going." So, you've got John Berry and all these experienced players in the team and they turned to Duncan Edwards as their saviour at just 19. That tells you everything about him' – Sir Alex Ferguson

'There is no doubt in my mind that Duncan would have become the greatest player ever. Not just in British football, with United and

England, but the best in the world. George Best was something special, as was Pelé and Maradona, but in my mind, Duncan was much better in terms of all-round ability and skill' – Tommy Docherty, who played against Edwards for Preston and Scotland.

There are so many tributes to Duncan from Sir Bobby Charlton, the player who knew him best, that one could easily fill ten pages but let's end with this encomium:

'Ask me who is the greatest footballer I ever played with. Ask me who is the greatest footballer I ever played against. Same answer: Duncan Edwards. Don't ask me how much greater he would have become. It defies imagination. What's bigger than a colossus? Think about that. Then remember that I played not only with George and Denis but with Bobby Moore. That I played against Pelé. They were truly great, but Duncan was the greatest.'

BUSBY'S TREBLE CHANCE
The 1956/57 Season

In the summer of 1953, as Matt Busby relaxed on the golf course, he reflected on a disappointing season. Since football had resumed after the war, under Busby's management, United had challenged for the top spot; runners-up four times and champions just a year before. After finishing eighth in the season just past, however, it was clear that his team was in decline.

The core of his team were now over 30. Rowley, Pearson, Carey, Cockburn and Chilton had broken into the first team before the war. The signing of Tommy Taylor in the spring for £29,999 had proved to be an instant success, but Busby resisted the temptation to rebuild through the transfer market and Taylor would be the last significant purchase until the arrival of Harry Gregg at the end of 1957.

Busby instead put his faith in youth. The academy would be the wellspring. Busby's lieutenant, Jimmy Murphy, was assisted by Bert Whalley, and Tom Curry looked after the kids. The scouting network was expanded. The club vetted and appointed local landladies to provide homes for the teenagers good enough to sign professional forms. Everything was in place.

Busby could see the youngsters blossom as the youth side won the first of five successive FA Youth Cups in 1953. He always hated the term 'Busby Babes' coined by *Manchester Evening News* reporter Tom Jackson, preferring to call them his 'Golden Apples'. Had schoolboy Matt somehow been taught the judgement of Paris back in the grimy mining village of Orbiston? No doubt about it; he prized his golden apples every bit as much as Aphrodite hers. It was now time to start harvesting the crop.

Against Huddersfield at the end of October and Arsenal the following week, United fielded a team including six players who were aged 21 or under. Duncan Edwards played his second senior game just four weeks after his 17th birthday. In the Charity Shield played in October, David Gaskell (at 16 years and 19 days) was summoned from the terraces to take the injured Ray Wood's place in goal moments before kick-off.

United were improving; they finished fourth in 1953/54 and fifth in a very tight title race the following year. The stream of home-grown talent was now in full flow. Mark Jones, Albert Scanlon and Liam Whelan debuted in 1954/55, Eddie Colman in 1955/56, and Bobby Charlton burst into the side in 1956.

United won the 1955/56 title at a canter, finishing 11 points clear of runners-up Blackpool; they were unbeaten from the end of January, winning nine and drawing four. Their victory was built on youthful energy and skill guided by Busby's principle of entertaining football played the 'United Way'. At the beginning of the season, only captain Roger Byrne and winger Johnny Berry had made more than 100 first-team appearances. The average age of the team was just 22.

They moved up a gear the following season. They started as they had left off, winning ten and drawing two of their first dozen league games. They scored goals for fun: 103 in the league; 25 in the European Cup including a 10–0 thrashing of Anderlecht at Old Trafford; and 15 in the FA Cup. Eye-catching results in the league included a 6–1 win against Newcastle, a 6–2 win over

Arsenal and a 5–1 away win at Charlton. Bobby Charlton took a liking to the Addicks, scoring twice on his debut and a hat-trick in the return fixture at the Valley.

The team was gelling into a formidable unit. Byrne, Foulkes and Jones at the back, Duncan Edwards and crowd favourite Eddie 'Snake Hips' Colman (so called because of his sinuous body swerve) the Little and Large in midfield alongside Jackie Blanchflower, and a dazzling array of attacking talent up front: pick any five from Berry, Pegg, Whelan, Taylor, Viollet, Scanlon, Doherty and Charlton depending on injuries and National Service obligations. Above all, they were a team moulded in Busby's image, bonded by the schooling from Murphy and his coaches into a collective bigger than the sum of its considerable parts.

By the end of March, United were thinking the impossible – a treble of Football League, FA Cup and European Cup. They were five points clear in the league, had just won their FA Cup semi-final against Birmingham, and were looking ahead to a European Cup semi-final against the holders Real Madrid.

The European challenge was undertaken in the teeth of the Football League's bloody-minded opposition whose secretary, Alan Hardaker, wanted nothing to do with foreigners. (His actual words don't bear repeating.) Busby, an admirer of the great Hungarian side of the 1950s and an enthusiast for the progressive style of European football, defied the Football League and petitioned Stanley Rous at the FA to grant permission to take part in the European Cup.

The tournament caught the public's imagination: 70,000 spectators saw United overcome Athletic Bilbao at Maine Road to set up the semi-final clash against mighty Madrid. Outkicked and outclassed by the streetwise Spaniards at the Bernabéu, United put up tougher resistance in the return, holding Di Stefano's team to a two-all draw under the newly installed floodlights. Defeat to *Los Blancos* was no disgrace, and it was a valuable lesson in the Babes' education. Next year they'd be stronger.

The treble may have gone, but the double was still on. By Easter the title was won; now only Aston Villa stood in their way. United had had the better of Villa in the league, taking three points of a possible four.

The final is remembered for one horrific, game-changing incident that took place after six minutes when Peter McParland's head collided with Ray Wood's cheekbone – or a blatant head butt in the eyes of Bill Foulkes and anyone who has seen the YouTube footage. The United keeper was knocked unconscious, and he was stretchered off, his place in goal taken by Jackie Blanchflower. Wood bravely returned to the pitch as an outfield player after treatment but, understandably, took little part in the game. The Villa(i)n, who would have been shown a red card by a modern-day referee, was not even cautioned, and he rubbed salt into the wounds by scoring two second-half goals. Tommy Taylor's late strike was little consolation as Villa ran out 2–1 winners.

Despite the disappointment, Busby had seen his team grow in maturity and stature; he could reflect on a season of progress and look forward to the next season with optimism. He was not to know that the season past was as close as United would come to a historic treble for 43 years and marked the high point of the Busby Babes. They had captured the imagination of fans not just in Manchester but all over England. Fans could only wonder how much higher they might have gone, how many more milestones they might have passed, when fate ripped the heart out of their young team at Munich airport just nine months later.

'THE GREATEST GAME EVER SEEN'
Arsenal 4 Manchester United 5
1 FEBRUARY 1958

By the beginning of 1958, Arsenal, league champions in 1948/49 and 1952/53, had seen a drop in standards but still retained an aura from the 1930s heyday of the great Herbert Chapman side. A league match against defending champions Manchester United was bound to draw a crowd, and 63,578 – Arsenal's biggest of the season – turned up at Highbury to enjoy a thrilling encounter.

United had won the title in the two previous seasons but now trailed in third place behind Wolves and Preston. But, still in the FA Cup and ahead in their European Cup quarter-final tie against Red Star Belgrade, they were moving through the gears; a win in their home fixture against Wolves the following week would cut their league deficit to three points. But first they had to beat the Gunners.

The game was a classic. United were scintillating in the first half, sweeping 'the field with movements based on precision passing and Scanlon at outside-left showing how he keeps the international David Pegg out of the Manchester team', gushed the *Sunday Times*. They scored three times without reply through Edwards, Charlton – tubby and with his socks round his ankles according to the *Daily Express* – and, following a 70-yard burst down the wing by Albert Scanlon, Tommy Taylor, who was 'the old England brand I once admired', according to the same reporter.

The match and the home crowd really came to life on the hour mark. In the space of three minutes Arsenal shattered United's complacency and pulled themselves back into contention with goals from David Herd, a United legend himself in later years, and a brace from Jimmy Bloomfield. The crowd thundered like a turbulent sea according to the *Times* report. United responded like true champions or, as the *Express* man had it: 'Those annoying experts from Manchester did the well-known switch from take it easy to get cracking.' In five short minutes, goals by Viollet, fed by Charlton, and Taylor from an acute angle gave United a 5–3 advantage. The home side pulled one back but United won the day.

The *Times* reporter admired the way United showed their mettle to restore their lead and praised their all-out attacking style: 'It matches the Hungarian outlook of four years ago [referring to the great side that humbled England at Wembley]. If you score three, four or five, we will score four, five or six.'

Standing at the Clock End that afternoon was the 15-year-old Terry Venables. He'd persuaded his father to take him along to see the team that had made headlines by thumping Bolton 7–2 the previous month. In particular he wanted to watch Duncan Edwards. 'It was a day I will never forget,' he later recalled. 'I couldn't take my eyes off Duncan. There were nine goals in a fantastic match, but it was Duncan I really remember.'

What makes this match so bittersweet is that it was the last time that great side played on English soil and they went out winning what was later described by the Arsenal match day programme as the 'Greatest Game Ever Seen'. It was the final flourish of the Busby Babes, who were maturing into one of the greatest teams ever to play the game. The same 11 players who took the field that day would be on the plane that crashed at the end of the Munich airport runway. Of the starting line-up, only Charlton, Viollet, Foulkes and Gregg would play again.

REMEMBERING MUNICH

Anyone visiting the Old Trafford ground will be reminded of the Munich air disaster through the memorials: the clock at the south-east stand, the Munich tunnel and the plaques.

This is not the place to go over the horrific details of the crash itself. But it is worth remembering the names of the dead and seriously injured who were on BEA flight 609 on that cold Bavarian winter afternoon, on 6 February 1958. Of the 44 passengers and crew on board, 23 died as a result of the crash, including eight journalists (one of whom, Frank Swift, was a former Manchester City and England goalkeeper) and supporter Willie Satinoff, a friend of Matt Busby who was due to join the club's board of directors.

From the Manchester United contingent eight players and three staff members were lost.

Players
Geoff Bent, full-back, aged 25
Roger Byrne, club captain, 28
Eddie Colman, wing-half, 21
Duncan Edwards, left-half, 21
Mark Jones, centre-half, 24
David Pegg, outside-left, 22
Tommy Taylor, centre-forward, 26
Billy Whelan, inside-forward, 22

Staff

Walter Crickmer, club secretary 1926 to 1958 and acting manager 1931/32 and 1937 to 1945, aged 57

Tom Curry, club trainer, 63

Bert Whalley, chief coach, 44

United survivors

Johnny Berry, 31, suffered terrible injuries and never played again.

Jackie Blanchflower, 24, like Berry, suffered serious injuries and never played again.

Bobby Charlton, 20, was hauled unconscious from the plane by goalkeeper Harry Gregg and was able to return to the team on 1 March, but sought medical advice after suffering survivor's guilt. He continued playing for United until May 1973.

Bill Foulkes, 26, sustained a mild head injury during the crash but struggled in later years, losing weight and being unable to sleep. He played in United's next match and remained at the club until retiring from playing in 1969. He said in an interview in 1988: 'There were three tremendous sickening thuds and everything was spinning around. A second later, I was sitting in my seat in the snow.'

Harry Gregg, 25, was often commended as the 'Hero of Munich', having pulled several passengers from the burning aircraft. He was the only other survivor able to play in United's next game; he remained at the club until 1967.

Kenny Morgans, just 18 at the time, was the last survivor to be found in the wreckage by journalists, five hours after the official search had been abandoned. His form never fully recovered and he left to join Swansea in 1961.

Albert Scanlon, 22, suffered serious injuries but recovered in time for the start of the 1958/59 season. He moved to Newcastle United in November 1960.

Dennis Viollet, 24, suffered head injuries but returned to the team for the 1958 FA Cup final. He joined Stoke City in January 1962.

Ray Wood, 26, suffered minor injuries. He joined Huddersfield Town in December 1958.

Matt Busby, 50, was so gravely injured that he was twice given the last rites. He spent two months in hospital and in recuperation in Switzerland, and almost left his job such was the guilt he felt. But he rebuilt the team and remained at the club, serving as club director and president.

The aftermath

A legal action brought by Manchester United Football Club against British European Airways was settled out of court for an undisclosed amount.

The German authorities' case against the plane's captain, James Thain, was finally dropped in 1968. He was cleared of any blame, after it was ruled that the crash was caused by slush on the runway.

A fund for dependents of the crash victims was set up in March 1958 by the Football Association and disbursed £52,000 in October of that year.

Real Madrid

Real Madrid's chairman Santiago Bernabéu was greatly moved by the disaster. He had enormous respect for the Manchester club after their epic European Cup semi-final tie the previous year, and he wanted to help. He made the generous offer to lend United the services of their talisman Alfredo Di Stéfano for the remainder of the season, only for the gesture to be blocked by the obdurate

Alan Hardaker at the FA. Bernabéu also suggested offering a free pass into the following season's European Cup only to fall foul of Hardaker again. But Real Madrid were able to help financially by organising a number of friendly games against United over the following four years.

The Manchester memorials

The team somehow picked themselves up under the guidance of Jimmy Murphy, who only missed the tie against Belgrade due to his international duties with the Welsh national team, and they played their way to the FA Cup final in May. The matchday shirt bore a symbolic memorial, the badge embroidered with a phoenix rather than the Manchester coat of arms worn the previous year.

The first official memorial at Old Trafford to the lost players and staff was unveiled on 25 February 1960. A plaque in the shape of the stadium with the image of a green pitch inscribed with the names of the victims was placed above the entrance to the directors' box. (The plaque has since been replaced and redesigned twice following stadium alterations.)

The second was a memorial to the members of the press who died at Munich, which consisted of a bronze plaque that named the eight journalists. The original plaque was stolen in the 1980s and replaced by a replica which is now behind the counter in the press entrance. The most public memorial is the Munich clock, a simple two-faced clock paid for by the Ground Committee and attached to the south-east corner of the stadium, with the date '6 Feb 1958' at the top of both faces and 'Munich' at the bottom. The clock has remained in situ since it was first installed.

And a memorial to supporter William Satinoff sits above the door to the offices of MUST (Manchester United Supporters Trust) on Sir Matt Busby Way.

The Munich memorials

In Munich, a plaque mounted on a simple plinth stands in Machesterplatz, a street near the old airport renamed in honour of the fallen. On the 62nd anniversary of the disaster Bayern Munich's chairman Karl-Heinz Rummenigge laid the foundation stone for a commemorative display case at the crash site.

The club's first testimonial in aid of the victims and survivors took place at Old Trafford in August 1998. Eric Cantona came out of retirement to play in his Europe XI select against United. In the match programme, Cantona wrote: 'As everybody knows, 1998 celebrates a sad anniversary in the club's history. Of course, I immediately agreed when Manchester United asked me to give the whole benefit of the game to the families of the victims of the February 6, 1958 tragedy.'

The 50th anniversary fell four days before the derby fixture against Manchester City. The game kicked off at 3.04 p.m. precisely, and the teams lined up in 1950s replica kit, without sponsors' logos as a token of respect.

To mark the same anniversary, the old players' tunnel, which is now flanked by the home and away team technical areas, and the only surviving part of the original stadium, was renamed the Munich Tunnel. A plaque of remembrance was unveiled by chief executive David Gill and Roger Byrne, and the tunnel now includes an exhibition about the disaster and its victims.

Every year, two annual events are organised by Munich 58. They are held beneath the memorial plaque on 6 February and before the home game nearest that date. These occasions attract large crowds of fans, honour the victims through the observance of a minute's silence and feature readings, prayers and songs, including 'Flowers of Manchester', the lyrics of which were written shortly after the crash by Eric Winter.

WHAT'S IN A NAME?
The Origin of the Red Devils

Football clubs around England have, for one reason or another, acquired nicknames which fans and journalists like to associate with them. Some are boringly obvious, like the Blues or Reds or City; others are anthropomorphic identities such as Magpies, Wolves or Canaries; some relate to the location: the Cod Army was an obvious one for Fleetwood Town, and the Sheffielders gave their team the Owls due to the ground's proximity to Olwerton (no, not Owlerton); there are also acknowledgements to past occupational associations – the Gunners comes from Arsenal's roots at the Royal Arsenal at Woolwich, the Hammers from the Thames Iron Works; and then there are the unfortunate ones such as the Cobblers (Northampton Town) and the Wombles (yes, Wimbledon).

There are some very peculiar ones. The Monkey Hangers of Hartlepool harks back to an episode in the Napoleonic Wars when locals hanged a monkey fearing it was a French spy. Charlton are known as the Addicks – their ground in south London was close to a well-known fish and chip shop and that's the way they like to pronounce the word 'haddock' in that neck of the woods. There are the more pious examples of the Saints in Southampton and the Pilgrims of Plymouth, which offer a stark contrast to the Heathens of Newton Heath where the provenance is not hard to guess and the more demonic Red Devils, a name by which Manchester United are known and the image of which adorns the club's logo and playing shirts.

For most of the 20th century United were known commonly as the Reds – due to their famous red shirt – or simply United. So far, so unsurprising, but how did United also come by the name the Red Devils?

In the 1950s, as Matt Busby introduced more and more players from United's youth team into his starting XI, they became widely known as the Busby Babes. Matt hated the name – in his opinion, far too cute a label in the manly world of football. Would the Cloggers of yesteryear feel overly concerned by opponents that sounded as cuddly as bushbabies? Matt preferred to call his young charges the Golden Apples, but that was never going to catch on. Footballing nicknames encompass birds, predators and insects, yes, but Bournemouth (the Cherries) apart, never fruit.

Following the trauma of Munich, the term 'Busby Babes' would only ever be used in a memorial or historical sense. Early in the new decade, Busby thought his new side needed a new name. He took inspiration from neighbouring rugby league club Salford. The red-shirted team were hailed by French journalists as '*les diables rouges*' after touring there in the 1930s. Busby declared publicly that Manchester United should also be known as the 'Red Devils', a name befitting the powerful, attacking group of players he was assembling. The name caught on. Soon the club began incorporating the devil logo into match programmes and scarves, and, in 1970, the club adopted the red devil below the ship on the club's crest, replacing the traditional red field with black stripes.

Back in the day, shirts were simple: plain red with perhaps a white collar. From the flamboyant 1970s on, shirt design became much more elaborate, and, in 1972, the club crest made its first appearance. Over the years, the crest has changed colour, typography and content – the words 'football club' disappeared – but the impish figure with the trident remained. The devil is always in the detail.

In the commercialised world of Premier League football, where clubs are reaching out to young supporters and encouraging a family-friendly image, club mascots are de rigueur. Outsized, ridiculous and frequently over-familiar, they provide pre-match entertainment and make themselves available for selfies with small children. So, while United chose as their mascot a devil in an XS first team strip, they wisely decided against giving him the shirt number 666, or indeed 17, but opted, for reasons unknown, for 55, and gave him a happy smile and the unthreatening name of Fred. And the name above the number on the back of the shirt? Rather than 'Fred the Red Devil', they plumped for plain, old-fashioned 'Fred the Red'.

HARRY GREGG, HISTORY MAN

Tobermore is a small, quiet village in the middle of Ulster. Not much happens there, or ever did, and few heroes hail from that part of County Londonderry. But one such is Harry Gregg, who in the space of three short months was at the centre of three historic events.

Gregg left Northern Ireland to play for his hero, Peter Doherty, then in charge of Second Division Doncaster Rovers. Gregg was a class act in goal and, aged 21, he received a call-up for the Northern Ireland international side. On 6 November 1957, in a team boasting the talents of Jimmy McIlroy, Billy Bingham and the Blanchflower brothers, Gregg starred in a historic win at Wembley, Northern Ireland's first on English soil since 1914 and only their second ever.

Busby had been on the lookout for a new keeper to replace Ray Wood, whose confidence had taken a knock after the horrific injury he suffered in the 1957 FA Cup final. Such was Gregg's ability that Busby was prepared to make history by breaking the world record transfer fee for a goalkeeper to bring him to Old Trafford, paying Rovers £23,500. Busby showed typical shrewdness in organising Gregg's arrival in Manchester, meeting him at Victoria station with his wife Jean and Harry's schoolboy international friend, Jackie Blanchflower, to welcome him into the United family.

The United fans took to him straight away. His physical presence and command of the penalty area, big hands and shot-stopping made him an instant star. Only 25, he could look forward to a decade of glory and honours playing with the Busby Babes. By the beginning of February, United were hot on the heels of league leaders Wolves, into the fifth round of the FA Cup and playing in the quarter-finals of the European Cup.

On 5 February, all seemed to be going to plan. In a hard-fought second leg against Red Star Belgrade, United secured the result they needed to progress to the semi-finals. Gregg was still getting acquainted with his teammates and, as fate would have it, with some he would never get the chance to know better.

The next day, the charter flight to Manchester, having stopped over at Munich, made its doomed third attempt to take off from the runway and suffered its fateful crash. 'I could feel the blood coming down my face and I didn't dare put my hand up,' he recalled as he came to. As his senses returned, he saw, just above him, light shining into the cabin, and Gregg kicked the hole wide enough for him to escape. A crew member, fearing the plane was about to burst into flames, shouted to Gregg to flee, but he considered the scene and shouted back, 'There are people alive in there!'

Returning to the wreckage, he first hauled out a young pregnant woman, Vera Lukic, and her 20-month-old daughter Vesna, then returned for Bobby Charlton and Dennis Viollet. Back in he went to find his friend Jackie Blanchflower. Blanchflower's arm was bleeding badly and Gregg used his tie as a tourniquet.

Gregg was uncomfortable with his hero status. Instead, this warm-hearted, courageous young man was scarred by the crash. Some said he'd vowed never to smile in public in case a newspaper cameraman caught him and printed the image. Although he had suffered head injuries – indeed he suffered from headaches for years afterwards – he was back at work 13 days after the crash, keeping goal in the sixth round FA Cup tie against Sheffield Wednesday.

Cruelly for Gregg, he never won any medals with United. Although they fought their way to Wembley three months after the crash, they lost to Bolton Wanderers. Gregg missed the 1963 triumph as an injury lay-off had given possession of the goalkeeper's jersey to David Gaskell. Injuries prevented him from playing enough games to qualify for a winners' medal in 1964/65 and he left the club midway through the 1966/67 season. In January 1962, he suffered the loss of his first wife, Mavis, to cancer.

His playing ability was recognised at the 1958 World Cup where he was voted the best goalkeeper of the tournament. During the trip his captain Danny Blanchflower said to him, 'Harry, you don't have to fight people any more . . . you have a crown on your head, you are the best.'

If the fates had been harsh, history has been kinder to Gregg's memory. Although he didn't wish it, Gregg was defined by the events of 6 February 1958. In the foreword to Gregg's autobiography, *Harry's Game*, George Best wrote: 'Harry, you are my hero – and I mean that.' And, of Munich, perhaps George's thoughtful words afford the best description of his fellow Ulsterman: 'What Harry did that night was more than just bravery. It was about goodness.'

JIMMY MURPHY, FIRST AIDE

Assistant managers do not lead a charmed life. Their jobs are at the mercy of managers, and they are often collateral damage of managerial sackings, or they are lured, for better or worse, by other clubs offering the status and salary of the top job on condition they leave their comfort zones and previous loyalties far behind. Sir Alex Ferguson lost Archie Knox – previously joined at the hip to his fellow Scot – to Rangers, Brian Kidd to Blackburn, Steve McClaren to Middlesbrough and Carlos Queiroz twice, once to Real Madrid and later to the Portuguese national side.

In the past half-century, United have had 12 assistant managers; in the previous quarter of a century, they had one. Although the position wasn't formalised until 1955, Jimmy Murphy was Busby's right-hand man from day one. In fact, the Welshman was Busby's first appointment on becoming United's manager. Busby later remarked: 'Jimmy and I worked together to bring greatness to Manchester United. He was my first and most important signing.'

The two met in Italy in the spring of 1945 when Busby chanced upon Murphy taking a training session and listened as he gave the assembled NCOs his thoughts on how football should be played. A natural orator, the Welshman's fierce passion for the game made an impression. Murphy was offered the assistant's job, looking after the reserves at the weekend and helping Busby with the first-team training during the week. Murphy didn't hesitate – and he would prove to be a perfect foil to Busby.

Busby had the vision for attacking football and the development of the youth system, but much of the implementation of his ideas on the training ground was left to Murphy and the coaching team. He and Busby would organise games with the youth team in the gravel car park behind the old Pop Stand, and Murphy – who earned the nickname 'Tapper' during his playing days – would put in a few strong tackles to harden them up and give them a taste of the senior game.

Absent on international duty as manager of Wales in February 1958, Murphy missed the trip to Bucharest and the subsequent disaster at Munich that took so many lives. Murphy hurried to the city to assess the situation and take charge of repatriating the bodies. Desolate, he was found sobbing uncontrollably on a back stair by Harry Gregg. It might have been the loss of friends, the ruination of the Babes or even survivor's guilt, but Murphy must have felt very alone and was clearly distraught.

With Busby critically ill in the Rechts der Isar hospital, it fell upon Murphy to lead United in their darkest hour. In the days after the tragedy, Murphy said: 'The Red Devils will rise again. It took Matt Busby, Bert Whalley and myself 13 years to produce the 1958 Red Devils. It was long, tiring, hard work. But we succeeded. We reached a perfect system. We had the best set-up in football.

'It will again be a long, tiring job to rebuild the Red Devils. This time we have to start practically from scratch. But we'll do it. But this I do know. United was and will again be a great club. We have the greatest club spirit in the world.

'Matt, I pray, will soon be back. Soon the world-famous partnership of Busby and Murphy will be reunited. Soon we will be working together again for the greatest club in the world.

'We have done it once. We will do it again in tribute to those wonderful Red Devils who tragically are no longer with us.'

It would take ten long years, but Murphy and Busby succeeded in rebuilding United and claiming the European Cup so cruelly denied to the Babes.

In Martin Edwards' words: 'Jimmy was an absolute giant. Without Jimmy we may well have sunk.' Throughout the months of Busby's recuperation, Murphy, now acting manager, had to keep the show on the road. He scrambled to put together a team from a couple of signings, the reserves, Gregg, Foulkes and, after a few weeks, Bobby Charlton. The weakened team did well to reach the FA Cup final at Wembley where Murphy proudly led out the patched-up XI to face Bolton. In the European Cup semi-final, a valiant win at Old Trafford was overturned in the San Siro by Inter Milan.

Impressed by the manner with which he had dealt with grievous adversity and his success at guiding Wales to a World Cup quarter-final in Sweden, Murphy was offered the managerial position at Arsenal as well as Juventus and Brazil. Murphy stayed loyal to the club and the number two he had served for 13 years, and would continue to do so for a further 13 as second-in-command.

Following Busby's retirement, he acted as a scout when the assistant's role was handed first to Malcom Musgrove and then to Paddy Crerand. Even at the end of his time at Old Trafford he still had an eye for young talent, spotting the wingers Gordon Hill and Steve Coppell, who did so much to revitalise Tommy Docherty's team.

Despite his long service, United weren't particularly generous to Murphy (nor anyone else in the pre-Premier League era for that matter). The club cancelled Murphy's taxi account, which made life difficult for someone who had never passed a driving test, leaving him no option but to take public transport on scouting missions.

However, the year after his death in 1989, the club honoured Murphy's memory by renaming the Young Player of the Year Award: the Jimmy Murphy Award is a fitting tribute to a man who had done so much to bring young players through the academy.

In the summer of 2021, following a proposal presented to the club by a coalition of United supporters' groups led by the Manchester Munich Memorial Foundation, the club agreed that plans should be developed to erect a statue at the rear of the Stretford End in lasting tribute to Murphy.

IT TAKES TWO (OR MORE)
Goal-scoring Partnerships

Often sides have to be content with a lone prolific goal scorer leading the line. For Newton Heath it was Joe Cassidy in the 1890s; United had Joe Spence in the 1920s, George Best in the late 1960s and early 1970s, and Zlatan Ibrahimović in 2016/17 scoring the lion's share of goals. When the efforts of front men such as Brian McClair or Mark Hughes in the 1980s could be supplemented from midfield by the likes of the prolific Bryan Robson – even better. But the great sides, ones that win titles, usually have a deadly strike partnership – usually they come in twos, but threes and even fours are not unheard of.

Sandy Turnbull and Enoch West

United enjoyed their first period of success in the years leading up to the outbreak of the First World War. Ernest Mangnall's side won their first title in 1907/08, greatly assisted by 25 goals from the Manchester City escapee Sandy Turnbull, who along with Billy Meredith and others had left on free transfers after the illegal payments scandal of 1906. The Scot formed an effective partnership with Enoch West aka 'Knocker', who signed from Nottingham Forest in the summer of 1910. In their first season together, the pair banged in 39 goals – with Harold Halse chipping in a handy 11 – on the way to United's second title. The following season, between the three strikers they managed a bigger haul of 52 – the only problem being that the rest of the United squad could only bag 14.

Jack Rowley and Stan Pearson

Trophies eluded United in the inter-war period, and by the late 1930s the club decided to put their faith in youth to improve their fortunes. Jack Rowley signed as a 17-year-old from Bournemouth in November 1937, while Stan Pearson, a year older, had joined the club's ground staff in 1936. Both would enjoy stellar careers after the war. In the seven seasons following the resumption of the Football League, the pair racked up an incredible 312 goals in all competitions, helping United to four runners-up spots and eventually the title in 1951/52. They also starred in the famous 1948 FA Cup final – both Rowley and Pearson were on the scoresheet – helping to secure the club's first major trophy in 37 years.

Tommy Taylor and Dennis Viollet

As Rowley and Pearson entered the twilight years of their careers, two young bucks made their first-team debuts. In March 1953, Tommy Taylor signed from Barnsley for a pound less than £30,000 and Dennis Viollet made his entrance the following month, scoring on his home debut.

Taylor was the archetypal number 9: pacey, powerful, good in the air. Viollet was a slimmer model: a clever, ball-playing number 10 with good positional sense inside and out of the penalty area.

They were both key members of the Busby Babes that swept all before them in the English game. In the five years before the Munich disaster, they managed 223 goals as a strike partnership. In the championship-winning side of 1956/57 their combined total was 60, and they even managed 45 in the following season before tragedy struck.

David Herd and Denis Law

Tommy Taylor was one of the fatalities of the crash, and with Viollet leaving in 1962 after an argument about wages, Busby needed new weapons in attack. He had already bought David Herd from Arsenal in 1961 before making his best-ever move in the transfer market by bringing Denis Law from Torino to Old Trafford in the summer of 1962 for a British record fee of £115,000.

In their first season together, in a side struggling in the league, the Herd/Law combination still managed to net 50 times. The underrated Herd was a fast, muscular number 9 with a ferocious shot, while the livewire Law was fearless and deadly in the penalty box – 'an electric eel' in the words of Gordon Banks. They made their mark in the FA Cup final of 1963 when Herd (scoring two) and Law put Leicester City to the sword.

The strike force, and United, flourished as they struck a combined total of 280 goals in five golden seasons – with a mighty haul of 67 in 1964/65 when the Reds pipped Leeds for the title. A broken leg in March 1967 effectively ended Herd's Old Trafford career.

With Herd's departure and Law's increasing absences through injury, United's front line lost some of its menace, leaving George Best to do most of the heavy lifting. The next title would be a long time coming.

Mark Hughes, Eric Cantona and the first double

In his second spell at United, Mark Hughes' link-up with Brian McClair promised much but fizzled out when the Scot moved back into a midfield role. It wasn't until the 1993/94 season, when Sparky teamed up with Eric Cantona, that United found the magic formula. Scoring 47 goals in 70 appearances between them, the pair rounded off a glorious season by scoring three of United's four goals in the FA Cup final and, fittingly, McClair got the last one to complete United's first double.

The partnership didn't last. Andy Cole's transfer from Newcastle for a British record fee of £7 million in January 1995 put Hughes lower down the pecking order and he duly left to join Chelsea at the end of the season.

Dwight Yorke and Andy Cole

Andy Cole had a difficult start to his United career. Any chance of forming a partnership with Cantona was thwarted by the Frenchman's post-kung fu suspension, and then there were his own injury problems, before the Frenchman said adieu after the 1997 FA Cup final.

Following the emergence of Wenger's new-look Arsenal, Alex Ferguson knew he had to strengthen his forward line. In the summer of 1998, he bought Dwight Yorke from Aston Villa. It was a slow burn, but then the partnership clicked. Gary Neville singled out the game away to Leicester when Yorke scored a hat-trick and Cole a double in a 6–2 rout. This was a turning point. They began to socialise together, and neither minded who scored.

In that glorious 1998/99 season, the pair helped themselves to 53 goals and also helped United to clinch a glorious treble. The following year saw them rattle in a further 43 goals, but the manager found it hard to ignore the claims of the back-up strikers, Ole Gunnar Solskjær and Teddy Sheringham – the guys who had come off the bench at the Camp Nou to win the European Cup.

The Three Rs and an Argentine

United enjoyed more success with their quartet of strikers, but the competition from Arsenal's 'Invincibles' and newly rich Chelsea was hotting up. Sir Alex's response was to pair up the goal machine Ruud van Nistelrooy with the teenage sensation Wayne Rooney signed from Everton in 2004 for a cool £27 million.

The two formed a good partnership, which developed apace with the growing maturity of the young Portuguese winger, Cristiano Ronaldo. By 2006, the Three Rs were menacing opposition defences, scoring 55 goals between them. But despite the potency of this forward line, the Dutchman was unhappy at Old Trafford. Unconvinced that the 20-year-old Rooney and 21-year-old Ronaldo were mature enough to win the biggest prizes, he engineered a move away to Real Madrid.

Ferguson had tried to argue that the pair would come good but came to realise that van Nistelrooy's abrasiveness was bad for team spirit. The following season, both Rooney and Ronaldo increased their tallies to 23 apiece, and 2007/08 would see Ferguson's faith in them totally vindicated. Ronaldo scored 41 times, and Rooney chipped in with a tidy 18, but the second-biggest contribution came from loan-signing Carlos Tévez with 19. Often used as an impact player, the tough, combative Argentine was a fan favourite.

Despite fans imploring, 'Fergie, Fergie, sign him up,' United weren't prepared to meet the Argentine's contractual demands, and Tévez moved to Manchester City, while Ronaldo made his dream move to Real Madrid in the summer transfer window. Although there would be more glory to follow for United, the departure of Tévez and, especially, Ronaldo signalled the beginning of the end of the great Ferguson era as momentum slowly shifted to the Etihad in the Premier League and to Spain in Europe.

THE KING OF THE STRETFORD END
Denis Law

The skinny kid from Aberdeen started his football career at Huddersfield Town as a teenager, prospered under the guidance of the Terriers manager Bill Shankly, and soon the big clubs were queueing up to sign him. Matt Busby, who in his capacity as manager of the Scotland team awarded Law his first international cap in 1958, offered £10,000; Shankly tried to buy him when he took the managerial reins at Liverpool but couldn't afford the British record fee of £55,000, and Law moved instead to Maine Road.

More transfer records followed as Law joined Torino for an unhappy season before he engineered a move back to England. Busby finally snared the striker for £115,000 in July 1962. The signing was an important step on the road to recovery after Munich.

Law was a born goal scorer. Fast, skilful and brave, he could score with either foot and was majestic in the air. And although he loved dropping deep for the ball and dribbling past opponents, he truly came alive in the penalty box, possessing a sixth sense for a scoring chance. In short, he was the all-round striker. He could be spiky, but he played with a smile and the fans adored him.

He quickly formed a striking partnership with fellow Scot David Herd, the pair combining to score United's three goals in the 1963 FA Cup final win over Leicester – United's first silverware since the Busby Babes era. It was not a one-off, merely the appetiser for the feast to follow.

From the FA Cup win to the return to Wembley to win their first European Cup five years later, United rode the crest of a wave. In a golden age for English football with fierce competition from their great rivals Liverpool, Everton, Spurs, Chelsea, Leeds and Manchester City, United won the league twice, were runners-up twice and, of course, became the first English team to win the European Cup. In those five glorious years, Denis Law was a scoring machine. In 1963/64, he scored 46 goals in 42 appearances; the following season he won the coveted Ballon d'Or and was the league's top scorer when United won their first title since Munich in 1965.

His partnership with Herd was special, but his chemistry with Bobby Charlton and George Best, the two other parts of the United Trinity, was electric. In those magical years in the mid-1960s, which coincided with the arrival of BBC's *Match of the Day*, United became the nation's team. Fans from all over England would flock to Old Trafford to get a chance to see the Red Devils in all their attacking glory and thrill to the sight of Law scoring, celebrating with his arm high, clutching the sleeve of his shirt with a solitary finger pointing to the sky. For the fans standing in the Stretford End, Denis was 'The King'. Their affection for him is embodied by the statue, unveiled in 2002, that graces the Stretford End concourse.

But injuries took their toll on the Lawman. Troubled by dodgy knees since his Huddersfield years, a botched cartilage operation was never properly repaired, and Law was forced to play on with the help of cortisone injections. He missed the European Cup final and most of the 1969/70 season through injury and, by then a shadow of his former self, he was put on the transfer list by new manager Frank O'Farrell. There were no takers.

United had entered a period of steep decline following Busby's retirement. O'Farrell's time at the helm came to an end in December 1972, and it was Law who recommended Tommy Docherty to United as the man to revive the club. In his brief spell as the national coach, the Doc had previously restored Law to the Scotland team and Law trusted him. Big mistake.

Docherty, anxious to clear out the old order, misled the board into thinking Law had requested a transfer and showed him the door. Only learning of his move back to Maine Road on television, Law was deprived of the testimonial he richly deserved, and needed, as one who earned a meagre £200 per week.

There was to be a sting in this 'tale', one that would wound Docherty. The King, wearing a sky-blue shirt, would return to Old Trafford one last time, in April 1974, to deliver the *coup de grace* to United's 36-year spell in the First Division.

A KNIGHT TO REMEMBER
Sir Bobby Charlton

In the pantheon of United legends, there are only a handful of greats whose association with the club spanned five decades: Walter Crickmer, Louis Rocca and Sir Bobby Charlton.

Charlton, who came from a North East footballing family – his mother's cousin was the Newcastle United star Jackie Milburn – joined United as a trainee straight after school. He grew up with the Busby Babes, playing alongside Duncan Edwards, and made his debut against, as chance would have it, Charlton. It was an auspicious start for the 18-year-old. He scored twice on his debut on 6 October 1956 and a hat-trick in the return fixture at the Valley four months later.

Although not yet a regular in the side, Charlton was a rising star and was picked for the second leg of the European Cup quarter-final against Red Star Belgrade in February 1958, scoring twice in the 3–3 draw that saw United through to the semis. He was fortunate to survive the crash at Munich airport on the return to Manchester. On the third attempt at take-off, he and fellow survivor Dennis Viollet swapped seats with David Pegg and Tommy Taylor, who thought it would be safer to sit at the rear of the plane. Charlton and Viollet were thrown clear of the wreckage, rendered unconscious, and it was Harry Gregg who, initially taking them for dead, nevertheless hauled them both to safety.

First to leave the Munich hospital, having suffered cuts to the head and in shock, Charlton recuperated at his parents' home in Ashington, coming to terms with the disaster and the loss of his friends, and at times doubting whether he could face playing again.

But he did come back. Resolved to help restore United's fortunes, he now became a key plank in the slow rebuilding process. He top-scored in the 1958/59 and 1960/61 seasons, and never really stopped scoring, amassing a total of 249 goals in his long United career. But he was more than just a goal scorer. In his early career, Busby would play him on the left wing or at inside-left in the old 2-3-5 system – his versatility was such that he could play in any position. His style combined athleticism, pace, incredible stamina, a superb range of passing and a thunderous shot off either foot – his long-range shots were the stuff of legend. Once the other two parts of the United Trinity were in place, Charlton became an attacking midfielder with a free role – some have described him as an early example of a false number 9. Playing scintillating football, with Charlton as its fulcrum, United won the 1965 and 1967 league titles.

He may have worn the number 9 on his shirt, but there was nothing false about the man. Regarded as one of the true gentlemen of the sport, Charlton only ever received two bookings in his 913 appearances for club and country: one as a result of a misunderstanding over a free kick, the other when trying to act as a peacemaker during the infamous brouhaha in the World Cup quarter-final against Argentina in 1966.

That World Cup saw Charlton achieve wider fame. He was the best player of the tournament, and his two goals against Eusebio's Portugal took England to the final. He received the Ballon d'Or that year and he was also voted the Football Writers' Player of the Year. He was the most recognised Englishman on the planet.

Back at Wembley two years later, Charlton enjoyed his greatest night. Captaining the side in the European Cup final, he scored twice – the first, a rare header – in the 4–1 victory against Benfica. Ten years after the Busby Babes' European campaign had ended in tragedy, Charlton, Foulkes and Busby had found redemption. Munich was a day they could never forget, but this was a night to remember.

Bobby's career went into a gentle decline. He was still England's finest player, and his withdrawal in the 1970 quarter-final against West Germany to conserve his energy for the semi led to his marker Franz Beckenbauer being set free to engineer England's defeat. He remained United's captain until his retirement in 1973; his tally of seven goals in that final season made him United's top scorer once again, but it was also a sad reflection of their decline. At least he was spared the humiliation of relegation that followed a year later.

His honours and achievements are legion. An OBE in 1969 and a CBE in 1974 were followed by a knighthood in 1994. His 249 goals for club and 49 goals for country were records only surpassed by Wayne Rooney in recent times; his record of 749 appearances for United was only eclipsed by Ryan Giggs in 2008. His inclusion in four World Cup squads remains a record.

From 1984, upon the retirement of Matt Busby from the United board, Bobby Charlton became a director of the club. He was influential in the decision to appoint Alex Ferguson as Ron Atkinson's replacement in 1986 and offered Ferguson support through the difficult early years. More than anything, he has been a symbol of continuity through changes in the club's ownership and football itself during the Premier League revolution, standing for decency and the values of the 'United way'.

He was delighted to be granted the freedom of the city of Manchester in 2009. After previously promoting the city's bid for the Commonwealth Games in 2002, the acceptable face of football was also enlisted to help London's successful bid for the 2012 Olympics – such was the respect and affection in which this modest and virtuous figure was held.

His contribution to the history of the club was marked in 2008 with the unveiling of a statue of the United Trinity in front of Old Trafford and then in 2016 when the South Stand was renamed in his honour. A fitting tribute to a long-serving legend who has stood the test of time.

SPRINGWATCH
The 1964/65 Title Race

Chris Packham was only four at the time, too young to have enjoyed the ecology of English football and the primordial battle that was taking place for superiority amongst England's top four sides.

The old order had been shaken up in the early 1960s. The newly promoted sides Liverpool (1962/63), Chelsea (1963/64) and Leeds United (hereafter referred to as simply Leeds), back in the top flight for the 1964/65 season, were challenging for all the major prizes. The previous season, Busby's side had finished runners-up to Shankly's Liverpool, but now two young teams with managers in their 30s were threatening the older alpha males.

As winter turned to spring in 1965, Chelsea had already claimed the League Cup (although it should be said that Busby didn't field a team in the competition), and on 22 March the Blues led the table on goal average from Leeds in second and United a further point behind. Since the turn of the year, United – with Best in his first full season with Law and Charlton – had enjoyed a good run in both the league and cup, enjoying a confidence-boosting 4–0 win against Chelsea just nine days before.

After a long campaign, the run of fixtures to the end of the season looked daunting. Over the next five weeks, United were due to play seven league games and an FA Cup semi-final against Leeds. The other semi featured Chelsea against league champions

Liverpool. The permutations for prize-giving day were intoxicating for the fans: both United and Leeds could win the double; Chelsea could lift an unprecedented treble; while Liverpool sought the consolation of winning their first-ever FA Cup.

The first hurdle for United was their semi-final clash against Leeds, played in front of 65,000 fans at Hillsborough on 27 March. It was a game that the *Times* reporter would later describe as the embodiment of Dante's *Inferno*. The tackles had been flying in from the start, but then it all kicked off on the hour mark. Denis Law went chasing after Jack Charlton to confront the Leeds centre-half; Charlton lost control of his temper and fists started flying. The flare-up was the signal for all players from both sides to pile in. The card was not for the faint-hearted: Crerand v. Bremner was followed by Stiles v. Hunter, who had to be physically separated.

It was several minutes before calm was restored, with Law's shirt torn to shreds and left dangling from his shoulder for the rest of the match. Astonishingly, referee Dick Windle took no action, choosing only to tick off Law and award a free kick to Leeds. The match ended goalless and with a sour taste for the *Times* reporter: 'This angry, shabby affair of naked intimidation and moments of physical violence should be held up as a permanent warning to all those who bow to Mammon at the expense of ethical standards.'

It was easy to characterise United as the good guys and Leeds as the baddies – George Best certainly did, saying: 'That Leeds team are now remembered as the most cynical football team of all time . . . I hated playing against them, I really did.' Recalling another occasion at Old Trafford, he wrote in *The Best of Times*: 'As the two teams walked down the tunnel, I felt a terrific pain in my right calf as someone kicked me with brute force. I turned. It was Bobby Collins. "And that's just for starters, Bestie."'

In one team talk before a game against Don Revie's boys, Busby indulged in a spot of colourful character assassination: 'Gary Sprake, the goalkeeper . . . on his day a nasty piece of work. Right-back, Paul Reaney . . . dirty b*****d. Left-back, Terry Cooper. . . even dirtier b*****d. Johnny Giles . . . dirty little b*****d. Centre-half, Jack Charlton . . . dirty big b*****d.' And, with not a little irony, he concluded: 'Right-half, wee Billy Bremner . . . good Scottish boy!'

For all that, in a strategy to get their retaliation in first, United were more sinners than sinned against; both Stiles and Law were booked, and United conceded 24 fouls to Leeds' ten. The replay followed four days later at the City Ground, and the Yorkshiremen returned to type. In a game dominated by United, Leeds nicked the tie in the last minute – Billy Bremner, the smallest man on the pitch, scoring a back header from two yards. It was sickening for United, and too much for the fans who invaded the pitch at the final whistle. The referee, the same Dick Windle who had turned a blind eye to the mayhem at Hillsborough, was felled by a punch from an angry fan.

Leeds had won the battle, but United would have their revenge. United travelled to Elland Road for a crunch game in the middle of the busy Easter programme. In their third encounter in three weeks, table-topping Leeds' double hopes were still looking good, but United were just three points adrift with Chelsea a point further back. But Leeds were without their inspiration – the 'good' Scottish boy had been in the referee's bad books and was suspended for the game. Ironically, the silky footballers were thankful that a scuffed effort from winger John Connelly that went through Norman Hunter's legs was sufficient to secure a crucial victory.

The uncertain glory of an April day,
Which now shows all the beauty of the sun,
And by and by a cloud takes all away!
(from *The Two Gentlemen of Verona*)

The sun now shone on United, who won their next three games convincingly as Leeds' hopes clouded and Chelsea's challenge evaporated; United's loss on the final day to Aston Villa was rendered irrelevant by their superior goal average, the decisive factor in a photo-finish to the title race with both United and Leeds finishing on 61 points.

But April wasn't to be the cruellest month for Leeds; on May Day they succumbed to Liverpool in extra time and had to settle for runners-up medals in the FA Cup final. No glorious summer for those sons of York. For United, they could enjoy the satisfaction of winning their first league title in the post-Busby Babes era. The young pretenders had been seen off, and the big beasts of Lancashire were monarchs of all they surveyed.

A STAR IS BORN
Benfica 1 Manchester United 5
9 MARCH 1966, ESTÁDIO DA LUZ

In winning the FA Cup in 1963, United had won their first silverware since Munich. The rebuilding process for Busby's shattered side was now well under way, and they could once again challenge for the league and, importantly for Busby, retake their place on the European stage. Three survivors of the crash – Charlton, Foulkes and Gregg – remained; in Denis Law they now had a world-class striker to partner David Herd – the two of them combining to score United's three Wembley goals. Paddy Crerand had joined from Celtic in February earlier that year, to add craft to Stiles' defensive graft in midfield and his slide-rule passing to supply ammunition to the front men; and, waiting in the wings, was a shy, skinny kid from Belfast.

George Best had been spotted by United scout Bob Bishop and invited to Manchester for trials in July 1961. Bishop sent a telegram to Busby saying simply: 'I have found you a genius.' Travelling with another promising Northern Irish teenager, Eric McMordie, Best, who had just turned 15 in May and never left the province before, was instantly homesick, and the two promptly returned to Belfast. Mercifully, Bishop and Busby persisted and coaxed the young Best into giving Manchester a second chance.

Best was a precocious talent who ate, drank and slept football. The watchful Mary Fullaway, his landlady at number 9 Aycliffe

Avenue, became a second mother to him and, in many ways, Busby became a second father and United a second family.

Best made his debut in September 1963 against West Bromwich when his fellow lodger, the young David Sadler, scored the only goal of the game; Mrs Fullaway must have been chuffed to bits. From January 1964 onwards Best was a regular in the first team, occupying the wing position. Quite apart from adding a new threat for opponents, Best's inclusion allowed Bobby Charlton to move inside to a more central position. The chemistry was transformative: the Trinity of Best, Law and Charlton was the alchemy that turned United from a good side into a great one.

United now shifted up a gear. From finishing a lowly eighteenth in the league the year before, they were runners-up in 1963/64. In the Cup Winners' Cup, after a good run to the quarter finals, they blew a 4–1 lead to lose 6–4 on aggregate to the eventual winners Sporting, causing the normally collected Busby to lose his temper in the dressing room.

The following season, the Trinity scored 71 goals between them. United won the league, reached the FA Cup semi-final, and enjoyed another fine season in Europe. Playing in the Inter-Cities Fairs Cup, they saw off Everton and put Borussia Dortmund to the sword, winning 10–1 on aggregate. In the semi-final, which went to a replay, Ferencvárosi gained revenge for their humiliation in their only previous game against United 57 years earlier, before winning the final itself.

Despite the disappointment, everyone could see the trajectory. Now, as league champions, United were back in the big time, competing in Europe's premier tournament for the first time since 1958. The early stages were straightforward enough as they eased past Finnish and East German opposition. In the quarters, the Red Devils now faced the mighty Benfica, twice winners and the losing finalist in 1965. The first leg, played at Old Trafford, ended in a narrow win for United; in a see-saw game, Benfica led on the half-hour before United scored through Herd, Law and Foulkes to take a handy 3–1 lead before Portuguese international Torres reduced the arrears.

It was a narrow advantage to take to Lisbon; few gave United a chance. In his pre-match talk, Busby urged his players to be cautious. Sixteen minutes later, he was eating his words. Looking up at the scoreboard, he must have rubbed his eyes to double-check he wasn't dreaming; it read Benfica 0 Manchester United 3. Benfica's defence had been torn to shreds. First, in the seventh minute, Best glanced in a header from a Dunne free kick; seven minutes later, Best surged past two statuesque defenders to rifle home his second; three minutes later, Law and Herd combined to set up Connelly for the third. Benfica needed an own goal from Brennan to gain a toehold in the game until, late on, Crerand scored a fourth before Charlton waltzed through the hapless Portuguese defence to put the icing on the cake.

It was a scintillating display. Kenneth Wolstenholme, in commentary, suggested that Benfica were playing in slow motion compared to United. The player who had caught the eye and taken the game by the scruff of the neck was Best. He was a game changer. His absence through injury was sorely felt in the semi-final as United, also missing Denis Law, went out 2–1 on aggregate to a rugged Partizan Belgrade who, in Paddy Crerand's words, 'kicked the s**t out of us'.

Comparisons across different eras are invidious, of course, but can sometimes offer insights. In the modern era, the player who most resembles Best is Lionel Messi. Graduates of their respective academies, they each had amazing close control and dribbling skill, they were fast and had the ability to accelerate past a defender over a couple of yards, both had a great passing range, and each had instinctive game intelligence. Slightly built, each possessed balance, agility and an eye for goal. Whereas Messi is predominantly left-footed, Best was equally good off either foot and also a fine header of the ball.

What Messi has over Best is his amazing longevity and consistency, but then he didn't have to contend with the muddy pitches of the 1960s, or the brutal tackling and lenient referees who tolerated the violence meted out by the likes of Norman Hunter, Ron Harris and Tommy Smith. Messi also had the help of an agent, a management team and a supportive club structure to look after him and help him deal with the pressures of stardom. On the field of play, George could rely on surrogate big brothers Paddy Crerand and Nobby Stiles to look out for him; off the pitch he had Mrs Fullaway.

United's win in Lisbon sent shock waves around European football. The result made not just the back pages, but also the front pages of the newspapers. A smiling Best, pin-up good-looking with fashionably long hair, was pictured wearing the sombrero he had picked up as a souvenir on the trip and was instantly dubbed 'El Beatle'. He had left Manchester a young kid relatively unknown outside football circles; now he was a superstar who fitted effortlessly into the glamorous world of Swinging Sixties popular culture.

Harry Gregg, in goal in Lisbon, could see that something momentous had happened. He said, 'That night George became a different person. A child that the world didn't know about that night became a legend.'

WHERE THEY WERE ON 31 JULY 1966
The 1966 World Cup Final

It's no secret that Denis Law was a fiercely proud Scot. His daughter tells the story of how her father, during his playing days, was so anxious to return to Scotland for Christmas and Hogmanay that he would deliberately get himself booked so that he would be suspended for the holiday season and be free to travel north. And his pride in his country also manifested itself in an antipathy to the England football team; it mattered not that the English national side usually included a number of his United teammates.

At the end of July 1966, as the sun shone on Wembley and the red-shirted English lions, it was pouring in Manchester. Out on the golf course, trying to take his mind off things and the possibility of his worst nightmare coming true, Denis Law was losing his game and his cool.

There had been no trouble getting a tee-off at that time of day as most of the members were huddled round the TV watching the biggest game of England's footballing history. As Law came off the course, they were all at the clubhouse window cheering, holding up four fingers to let him know the score. He later confessed, 'I thought it was the end of the world.' Some say the story is apocryphal, but it wouldn't be like Denis to embellish the truth for the sake of a good story, would it?

Meanwhile in the Wembley stands, two young Manchester footballers were sitting together. Close friends George Best and City's Mike Summerbee were enjoying the occasion – and perhaps taking the opportunity to discuss their plans for going into business together (their menswear boutique Edwardia opened the following year). Closer to the action, sitting behind what passed for the technical area, amongst the suited and booted of England's non-playing World Cup squad, was United winger John Connelly. Many remember Jimmy Greaves as the England player who appeared only once in the tournament, but Connelly was another, along with two other wingmen: Southampton's Terry Paine and Liverpool's Ian Callaghan. After the group stage, width gave way to Ramsey's 4-3-3 system – the 'wingless wonders' – one that proved to be a winning formula. No one had thought to invent Red Bull in the 1960s.

For the final, Ramsey did select two United legends: Bobby Charlton, whose goals had done so much to get the team through to face West Germany, and Nobby Stiles, the tireless dynamo who kept the midfield engine ticking over. Charlton had, for him, a quiet game – his job was to contain the dangerous Beckenbauer – but in the images of that famous day you see him overcome with emotion. After the final whistle, his teammates laughing and cheering as the cup is held aloft, Bobby is in tears. By contrast Stiles is a figure of impish joy: socks down at his ankles, with a huge gap-toothed grin, he holds his false teeth in one hand and the Jules Rimet trophy in the other, jigging his way round Wembley in a glorious lap of honour.

THE RULE OF THREE
West Ham United 1 Manchester United 6
6 MAY 1967

After the glory of winning the league title in 1965, the following year had been something of an anticlimax for Busby's team. They finished a distant fourth behind Liverpool in the league, and lost at the semi-final stages of both the FA and European cups. And they stuttered at the beginning of the 1966/67 season, losing four of their first ten First Division games and suffering an embarrassing 5–0 exit from the League Cup at the hands of Blackpool.

By the turn of the year, United were at the top of the table, but Liverpool were breathing down their necks. From that point on, despite a shock FA Cup defeat at home to Norwich, United went unbeaten in the league. With two games to go, the title was theirs to lose. But in all that time, United hadn't managed an away win, having drawn eight in succession.

They were at near full strength for the match at Upton Park. Only David Herd, who suffered a broken leg playing Leicester City in March, was missing from Busby's strongest XI. The Hammers fielded their three World Cup winners: Geoff Hurst, Martin Peters and Bobby Moore. But United had their own Trinity, who by the end of that season were playing at their absolute peak collectively – it was the rule of three. For modern equivalents, think Neymar, Suárez and Messi at Barcelona;

or Benzema, Bale and Ronaldo in their prime at Madrid. They were sensational. Bobby Charlton, the star of the 1966 World Cup, combined experience with skill and phenomenal athleticism; Denis Law was relatively injury-free and scoring for fun; and George Best, still only 20, was putting his energies into becoming the world's greatest footballer rather than the lifestyle distractions that would later chain football's Prometheus. Between them, Best, Law and Charlton scored 45 of United's 84 league goals that season.

The Trinity was born in January 1964 when all three featured in the same starting line-up for the first time in a 4–1 victory against West Bromwich in which all three scored, with Law bagging two.

All three would be voted as the winner of the Ballon d'Or, the trophy awarded to the world's best player. Law won in 1964, Charlton in 1966 and Best in 1968. Combined, the players scored 665 goals in 1,633 games. Liverpool manager Bill Shankly spoke of how he once psychologically built up his team ahead of a game against United: 'I took the models of Bobby Charlton, Denis Law and George Best off the model pitch and put them in my left-hand pocket. Then I told our players: "Don't worry about them, they can't play at all." It was psychology, of course. Charlton, Best and Law were three of the best players in the world.'

And as they took the field that Saturday afternoon, facing in Bobby Moore one of the best defenders who ever played the game, they were confident of victory, knowing West Ham had the third worst defensive record in the league.

The outcome of the game, and the season, wasn't in doubt for long. Within 20 minutes United were four goals up and the game finished in a 6–1 rout. The scorers? Law (two), Charlton and Best (but of course) with Paddy Crerand and Bill Foulkes also finding the net. It was United's biggest win of the season. It was a fitting climax to clinch Busby his fifth championship title. But as important as the title was to the manager, more than anything he was delighted to be granted another chance to win the prize he coveted above all: the European Cup.

IT'S A WONDERFUL WORLD
Benfica 1 Manchester United 4
(after extra time)
29 MAY 1968, WEMBLEY

In May 1968, before 100,000 spectators and a worldwide television audience of 250 million, United became the first English team to lift the coveted European Cup. The Red Devils, appearing in their first final, were up against the mighty Benfica, playing in their fifth final in seven years, whose line-up included the dazzling talent of Eusebio, one of the stars of the 1966 World Cup.

United's path to European glory came just ten years after the Munich air disaster cast its terrible shadow over the club. The Busby Babes had been pioneers for English football in Europe. The Football League had shown little interest in the competition and offered no concessions to English participants; the 1955 champions, Chelsea, were actually forbidden from taking part. United, as champions the following season, were the first team to enter.

The English football establishment's arrogant view of its own importance, dented by defeats to the USA in 1950 and to Hungary three years later, would take years to shake off. The Football League continued to take a dim view of European competition; no allowance would be made for sides' travel and recuperation after away games – the league's Saturday fixture schedule was sacrosanct.

But the new tournament quickly grew in popularity. In Britain, the 1960 final made a huge and lasting impression on the 128,000 captivated fans at Hampden Park in Glasgow who watched the great Real Madrid side thrash Eintracht Frankfurt 7–3. Amongst those in the crowd that day was a wide-eyed Alex Ferguson.

Meanwhile, the painful rebuilding process at United had begun. Success in the 1963 FA Cup was followed by the league title in 1965, which gave United passage back into the European Cup. The highlight of the campaign was a thrilling success at Benfica's Stadium of Light when the teenage Best lit up the evening, scoring twice in a memorable 5–1 victory. United eventually fell at the semi-final stage.

English football was entering a golden era. Alongside United, Leeds, Liverpool, Everton and Manchester City were producing great sides; Spurs and West Ham had both won the Cup Winners' Cup in recent years. And, in 1966, the national team, inspired by Bobby Charlton, won the World Cup.

Winning the league for the second time in three years, United were now back in the European Cup for the 1967/68 season. After conquering tough opponents in Górnik Zabrze in the quarters United needed a brave 3–3 draw at the Bernabéu to reach their first European final, winning 4–3 on aggregate. Coming back from a 3–1 deficit at half-time, it was Munich survivor Bill Foulkes who was the unlikely scorer of the decisive goal. After the match, both Busby and Charlton were in tears – they were one step closer to the prize they had dreamt of for so long. Now only Benfica stood in their way.

The final was a return match for Charlton and Eusebio at the venue which saw one of the great World Cup semi-finals when

Bobby scored twice to defeat a talented Portuguese team. The Benfica XI that faced United that May evening contained no fewer than six of the Portugal side that played two years before. But United had their own stars, none brighter than George Best, whose exploits in Lisbon two years before were still fresh in the memories of the Benfica players.

Denis Law missed the game through injury, but United had teenage sensation Brian Kidd up front to partner Best and winger John Aston Jr, with Charlton and fellow World Cup-winner Nobby Stiles in midfield alongside Paddy Crerand. The game was a tight affair: Alex Stepney made a crucial save as the game approached injury time at 1–1; United's opener was remarkable for being a rare headed goal by Charlton.

In extra time there followed a virtuoso goal from Best, who rounded the Portuguese keeper to restore United's lead, then Kidd, on his 19th birthday, bagged a third, before the captain scored his second to make it a 4–1 victory.

In winning the trophy, Busby's side had reached the pinnacle of success in club football. It had taken ten years to pick the club up from the depths of despair to conquer first the English First Division and now the best that Europe had to offer. It was redemption for Busby, Charlton, fellow survivor Bill Foulkes and the thousands of United fans who had mourned the loss of Edwards, Coleman, Taylor and the other Babes and wondered what might have been. Winning could never erase the memories of Munich, but winning the crown would help heal some of the scars. When Busby sang Louis Armstrong's 'It's a Wonderful World' at the after-match banquet, with a catch in his throat, he encapsulated the bittersweetness of the occasion.

For the younger players – Best, Kidd and Ashton Jr – Wembley should have been a springboard, but for the older guard it was mission accomplished. Busby retired from a post he had held for 24 years at the end of the following season. Wembley proved not to be a stepping stone to greater prizes but the high-water mark of this United vintage. It would be more than a quarter of a century before United won the English title again and three decades before they could once more call themselves champions of Europe.

SIR MATT BUSBY
Quote Unquote

Sir Matt Busby may not be able to match the wise-cracking Tommy Docherty or Ron Atkinson for quips but he spoke with conviction, passion and a simple dignity. Although the famous quote that 'there is no football without fans' is misattributed to him – it probably belongs to Jock Stein – he would no doubt have agreed with the sentiment and would have happily repeated it.

On high standards

'I never wanted Manchester United to be second to anybody. Only the best would be good enough.'

'At United we strive for perfection. If we fail, we might just have to settle for excellence.'

'In all modesty, my summing up of 1955/56 and 1956/57 must be that no club in the country could live with Manchester United.'

'I should like to see the honours in England won by a pure footballing side, the sort of team that concentrates on ball skills above all else. Such a team would inspire the other ninety-one clubs. But for the

disaster I like to feel that others now would be copying United to the benefit of the whole league.'

On Manchester United

'Manchester is my heaven' was Busby's response to Santiago Bernabéu when told managing Real Madrid 'would be like paradise'.

'United is no longer just a football club; it is an institution. I feel the demands are beyond one human being.'

On attacking football

'I do not worry about conceding goals because I know my forwards will double it at the other end.'

'All those lads you see going to the factories in Trafford Park, they come to watch you on Saturday. They have boring jobs, so you have to give them something, something they will enjoy. Give that man something he can't do himself, something exciting. That's why Manchester United always play attacking football.'

On his faith in youth

'If you don't put them in you can't know what you've got.'

'If you want football's finest fruit, grow your own.'

On great players

'We encourage individualism especially that of Best, Charlton and Law. Unless you encourage that sort of individualism you have nothing.'

Busby used to tell Best not to bother coming to pre-match team meetings. 'It was a very simple team talk. All I used to say was, "Whenever possible give the ball to George Best."'

'We had our problems with the wee feller [Best], but I prefer to remember his genius.'

'Every manager goes through life looking for one great player, praying he'll find one. Just one. I was more lucky than most. I found two – big Duncan and George.'

'Nobby Stiles a dirty player? No, he's never hurt anyone. Mind you, he's frightened a few!'

On staying humble

'Sometimes it does you good to look back at the days when the living wasn't so good. I remember 1945, the dressing rooms were gone, the park was in ruins, no stand, nothing.'

'Winning isn't everything. There should be no conceit in victory, no despair in defeat.'

And what they said about him . . .

'[United were] playing the finest football in the country and by rights they should be known as Matt Busby United.' – News of the World report on the 1948 Cup-winning side

'Bloody hell, the way your lot were playing, you could win the Boat Race.' – Bill Shankly, in 1949, playing for Preston North End, as recounted by Charlie Mitten

'When I first signed for Manchester United I wasn't even shown a contract. I just signed. That's the kind of charm that Busby had. He had a great sense of humour. He was a funny man. He was a great man. A gentleman of the highest quality.' – Paddy Crerand

'I played with some marvellous players at Manchester United and a great manager in Sir Matt Busby. When you think after the crash, Sir Matt lifting the European Cup at Wembley was just wonderful for everybody.' – Denis Law

'The United Way was born under Matt Busby.' – Eric Cantona

'I'm privileged to have followed Sir Matt because all you have to do is to try and maintain the standards that he set so many years ago.' – Sir Alex Ferguson

SIX OF THE BEST

Northampton Town 2 Manchester United 8

FA CUP FIFTH ROUND, 7 FEBRUARY 1970

As the 1969/70 season kicked off, Manchester United had their first new manager for nearly a quarter of a century. By the beginning of February Wilf McGuinness's side were well adrift of joint league-leaders Leeds United and Everton but had progressed to the fifth round of the FA Cup at the expense of their city neighbours.

In the fifth round, United were drawn away to Northampton Town. The Cobblers had been a top-flight side just four years before but had rapidly dropped down the divisions to the fourth: the natural order of things had been restored.

Nonetheless, Northampton must have fancied their chances with 20,000 fans packed into the ground and the pitch, a quagmire, promising to level the difference in class between the two sides. They had not reckoned on George Best.

Goalkeeper Kim Book later recalled: 'The trouble was that when the scout watched United, George Best was suspended so he didn't mention him. We actually managed to kick [Bobby] Charlton out of the game early on and at half-time I thought we were still in it. [United led 2–0 going into the break.] But then George put his scoring boots on.' Not just his boots. That afternoon he scored three with his right foot, one with his left and two with his head. Northampton's full-back Ray Fairfax was left chasing shadows. He told the *Daily Telegraph*: 'I think the closest I got to him was when we shook hands after the final whistle.'

Best's sixth goal saw him go one on one with the Northampton goalkeeper. Best feinted to go right, putting Book on his backside, before he went left and walked the ball into the net. Book later recalled: 'It's been a joke on the circuit ever since. You know, I'm on one side of the street, George Best is on the other. He nods to me and I dive under a bus.'

His tally of six goals remains a record for the club, which is held jointly with Harold Halse, who hit six past Queens Park Rangers in the 1911 Charity Shield. United went into the second half 2–0 up and won the tie 8–2.

Best's six-goal performance captured the public imagination and even earned him an invitation to 10 Downing Street from Prime Minister Harold Wilson, who had also regularly written fan letters to him.

This was Best at his best. He was still only 23 years old; alcohol and womanising had not yet dimmed his love of playing the game – the beautiful one, that is. He was now the undoubted star of a United side that had not yet entered terminal decline. Following the mission statement laid down by Matt Busby, he loved playing the 'United way' – charged with the duty to entertain the spectators and given a licence to thrill.

Speaking after the match, Best was adamant that he wanted to make the fans smile. 'I don't really class myself as a footballer,' he said. 'I call myself an entertainer. I know a lot of people have paid to see me do something spectacular and that's what I was trying to do on Saturday. It's my job to do something that will send people away feeling that they'd like to see me play again.' For George it was the best of times – before long they would become the worst.

TALKING REDS
Paddy Crerand, Pioneer TV Pundit

There was a time, not so long ago, when television and radio seemed to be a Liverpool old boys' club. Not to take anything away from Messrs Hansen, Lawrenson, Redknapp, Souness et al., but for the armchair United fan it would have been nice to hear another point of view.

Mercifully, times have changed. Now it is possible to flick channels and enjoy the opinionated Gary Neville, the laid-back Rio Ferdinand, the combustible Roy Keane or the calmer voice of Owen Hargreaves and blunt views of Paul Scholes. Turn on the radio, and you can listen to the motormouth phone-in expertise of Alan Brazil or Class of '92 graduate, Robbie Savage.

At the turn of the century, one United old boy, the charismatic Ron Atkinson, was one of the big beasts of TV punditry, dishing out drollery and discernment from his co-commentator's perch during the big games. Unfortunately, in 2004, Big Ron made a wildly inappropriate racist remark about Chelsea defender Marcel Desailly (when he thought he was off air), which was broadcast in Dubai and the Middle East. Desailly later said, charitably, that he felt sorry for Atkinson: 'I am not angry or bitter. I have been asked to react, but I have stayed quite cool . . . He had a great image, but he is 65 years old now and he has broken that . . . He has made the mistake and it is him who is going to pay for that mistake.' Indeed he did: that was the end of Atkinson's broadcasting career.

But the granddaddy of them all is Patrick Timothy Crerand. Known to many United fans as the voice of MUTV, Crerand's history in broadcasting goes back more than half a century, including work as a summariser for United games on Piccadilly Radio. But his media career began way back in 1970 when he was a panellist on ITV's ground-breaking coverage of the Mexico World Cup.

Before the tournament, TV punditry was rare, muted and deferential. England, the current holders, were expected to cruise through to the final with only Brazil standing in the way of their rightful prize. ITV decided to put together a panel of four experts plus Jimmy Hill as convener and lock them away at Hendon Hall Hotel for the duration. The panellists – all either current players or a successful coach – divided into two camps: the nice guys, the voluble Derek Dougan who was hard to shut up and taciturn Bob McNab; and the contrarians, the debonair, cigar-smoking Malcolm Allison and the cantankerous Crerand – no doubt Paddy's Scottish background made him all the more abrasive when discussing England's shortcomings.

In a time before Opta stats and endless post-match tactical analyses, the science of football was a mystery to the average fan. Now all of a sudden, this group of articulate, argumentative, stylishly dressed football men were enthralling viewers and making the sport easily accessible to football followers who might only catch the one live game shown each season: the FA Cup final. Fan letters flooded in and autograph hunters sought them out; and in a restaurant one night, Michael Caine asked to join them, saying he wanted to 'have a drink with the lads'.

Cheers!

'MACCHESTER UNITED'
United's Tartan Army

In a land of fierce warriors and dusty wallets, of mountains, flood and ice, the people of Scotland have often punched, sometimes literally, above their weight as a country. The world is richer thanks to the industrious Scots who have produced a steady production line of crime writers, poets, whisky distillers, Enlightenment philosophers, doctors, scientists, engineers, politicians and footballers. Just as Tony Blair's cabinet was chock-a-block with Scots, so the sport of association football has been blessed with its own Caledonian cohort.

Before the globalisation of football and the deluge of TV money in the Premier League, English teams looked to Scotland to add flair, industry and devilment to their playing sides, and steel and obsessiveness to their management. It was said that any team aspiring to win the title required a quota of three Scots to ensure success.

No fewer than 153 players of Scottish nationality have made at least one appearance in a competitive fixture for United's first team. Early pioneers included: the Heathen Joe Cassidy (1893–1900), the first to score 100 goals for the club; Sandy Turnbull, one of the four escapees from United's city rivals in 1906, who forged the deadly partnership with Billy Meredith that helped to secure the first league title in 1908; Jimmy Delaney, a Busby favourite, who was part of the team that won the FA Cup in 1948. Delaney was one of a number of former Celtic players who made the move to Old Trafford; other recruits from Parkhead included Paddy Crerand, Lou Macari, Brian McClair and, all too fleetingly, Henrik Larsson.

But the main invasion took place in the 1970s. There had been portents in the preceding years. In the aftermath of the Munich disaster, much of the home-grown talent had cruelly perished and new players had to be brought in. In the early 1960s, Busby signed three influential Scots: the prolific David Herd, midfield general Paddy Crerand and, best of all, Denis Law, 'The King'. Here was the requisite trio needed for a title-winning side.

And a word about Scottish managers. Busby and Ferguson, with over half a century of leadership between them, overshadow not just the other four Scots but, arguably, the rest. Of the others, David Moyes, 'the chosen one', was given a very short straw; John Chapman and Scott Duncan presided over struggling sides in the inter-war era. It should be said that Duncan did manage a Second Division title before going on to success at Ipswich Town, where he mentored Sir Alf Ramsey in the art of management. That leaves Thomas Henderson Docherty, 'The Doc', another Celtic old Bhoy.

Docherty liked to say he had had more clubs than Jack Nicklaus, but when the call from United came late in 1972, the Doc was in charge of the Scotland national team. So maybe it wasn't surprising that he looked to his compatriots to add recruits to an ageing United squad.

In the first month of his tenure, Docherty picked a starting XI that included no fewer than eight of his fellow countrymen (italicised here). The side that drew against West Ham on 20

January 1973 consisted of Stepney, Young, *Forsyth*, *Law*, *Holton*, *Martin Buchan*, *Morgan*, *MacDougall*, Charlton, *Macari* and *Graham*. Macari was one of the Doc's first signings, and the Scottish contingent was soon supplemented by the arrival of Jim McCalliog and Stewart Houston, while debuts were given to George Buchan (Martin's brother) and Arthur Albiston. No wonder they were cheekily nicknamed 'MacChester United'.

The trauma of relegation followed in 1974. Many of the Scots left Old Trafford through transfer (Law, MacDougall), injury (Holton) or a falling-out with the manager (Morgan). But Macari, Albiston and Buchan were the bedrock of the resurgent side that won promotion in 1975 and the FA Cup in 1977. They were joined by two more compatriots: Joe Jordan and Gordon McQueen, who crossed the Pennines in early 1978 to add steel to Dave Sexton's squad.

Gordon Strachan and Graeme Hogg became regulars in the 1980s, and then there was a spate of Scots who appeared shortly after Alex Ferguson's appointment when Brian McClair, Ralph Milne and Jim Leighton were lured south.

The emergence of the Class of '92 and the influx of foreign talent stemmed the Scottish tide. Since the turn of the last century, only Darren Fletcher and Scott McTominay could be called established first-team players. The flood had become a trickle as the Scottish talent pool dried up.

As the Scots would say, 'It's a sair fecht.'

PAST HIS BEST
George Best's Decline, 1971 to 1974

At the end of 1970, the prospects for United looked bleak. Languishing near the foot of the table, the board put out-of-his-depth Wilf McGuinness out of his misery and reappointed Matt Busby as a caretaker manager.

George Best was restive. While bravura performances against Northampton in the FA Cup and then an Indiana Jones-like slalom through a scything Chelsea defence in the League Cup caught the eye, his behaviour and form were becoming more erratic. On the pitch he was getting into trouble with referees and incurring a number of suspensions. He admitted later: 'My goals became all important, because others weren't scoring them so frequently. Instead of revolving around me, the team now depended on me, and I lacked the maturity to handle it. I began to drink more heavily and, on the field, my list of bookings grew longer as my temper grew shorter.'

Off the field he was even more wayward. Before the FA Cup semi-final replay against arch-rivals Leeds, Best breached team discipline by luring a young woman to his hotel room. He was discovered by Wilf McGuinness, who had the hotel manager unlock the door to catch him in the act. He wasn't dropped for this indiscretion but was guilty of missing United's best chance to win the replay the following day.

Worse was to follow in January 1971. George failed to rendezvous with the United squad and missed the train to London ahead of their fixture with Chelsea. Although he caught a later train, there was a change of plan. Instead of hitching up with his girlfriend, the actress Sinéad Cusack, after the match he went straight to her Islington flat without stopping off at Stamford Bridge.

Best described the escapade in his autobiography *Blessed*: 'Chelsea was the fixture I loved playing more than any other. Big club, big players, but it didn't interest me at all although I did fancy a weekend in London. It was utter madness. Here I was, one of the world's most famous footballers and I just decided not to play an important game and instead went out on a date. It's hard for me to explain what state of mind I was in to do such a thing.'

Best's absence had piqued the interest of the press pack, who tracked the Northern Irishman to Cusack's flat and laid siege to the couple for the next four days. Best was now plastered all over the tabloids and the subject of bulletins on television news.

A two-week suspension was administered by the indulgent Busby, and Best knuckled down, scoring 14 times in the remainder of the season. Busby relinquished his caretaker role in the summer, the board appointing Frank O'Farrell to the hot seat.

O'Farrell's first season started well. Before the end of November, Best had scored 17 times, including hat-tricks against West Ham and Southampton; the memorable individual goal against Sheffield United when he ran 40 yards past four defenders before firing into the net was so good it was replayed in *Match of the Day*'s opening credits. United led the league as the year drew to a close, and O'Farrell knew who to thank: 'Every night I'd say one simple prayer. Thank God for George.'

But trouble was never far away for the superstar footballer. Following a New Year's Day defeat to West Ham, George went missing again. This time, punishment was probationary: he was sent back to his old digs at Aycliffe Avenue under the watchful eye of Mrs Fullaway. It didn't work. He was now drinking heavily – he frequented the Brown Bull, a haunt for serious boozers – and would often sleep off a session on a filthy mattress in the room above the bar. As his addiction to alcohol increased, so his appetite for the game diminished.

In April, George quit for the first time. Unfit, drinking to excess and unhappy with the state of the club, he said, 'Sod it, I'm off to Marbella.' From there he went downhill faster than a Jamaican bobsleigh. He came back for the start of the 1972/73 season but, come December, disappeared once again into the London nightclub scene, incurring another suspension and being placed on the transfer list. As O'Farrell made way for Tommy Docherty, Best once again walked out.

There would be one last brief hiccup in this rake's progress. Having come back a third time into a barely recognisable United team – Charlton and Law had now departed – Best was a shadow of his former self. Following a 3–0 defeat at Queens Park Rangers on New Year's Day, 1974, he pitched up late for the cup tie against Plymouth, reeking of alcohol and with a young woman in tow. The Doc sent him home. The humiliation of being dropped for a game against the lowly Pilgrims was too much to bear and this time he didn't come back.

He was 27 years old, an age when most footballers should be at their peak. He did play again: for fun at Fulham and Hibernian, and for financial reward and success in the US for the Los Angeles Aztecs, Fort Lauderdale and San Jose Earthquakes. His disciplinary record remained patchy: he once cried off a cup game for Hibs against Ayr United after an all-night drinking session with French rugby legend Jean-Pierre Rives and Blondie's Debbie Harry that only ended four hours before kick-off. Ayr United or Debbie Harry? Hmm. . . even the 'Honest Men' might struggle to answer that truthfully.

Even in those twilight years of his playing career, Best could still draw a crowd. He answered his old friend Barry Fry's appeal to help out struggling Dunstable Town. George remembered how the young Fry had looked after him when he first arrived at Old Trafford. Creasey Park's attendance shifted from 34 dutiful fans to an astonishing 10,000 in the first of Best's three appearances.

United fans can be greedy; they wanted to see more of his genius. But they had the best years. He spent 12 years at Old Trafford, played 470 times for the Reds (nine more than Bryan Robson), was United's sixth-highest scorer with 179 goals, and helped the club win two titles and the European Cup. George once asked that he be remembered for his football rather than his lifestyle. Of course, it's impossible to separate the man from his unique ability, and the endless books, films and newspaper articles that continue to appear, half a century after his messy departure from Old Trafford, bear testimony to the enduring legacy of this flawed genius.

GEORGE BEST
Quote Unquote

George Best, the first celebrity footballer with a God-given talent, was blessed with devilish good looks and an exuberance of charm. He also possessed a sharp wit and here are a few choice examples.

On being born with a gift

'I was born with a great gift, and sometimes with that comes a destructive streak. Just as I wanted to outdo everyone when I played, I had to outdo everyone when we were out on the town.'

On lifestyle

'I used to go missing a lot . . . Miss Canada, Miss United Kingdom, Miss World.'

'I spent a lot of money on booze, birds and fast cars. The rest I just squandered.'

'In 1969 I gave up women and alcohol – it was the worst 20 minutes of my life.'

'I might go to Alcoholics Anonymous, but I think it would be difficult for me to remain anonymous.'

On enjoying the best of both worlds

'If you'd given me the choice of going out and beating four men and smashing a goal in from thirty yards against Liverpool or going to bed with Miss World, it would have been a difficult choice. Luckily, I had both.'

On other footballers

David Beckham
'He cannot kick with his left foot, he cannot head a ball, he cannot tackle and he doesn't score many goals. Apart from that, he's all right.'

Kevin Keegan
'He's not fit to lace my boots as a player.'
(This quote was memorably parodied by John Roberts of the *Daily Express* who wrote: 'Kevin Keegan is not fit to lace Best's drinks.')

Paul Gascoigne
'I once said Gazza's IQ was less than his shirt number and he asked me: "What's an IQ?"'

Cristiano Ronaldo
'There have been a few players described as the new George Best over the years, but this is the first time it's been a compliment to me.'

Pelé

'Pelé called me the greatest footballer in the world. That is the ultimate salute to my life.'

Eric Cantona

'I'd give all the champagne I've ever drunk to be playing alongside him in a big European match at Old Trafford.'

On scoring in the 1968 European Cup final

'I used to dream about taking the ball round the keeper, stopping it on the line and then getting on my hands and knees and heading it into the net. When I scored against Benfica in the 1968 European Cup final I nearly did it. I left the keeper for dead but then I chickened out. I might have given the boss a heart attack!'

And, finally, on his legacy . . .

'They'll forget all the rubbish when I've gone and they'll remember the football. If only one person thinks I'm the best player in the world, that's good enough for me.'

And here's what the football world had to say about him . . .

'George inspired me when I was young. He was flamboyant and exciting and able to inspire his team-mates. I actually think we were very similar players – dribblers who were able to create moments of magic.' – Diego Maradona

'George was as good as anyone you will see; he used to embarrass players time and time again. It was paradise watching George play football.' – Sir Bobby Charlton

'The complete player.' – Denis Law

'After his first training session in heaven, George Best, from the favourite right wing, turned the head of God who was filling in at left-back.' – Eric Cantona (following George's death in 2005)

'We had our problems with the wee fella but I prefer to remember his genius.' – Sir Matt Busby

'What he had was unique, you can't coach it.' – Johan Cruyff

'The great football critics said that because of his technical skills he didn't seem like a European athlete but rather like a Brazilian athlete who danced the samba with the ball at his feet.' – Pelé

'George was unique, the greatest talent our football ever produced – easily.' – Sir Alex Ferguson

'He was the first true modern footballer – the one every mediocre millionaire of the modern game should get down on their knees and thank.' – Jimmy Greaves

Life after football

Many fans felt that Best had wasted his great gifts. Best, however, never saw it that way. He recounted the story of how, shortly after retiring from football, he went on a date with the woman who had just won the Miss World contest. They went to the races and won several thousand pounds.

That evening as Best and Miss World spread the money out on the bed of their hotel room to count it, a hotel waiter knocked on the door to bring them the two bottles of champagne they'd ordered to celebrate.

The waiter, mindful of Best's early retirement, handed over the champagne, looked at the beautiful Miss World, looked at the thousands of pounds, and then said to Best, 'Mr Best, where did it all go wrong?'

NOT TOO GOOD TO GO DOWN
The Slow Fall from Grace, 1968 to 1974

The causes of United's steady but inexorable decline from the pinnacle of European Cup success to relegation candidates in a few short years go back to that glory night at Wembley. The European triumph represented everything that Busby had strived for; inevitably, there was bound to be a sense of anticlimax thereafter.

Busby, whose 60th birthday fell in May 1969, decided to withdraw from day-to-day management of the team, appointing a former Busby Babe, Wilf McGuinness, as his successor. McGuinness was barely half Busby's age with no experience of senior management. It was a short-lived experiment that proved to be a failure: after 18 months McGuinness was put out of his misery as Busby took the reins for the second half of the 1970/71 season. The experience was so traumatic for the younger man that his hair fell out, leaving the popular Wilf looking like an amiable Nosferatu.

Busby temporarily stopped the rot, but the signs of the team's decline were becoming increasingly obvious. In the summer of 1971, they said goodbye to the battle-scarred midfield engine room of Crerand and Stiles to retirement and Middlesbrough respectively. Law and Charlton were now in their 30s and they increasingly relied upon the sporadic genius of Best to get results.

The new man in charge, Frank O'Farrell, got off to a flyer as United stormed to the top of the table, five points clear at the beginning of December. But the fundamental problems remained: the squad was a mixture of ageing legends, callow youth and impulse buys. In the background, Busby's presence undermined O'Farrell's authority. Then their talisman upon whom they leaned so heavily proved to be unreliable; at the end of the season Best walked out of the club, swapping the pressures of football and paparazzi for the sunshine of Spain.

O'Farrell's luck was out, and he departed Old Trafford just before Christmas 1972 with United deep in relegation trouble. The quietly spoken Irishman was in stark contrast to his replacement, the inimitable Thomas Henderson Docherty.

The club needed a shake-up, but, instead, they suffered an earthquake. Bobby Charlton retired, Law was moved on to Manchester City, and in came an army of Scots as Docherty, who had until his appointment been manager of the Scotland national team, wielded the cheque book as swiftly as the axe. He kept United up, but not by much; they finished eighteenth.

The direction of travel was clear, and the Doc put his foot on the accelerator. By the end of 1973, they were once again eighteenth, a point above the drop zone. They brought in the New Year with a heavy defeat at Loftus Road, and a week later Best walked out for the last time. In a winter of discontent, United only managed to pick up five points from their next ten games. The defence was sound enough; they just couldn't score. It was as if the forwards had gone on strike in sympathy for Arthur Scargill and the miners. By the end of March, United were rooted to the foot of the table, five points from safety.

Worse was to follow. First, there was false hope. On transfer deadline day, the Doc signed the attacking midfielder Jim McCalliog from Wolves. Busby told Docherty to take United off the leash, saying, 'Tom, if we are to go down, let's do it with dignity.' United went on a run, taking eight points from five games, scoring ten times in the process.

The final act of a dramatic season that started as farce ended with a Greek tragedy. Any hope of a great escape was dashed in their last home game when, in the 82nd minute, their former king, Denis Law, back-heeled the ball past Stepney to score the game's only goal. Law, whose twelfth goal of the season was equal to the combined efforts of United's diminutive attack of Macari and McIlroy, was shocked and refused to celebrate. Then, all hell broke loose as fans invaded the Old Trafford pitch in a vain attempt to have the match abandoned.

In the end, the goal was not decisive. Birmingham's victory against Norwich had rendered the defeat to City academic. But that was little consolation to the fans or to Law. In 2010, Denis told the *Daily Mail*: 'I was inconsolable. I didn't want it to happen. How long did the feeling last? How long ago was the game? Thirty-odd years. There is your answer.' United, European Cup winners just six years before, were now consigned to Second Division football; rather than enjoying matches at Highbury or the Bernabéu, travelling fans would be consulting their road maps to locate Brisbane Road and Bootham Crescent.

In its match report of the derby game, the *Guardian* summed up well the mood of United fans when its correspondent wrote: 'Saturday's greatest irony at Old Trafford was, without doubt or exception, Denis Law's goal. It was "the most unkindest cut of all" in the words of Marcus Antonius, who in the same speech said: "If you have tears, prepare to shed them now."' There was not a dry eye in the house.

BUCHAN'S *THIRTY-NINE STEPS*
FA Cup Final, 21 May 1977, Wembley Stadium

At the end of the 1976/77 season, much was at stake. After the heartbreak of the previous year when United came so close to winning the league and lost to Second Division Southampton in the FA Cup final, United had a chance to redeem themselves back at Wembley 12 months later. But they were up against Bob Paisley's Liverpool team who were reigning league champions, going for not just the double but a unique treble: they had already won the league and they had the European Cup final to look forward to the following week.

Vowing to disappointed fans that United would win the cup in '77, United's manager, Tommy Docherty, wanted revenge for the calamitous defeat against the Saints, and returning to Wembley became his main goal after an indifferent league campaign, the team suffering a loss of form after the talismanic Martin Buchan was injured. And he enjoyed the satisfaction of beating Southampton in a fifth-round replay before, even sweeter, getting the better of Leeds United in the semis.

There was history between Revie's team and United. In 1965 and 1970, the two sides slugged it out – as did their fans, literally – at the semi-final stage. Both times Leeds prevailed after replays. Now they were to meet once again. But the great Leeds ship had sailed: many of their key players including Charlton, Bremner and Giles had retired or moved on, and Admiral Revie was now in charge of the England team.

Liverpool went into the final as firm favourites. United fretted over the fitness of their skipper and defensive lynchpin, Martin Buchan, who had suffered a bad knee injury just days before. Although he was nowhere near match fit, Buchan was imperious that day, shackling the mercurial Keegan, while at the other end of the pitch, the strike partnership of Stuart Pearson and Jimmy Greenhoff were giving Liverpool's back line a 90-minute headache. Greenhoff, now in his 30s, had only signed six months before, having accepted a big pay cut to leave Stoke City (yes, Stoke) to join the team he supported as a boy. He brought footballing intelligence to the forward line in much the same way that Teddy Sheringham would some 20 years later.

The first half ended goalless, but three goals in four dramatic minutes early in the second half decided the match. The United strike pairing combined to put Pearson through on goal and the number 9 beat Clemence at his near post only for Jimmy Case to score an equaliser two minutes later. The winner was scruffiness itself with Macari's effort deflected into the net via Greenhoff. It was not a thing of beauty to behold for anyone except the thousands of United fans and the jubilant Docherty.

Victory was sweet for the man from the rough East End of Glasgow. His managerial career had promised much but never quite delivered. The man was cruelly dismissed as 'the most successful failure in football'. Now, after a turbulent start at Old Trafford, he had won the cup, beaten rivals Liverpool and prevented them from winning the treble. As he wandered round Hyde Park in the early hours of Sunday morning, still in his cup final suit and champagne bottle in hand, it must have seemed like the dawn of a golden age, the start of something big for his young, buccaneering side. But it turned out to be a false dawn. Shortly after the final, Docherty's affair with Mary Brown, wife of the United physio, became public, and the United board gave him the sack.

*

Buccaneering was not one of the qualities ascribed to United's captain, a former pupil of the prestigious Robert Gordon College in Aberdeen, Martin Buchan. A club-record signing in 1972, United paid £120,000 for the cool, classy defender who quickly became an influential leader on the pitch, assuming the captaincy aged just 24 on Bobby Charlton's departure. Three years previously, he had captained Aberdeen to Scottish Cup success in 1970 and now he was to become the first player to lift the cup on both sides of the border. It was United's first major trophy since winning the European Cup in 1968, the first of the post-Busby era.

So, on that sunny Saturday afternoon, barely able to walk on the Friday before the final – 'I was just able to hobble' – Buchan now had to climb the Wembley steps to collect the prize. As the TV legend John Motson said in commentary, 'How fitting that it should be a man called Buchan who climbs the thirty-nine steps that lead from the pitch to the royal box.' A fitting tribute indeed to a Scotsman who was smart enough to enjoy the literary allusion.

THE DOC
Quote Unquote

Tommy Docherty, manager from December 1972 until the summer of 1977, was a larger-than-life character who was always quick with a quote and never one to mince words.

On management

'Of course we tell lies. We are the biggest hypocrites. We cheat. In our business the morals are different.'
(From an address at a Football Writers' Association dinner.)

'When one door closes, another slams shut in your face.'

'I must be the only man to lose his job for falling in love.'

On the directors of football clubs

'The ideal board of directors should be made up of three men, two dead and the other dying.'

'I don't think Henry Kissinger would have lasted 48 hours at Old Trafford.'

On the press

'I've always said there's a place for the press but they haven't dug it yet.'

On rivals Manchester City (in 1998, it has to be said)

'There are three types of Oxo cubes. Light brown for chicken stock, dark brown for beef stock and light blue for laughing stock.'

On the greatest footballer of all time

'You can keep your Bests, Pelés and Maradonas. Duncan Edwards was the greatest of them all.'

On his brushes with the law

'I've been in more courts than Björn Borg.'

'I will take you places no other man could. First stop, the Old Bailey.'

(His promise to Mary Brown, the love of his life. Mary was the wife of Laurie Brown, United's physiotherapist. Back in 1977, their affair became public. It was a different age with different standards of morality, and the club couldn't countenance Docherty staying in post. He blamed the prevailing conservatism of the United board for depriving him of fulfilling the promising potential of his buccaneering United team. The final irony is that the relationship was one that lasted: Mary and the Doc were happily married for more than 40 years until Tommy's death in 2020.)

On growing up in the East End of Glasgow

People assume that the tough-talking Docherty must have come from the Gorbals, but he hailed from an even rougher part of Glasgow – the East End, close to the home of Celtic. He once described how his mother struggled to make ends meet and had to rely on charity shops.

'You want to try walking to school wearing a third-hand Japanese admiral's outfit.'

On growing old, as told by his great friend Bill Shankly

'First they play bowls, then snooker and then golf,' said Shankly, adding, 'which just goes to prove that your balls do get smaller as you get older.' He would add the same punchline: 'So, Tommy, how about a game of marbles?'

What they said about the Doc . . .

'A liar and a bullshitter.'
(George Best in his infamous BBC *Wogan* chat show interview.)

'The worst manager there has ever been.'
(This quote, taken from a TV interview with Willie Morgan,

shortly after Docherty's sacking, so outraged the Doc that he sued the former player for libel in 1978. Unsuccessfully.)

'Tommy Doc? Come on, I'd rather go to the dentist than talk about Tommy Doc.'
(Paddy Crerand, Docherty's assistant from 1972 to 1976)

Ron Atkinson was dismissive . . .

'All I do know is that I'll never be able to achieve what Tommy Docherty did. And that is take Aston Villa to the Third Division and Manchester United into the Second Division.'

But the Doc had the last laugh . . .

'The sacking of Ron Atkinson is the best thing that could happen to Man United, and it didn't come a day too soon . . . his downfall has been all of his own doing. I dislike him because of his flash personality. And to my mind it's that sort of attitude which has finally got him the sack.'

Others remember him more charitably.

'There was no bigger character in the game than the Doc and there has never been one of such character since. He was funny, he could argue with you, but if you had a raging argument with him, he would make up with you the next day – it didn't affect your position in the team. I had Jock Stein, who changed my life by taking me to Celtic as a young boy, and then I went to Old Trafford with the Doc. He was an entertainer, a law unto himself and a great guy.'
(Lou Macari)

'For about four to five years, we were an unbelievable side and that was all down to the Doc . . . we were very, very attack-minded. The fans loved it at Manchester United. If the opposition scored two, we scored three . . . the words he used most in his team talks were: "Please the fans, excite the fans"'
(Sammy McIlroy)

THE QUIET MAN
Dave Sexton, United Manager, 1977 to 1981

July 1977. It was the second time in the space of ten years that Dave Sexton stepped out of Tommy Docherty's shadow and into the limelight. First, it was Chelsea; now, in the wake of Docherty's dismissal following his affair, it was United. The two men were chalk and cheese. One, shy and retiring, was happy to use the chalk for his blackboard coaching lessons; the other was finding his cheese to be hard and difficult to swallow.

Sexton hated the media circus. He was far happier on the training ground and was one of the most respected coaches around. He had coached at Chelsea and Arsenal before taking over at Stamford Bridge, where he developed Docherty's fledglings into a successful and attractive team that won both the 1970 FA Cup and European Cup Winners' Cup the following year, prompting Busby to offer him the manager's position at Old Trafford. That time Sexton demurred, staying with Chelsea before taking charge of Queens Park Rangers. Under Sexton, QPR, a team that had spent most of their history in the lower divisions, through an assortment of old rejects, mavericks and youngsters were elevated to a second-place finish in Division One in 1975.

With an impressive CV and a quiet and polite demeanour, he was seen as a safe pair of hands to take over United after the rollercoaster ride of the previous five years. The bookish Sexton enjoyed reading philosophy and poetry, and was a keen student of the tactical side of football, bringing video technology to Old Trafford for the first time.

His first job was to beef up a threadbare squad whose shortcomings were exposed if key players were injured. He added steel too by buying two of Leeds United's young stars: Gordon McQueen and Joe Jordan. On signing, McQueen instantly won over the United fans with his immortal quote: 'Ninety-nine per cent of footballers will tell you they want to join Man United. The other one per cent are liars.'

Sexton's modern tactical approach didn't go down well with everyone. Gordon Hill, a favourite of the Stretford End, didn't get the hang of the tracking-back business. The carefree 4-2-4 system preferred by Docherty morphed into a more cautious 4-4-2 under Sexton. The winger, feeling unloved, left to team up with his old boss at Derby County at the end of the season.

United struggled in the league but enjoyed a run in the cup. In words that summed up not just Sexton's era but that of his predecessor and successor, Lou Macari astutely observed, 'Whatever our struggles in the league, we always fancied ourselves in the cup. In a way you could say that was our problem, we had become a cup team.'

Which was fine as long as you won silverware. Unfortunately, under Sexton, United's one appearance at Wembley in 1979 ended in heartbreak after two goals in a late, late rally saw the Reds draw level with Arsenal, but as quickly as United hopes were raised, they were cruelly dashed when Alan Sunderland scored in the last minute to win it for the Gunners.

In the summer clear-out that followed, old stalwarts Stuart Pearson and Brian Greenhoff left the club with Sexton's Chelsea protégé Ray Wilkins joining for £825,000. Wilkins brought poise and vision to United's frenetic midfield, but the crowds didn't warm to him immediately; like Michael Carrick some 30 years later, he was unfairly accused of negativity, of being a master of the square pass.

The 1979/80 season held out yet more hope, this time in the league. In November, United topped the table, and a late run of eight wins on the trot the following spring saw them pushing hard for the title. Sexton must have been doing something right. So close, but once again, no cigar.

What was needed to squeeze out that extra 1 or 2% to go from nearly men to winners? Would Sexton throw caution to the wind? Would he hell. The following season was a borefest; United only managed to score 51 goals, featuring in eight goalless draws. This was poor fare to fans brought up on the attacking flair of the great 1960s side and the swashbuckling Docherty team of not so long ago. The team, like their manager, were just too quiet.

Sexton turned to the transfer market to address the problem, making Garry Birtles United's record signing, paying Nottingham Forest £1.25 million for their striker in October 1980. Unfortunately, United had not struck gold; rather, Sexton seemed to have turned gold into base metal. As hard as he tried, the luckless Birtles couldn't find the net.

There was a joke at the time, retold in Jim White's engaging *Manchester United: The Biography*, which captured the mood of United fans. When, in January 1981, the hostages were released after being held captive for six months in the American embassy in Tehran, what was the first thing the hostages asked when they were set free? Had Garry Birtles scored yet? (And, since you ask, no, he hadn't.)

Time was running out for Dave Sexton. He had brought stability and much-needed integrity to Old Trafford, and in Wilkins, Jordan and McQueen the spine of a good side. But the style of play was stultifying. The new chairman, Martin Edwards, mindful of the bottom line, was worried about the drop in attendances. He wanted box office, and that was not Sexton, the man dubbed 'Whispering Dave' by the press pack.

Edwards said, 'It wasn't happening, we weren't progressing, and the crowd was getting restless. But mostly I didn't feel the tradition was being upheld. There is such a thing as the United way. That is the character of the club and the supporters demand it.' Edwards wanted attacking football on the pitch and a big personality off it to take charge of the team.

And, in April 1981, the fans got what they wanted. Dave Sexton quietly left the stage to make way for a bigger player to strut upon it. It would be a case of *All's Well That Ends Well* if Edwards found 'a medicine that's able to breathe life into a stone, quicken a rock'. The prescription was Ron Atkinson.

CAPTAIN MARVEL TO THE RESCUE
Manchester United 3 Barcelona 0
21 MARCH 1984

In the 15 years since United exited at the semi-final stage of the European Cup in 1969, fans had been starved of European competition; with only two rounds of the 1977/78 Cup Winners' Cup they had precious little to enjoy.

Now, following their FA Cup triumph against Brighton in 1983, they were back in Europe. After seeing off the Bulgarians of Spartak Varna in the autumn, they had advanced to the quarter-final stage and could look forward to the mouth-watering prospect of a tie against Barcelona. United came into the match in good form; they had embarked on a 16-game unbeaten run in the league and were neck-and-neck with Liverpool at the top of the table.

The Catalans may not have been as formidable as they would later become; not unlike United, they had found winning cups easier than their domestic league. But they did boast a strong squad and, in Diego Maradoña, they had one of the most gifted players on the planet. At the Camp Nou, United had defended bravely but when Rojo blasted a late, late worldie, Barca took a two-goal advantage going into the return leg.

Chairman Martin Edwards warned Ron Atkinson to prepare himself for a special night, saying, 'You won't have heard anything like it.' Meanwhile, Atkinson had been making his own plans to create a noisy distraction for their visitors, hoping to disturb their night-time ease: 'We made sure they [Barcelona] were in a city hotel, with plenty of noise going on. Maradona liked all that and he joined in.'

Old Trafford was packed for the second leg. League attendances that season averaged 42,000, but that night more than 58,500 were crammed into the stadium. As the captains, Bryan Robson and Maradona, exchanged team colours before kick-off, fans roared in anticipation. Few gave United much chance of rescuing the tie from a two-goal deficit but they were about to witness something extraordinary. And the orchestrator-in-chief would be Robson.

Paul Davies, editor of *United Review*, would later capture the superhero qualities of Captain Marvel in this summary: 'He tackled like Nemanja Vidić; tore about the pitch with the intensity of Roy Keane (with slightly less snarling); timed runs into the box like Paul Scholes; and slung passes round the pitch like David Beckham.' He might have added that he could also head the ball like Denis Law and was as brave as a lion. Above all, he was an inspirational captain, not only leading by example but also driving his team on to ever greater efforts.

All those qualities were on display that evening. He gave United the lead on the night in the 23rd minute with a diving header. In two crucial minutes early in the second half, he scored the equaliser from close range and played a key role in setting up the third and winning goal for Frank Stapleton. At the final whistle, the crowd swarmed onto the pitch and lifted Robson shoulder-high.

It is still regarded as one of the loudest nights ever at the ground, with Robson later saying, 'It was the best atmosphere I have ever witnessed at Old Trafford,' and Sir Bobby Charlton commenting that he had rarely known a noisier crowd. The manager, beaming with delight, said, 'That was one of the great Old Trafford nights, that's what European football is really about.'

The Marvel scriptwriters would have liked Robson, but I suspect they'd have added one more quality: durability. When he played, United won more often than not; his games-to-victories ratio is better than those of Best, Law or Charlton. Maybe it's not surprising that he suffered so many injuries given his all-action playing style. Brian Clough said of Robson: 'Afterwards, he sometimes says, "I don't really know why I went for it." And he'll be asking that when he's lying in the treatment room. But that is Robson, end of story.'

Sure enough, from early April, at the crunch time of the season, Robson was sidelined for three critical weeks, missing both legs of the semi-final of the Cup Winners' Cup against Juventus, which United lost 3–2 on aggregate. Their form dipped in the league too with United only picking up seven points from their last eight games to finish fourth, six points behind champions Liverpool. Ah, what might have been if only he had stayed fit.

Let's leave the last word to someone who would eventually help Robson to win the coveted league title, Sir Alex Ferguson. 'An influential person in the dressing room, well-liked by the players, a great captain – and courage? Well, three broken legs, a broken collarbone, a hundred and one hamstring injuries, ankle injuries, and still played till 37 years of age! So that tells you something about the man. Oh . . . fantastic.'

A fitting tribute to United's marvel, their longest-serving captain, and a great servant to the club.

LEADING MEN
The Longest-serving and
Most Successful United Captains

It is unclear who led Newton Heath in their inaugural season. The first record of the captaincy appears on the 1882/83 fixture card, listing a Mr E. Thomas as captain about whom next to nothing is known. In the years spanning the club's accession to the Football League in 1892 as Newton Heath to the 2021/22 season, United have had 46 captains.

Defenders take well to captaincy – who'd want to argue with the likes of Frank 'Hard but unfair' Barson or Nemanja Vidić? But box-to-box midfielders like Bryan Robson or the uncompromising Roy Keane can inspire their teammates through their actions on the pitch, or to quote Sir Alex Ferguson, 'Roy is a natural, he leads by example. He's just like Bryan Robson.'

Longest-serving captains

Bryan Robson (1983–1994): midfield dynamo, nicknamed 'Captain Marvel', led United under Ron Atkinson, who bought him for a record £1.5 million fee from West Bromwich Albion, and Alex Ferguson. He shared the captaincy duties with Steve Bruce in his last two years.

Johnny Carey (1945–1953): Busby's first captain. Mr Versatility joined United as a teenager, making his debut before the war. He could play in any position on the field but he started most of his games at right-back. Captained the winning side in the 1948 FA Cup final and led the team to its first league title in 41 years in 1952.

Charlie Roberts (1905–1913): the first United captain to lift the League Division One trophy. Part of a famous back line alongside Dick Duckworth and Alex Bell, Roberts was a leader off the field as well; he and Billy Meredith were instrumental in setting up the Professional Footballers' Association in the face of hostility from the football authorities.

Roy Keane (1997–2005): United's most successful captain. An intimidating and aggressive presence on the pitch and in the dressing room, his energy and total commitment made him the perfect captain for his manager. They fell out badly over an interview Keane gave to MUTV, never publicly broadcast, where he was critical of some of his teammates; consequently, the Irishman left the club shortly thereafter.

Martin Buchan (1975–1981): having captained Aberdeen at the age of 20 to a shock Scottish Cup final victory over European Cup finalists Celtic, Buchan was bought by United in 1972 for a club record fee of £125,000, perhaps manager Frank O'Farrell's best decision during his time at Old Trafford. He led United to promotion from Division Two in 1975 and appeared in three FA Cup finals, winning the trophy in 1977.

Frank Barson (1922–1928): legendary hardman, a tough

centre-half who was sent off a dozen times in his career. In 1925, chairman J.H. Davies, owner of a successful brewing empire, promised to gift him a pub if he could guide United to promotion from the Second Division and Barson duly obliged. It was a rare moment of glory in a dismal period in the club's history.

Gary Neville (2005–2011): another right-back and graduate of the Class of '92. Earned the nickname 'Red Nev' after fighting his teammate's corner after England dropped Rio Ferdinand for missing a drugs test, threatening to call the players out on strike. United through and through, Neville emulated Keane's achievement of winning Premier League titles in three successive years.

Most successful captains

Roy Keane: four Premier League titles in 1998/99, 1999/2000, 2000/01 and 2002/03; two FA Cups in 1999 and 2004; the European Cup in 1999; the treble in 1999.

Gary Neville: four Premier League titles in 2006/07, 2007/08, 2008/09 and 2010/11; three League Cup wins in 2006, 2009 and 2010; the Champions League in 2008.

Steve Bruce: three Premier League titles in 1992/93, 1993/94 (both shared with Robson) and 1995/96; two FA Cup wins in 1994 and 1996; the double in 1993/94 and 1995/96.

Bryan Robson: two Premier League titles (both shared with Steve Bruce) in 1992/93 and 1993/94; three FA Cups in 1983, 1985 and 1990; the European Cup Winners' Cup in 1991; the double in 1993/94.

Charlie Roberts: two First Division titles in 1907/08 and 1910/11; the FA Cup in 1909.

Roger Byrne: two First Division titles in 1955/56 and 1956/57.

Denis Law: two First Division titles in 1964/65 and 1966/67.

Johnny Carey: the First Division title in 1951/52 and the FA Cup in 1948.

THE FOREIGN LEGION
United's First Foreign Players

Players from 45 different countries including the home nations have appeared for United. Excluding those with British or Irish nationality, 117 overseas players have made at least one first team appearance. But who were the early pioneers?

From 1930, following Arsenal's attempt to sign an Austrian goalkeeper, the ever-blinkered Football League imposed a ban on non-British-born nationals playing professional football in England unless they qualified through two years' residency in the country. The ban, supported by the Ministry of Labour, stayed in place until February 1978 when the European Community ruled it unenforceable. But in the intervening years, a few overseas players slipped through the net, with a couple finding their way to Old Trafford.

Two United States internationals who starred in the World Cup could make a claim to being United's first foreign players. Jim Brown, scorer of the Americans' only goal as losing semi-finalists to Argentina in the inaugural tournament in 1930, was born in Scotland but moved to America where he began his football career. As the game fell into decline in the US, Brown decided to try his luck in Britain, returning in 1932. A number of clubs were interested in signing him, but it was the quick thinking of manager Scott Duncan that ensured he became a

United player. As Brown's ship neared port at Londonderry, Duncan took a tugboat out to the liner and signed Brown on board, pipping his rivals. Brown was a success in his two years at Old Trafford, scoring 17 goals in 40 games. But was he American? He qualified to play for the US national team through his father's citizenship, while his own was not conferred until the mid-1930s. It is almost certain that he was a British subject at the time of his signing.

Ed McIlvenny was another 'American' escapee. A Scot by birth, he emigrated to the US in 1949. During United's summer tour of North America in May the following year, he turned out for the Kearney-Philadelphia All Stars, catching Matt Busby's eye in the only game of the tour that United failed to win. After promising to apply for American citizenship, McIlvenny was eligible to play for the national side in the following month's World Cup in Brazil and he was picked to captain the team against England. The game ended in a shock 1–0 victory for the USA in what became known as the 'Miracle Match' of Belo Horizonte. He stayed at Old Trafford for two years but only ever managed two appearances for the first team. He never did become an American citizen.

The first foreign-born player to appear for United was Carlo Sartori, who was spotted while turning out for, er, Manchester Schools, having arrived in England as a boy. The ginger-haired Sartori joined the Reds aged 15 and made his debut in 1968, making a further 55 appearances before being transferred to Bologna for a fee of £50,000 four years later. His Italian passport would have come in handy.

Finally, we come to the first proper example of an 'import' as such players are commonly known. After the EC ruling, Tottenham made the headlines with the signing of the two

Argentinians, Ossie Ardiles and Ricky Villa, after the 1978 World Cup, while Ipswich brought in two Dutchmen, Arnold Mühren and Frans Thijssen, from FC Twente. It would take United until 1980 to make a move when Dave Sexton signed the Yugoslav Nikola Jovanović from Red Star Belgrade for a cool £300,000. Injuries and national service limited the imposing defender to just 26 appearances before he returned home – by road, in his Man United company car.

It was Arnold – or, to give him his glorious full name, Arnoldus Johannes Hyacinthus Mühren – who would be the first foreign player to make an impact at Old Trafford. Moving from Portman Road in 1982, the classy midfielder complemented Bryan Robson's energy with passing ability and astute distribution. He scored in the 1983 FA Cup final replay win over Brighton, but injuries took their toll on his United career. His playing opportunities were further restricted by the arrival of the next exciting overseas star to join the club, the Danish winger Jesper Olsen, who arrived in 1984 from Ajax for £700,000.

Foreign players were still as rare as exotic birds until the 1990s. It's at this point that the English game takes off with the return of English teams to European competition in 1991, new money coming into the game from terrestrial and satellite television, and all-seater stadia drawing bigger crowds. The new Premier League was beginning to attract a global audience. With the funds coming in from an increasingly commercialised game, Premier League teams were now looking to recruit talent from abroad. And for United, slow starters in the import business, the arrival of Peter Schmeichel, Andrei Kanchelskis and Eric Cantona gave them the panache that helped transform Fergie's also-rans into serial title winners.

THE 1985 FA CUP
Manchester United 2 Liverpool 0

The Ron Atkinson era had proved to be a step up from the underachieving Sexton years – United were now offering fans excitement and attacking verve. On his arrival, Big Ron persuaded Martin Edwards to spend big in the transfer market; the signing of Bryan Robson and Remi Moses brought steel and energy to the midfield while Frank Stapleton added a goal threat up front.

But United faced a daunting challenge in the shape of the Liverpool juggernaut. Liverpool had enjoyed unprecedented success under Busby's old teammate Bob Paisley and his Boot Room successor Joe Fagan, winning three consecutive league titles from 1981/82 to 1983/84. And now a new threat emerged: Liverpool's neighbours Everton, winners of the 1984 FA Cup, had romped away with the 1985 league title and on 15 May lifted the European Cup Winners' Cup.

United were what we now call a top-four side – good but not quite good enough to dislodge their Merseyside rivals in the league. But in a one-off game, United were a match for anyone. To add to their midfield energy, they now had the attacking flair and threat of two academy players, Norman Whiteside and Mark Hughes; and in the summer of 1984 a threat from wide areas in the form of wingers Gordon Strachan and Jesper Olsen. In the league fixtures, United got the better of Liverpool

– as they usually did in the Thatcher decade – winning one and drawing one, but Everton thrashed United twice in the space of three days in the autumn, deflating United's league chances and dumping them out of the League Cup.

United's only realistic chance for glory at the end of the 1984/85 season lay in the FA Cup. Their passage to the semi-final had been smooth enough but standing in their path to Wembley were arch-rivals Liverpool. In the other semi, Everton faced the easier task of overcoming mid-table Luton Town. Could United prevent an all-Merseyside final? Could they upset the Scouse duopoly and win the trophy?

The first hurdle would require two attempts to clear. The first game at Goodison ended in a 2–2 draw with Liverpool riding their luck and the referee missing the linesman's flag in the build-up to Liverpool's second equaliser.

In the replay, United were behind at half-time to a McGrath own goal and in need of inspiration. Cue Captain Marvel. If ever there was a man for the big occasion, it was Bryan Robson. In his time at Old Trafford, he scored five goals in eight semi-finals and three goals in five finals. And if Liverpool were the best team of the 1980s, arguably, in their captain, United had the player of the decade.

United had come charging out of the blocks for the second half. In the 46th minute, Robson played a neat one-two with Gordon Strachan and cut through the Liverpool defence. Then, sensing Mark Lawrenson was catching him, he decided to let fly from 25 yards out. His stunning left-foot shot flew into the top corner giving Grobbelaar no chance. Eight minutes later, Strachan was the provider, sliding the ball through to Mark Hughes to score the deciding goal. It was an epic encounter. The *Guardian* wrote: 'If the atmosphere at Goodison Park had been electric, then Maine Road on the Wednesday night was simply nuclear.' And in the same paper, Rob Smyth wrote in 2011: 'This was football as nature intended, a relentlessly attacking slugfest played by proper men in front of proper men, in an atmosphere that, 26 years on, effortlessly shivers the spine.'

If the semi-final had been a classic, the final itself, as was often the case, failed to live up to expectations. The big talking point was the controversial sending-off of Kevin Moran in the 77th minute, 'A savage injustice,' railed the *Mirror*'s Frank McGhee. With the game deep into extra time, the ten men stood firm against a tiring Everton side who, just three days before, had been victorious in Europe. Then came a moment of genius: out on the right wing, Norman Whiteside, backed van den Hauwe towards goal and, using the defender as a shield, curled a superb left-footed shot off the inside of the post and past Neville Southall.

Steve Curry of the *Express* later described the shot as 'lethal as an Exocet missile'. Put simply, it was a goal worthy of winning a Cup final.

Atkinson had triumphed over both halves of Merseyside. But 1985 was as good as it would get for Big Ron. For while the new league season started with fireworks, United's title challenge fizzled out like a Hogmanay party on a rainy January morning and 1986 proved to be one long hangover. The Scousers would enjoy popping the champagne corks a while longer.

THE LONGEST WINNING STREAK
August to November 1985

Following on from their 1985 FA Cup triumph, United were off their blocks at a blistering pace at the beginning of the new season. Let's ignore the Charity Shield defeat to champions Everton, but starting with a home game against Aston Villa on 17 August, United began an 11-game winning sequence:

Manchester United 4 Aston Villa 0
Ipswich Town 0 Manchester United 1
Arsenal 1 Manchester United 2
Manchester United 2 West Ham United 0
Nottingham Forest 1 Manchester United 3
Manchester United 3 Newcastle United 0
Manchester United 3 Oxford United 0
Manchester City 0 Manchester United 3
West Bromwich Albion 1 Manchester United 5
Crystal Palace 0 Manchester United 1 (League Cup Second Round, first leg)
Manchester United 1 Southampton 0

After the Southampton game, United fans were entitled to believe that the long 18-year wait to lift the league title was finally ending. As they consulted their Sunday papers on 29

166

September they would have found the top half of the table looking like this:

	P	W	D	L	F	A	GD	Pts
1. Manchester United	10	10	0	0	27	3	24	30
2. Liverpool	10	6	3	1	25	11	14	21
3. Chelsea	10	5	3	2	14	10	4	18
4. Newcastle United	10	5	3	2	17	14	3	18
5. Everton	10	5	2	3	18	12	6	17
6. Arsenal	10	5	2	3	12	10	2	17
7. Sheffield Wednesday	10	5	2	3	15	18	-3	17
8. Tottenham Hotspur	10	5	1	4	22	12	10	16
9. Watford	10	5	1	4	22	16	6	16
10. Birmingham City	10	5	1	4	10	14	-4	16

Alas, it was not to last. A 1–1 draw at Luton ended the winning run, but United stayed unbeaten until early November when they travelled to Hillsborough, having increased their lead over Liverpool to ten points, having won 13 and drawn two of their 15 league games. Then Big Ron's tyres got a puncture after losing 1–0 to third-placed Sheffield Wednesday before the wheels truly came off. The season that had promised so much ended in bitter disappointment. Uncertainty over Hughes' future at the club and injuries to their inspirational captain Robson affected United's form. From their next 26 games they could only muster 35 points, finishing a distant fourth behind, yes, Liverpool.

What a difference a year makes. The young Mark Hughes, top scorer that season and the season before, had departed in the summer to join Terry Venables' Barcelona and Atkinson's forward line lacked its spark. A year on from the defeat to Wednesday, United languished just above the relegation places, and time was called on Atkinson's five-and-a half-year reign. At least his record for the longest winning sequence still stands, bearing testimony to a broken dream of what might have been.

ROBINS, THE BOY WONDER, SAVES THE DAY

Nottingham Forest 0 Manchester United 1

7 JANUARY 1990

It's the first Sunday of the new decade. It's the third round of the FA Cup and it's live on TV. Struggling Manchester United are away to Brian Clough's classy Nottingham Forest, the team that dumped United out of the cup the previous year. The sense of anticipation is tangible. There's going to be a public execution, and the head that is going to roll belongs to Alex Ferguson, who after more than three years in charge – an eternity by today's standards – is guilty of being a serial under-achiever. His neck is on the block . . .

The tabloids had had a field day in the run-up to the big match, the *Sun*'s headline reading: 'Troubled Boss Ferguson Reconciled to Trial by TV as Another Crisis Grips Old Trafford'. Ex-United captain Willie Morgan chipped in, bemoaning how Fergie had 'wasted £13 million on inexperienced players like Gary Pallister who are not up to the job'.

It had been a dismal season for United. They were languishing in fifteenth place in the league, had suffered a 5–1 pasting at the hands of their city neighbours in the autumn, and were then unceremoniously dumped out of the League Cup by Spurs. Fans were growing impatient. After early progress in his first full season, Ferguson's team seemed to be regressing. Many supporters who craved success had seen enough and wanted the manager to 'f**k off back to Scotland'.

The pressure was building. The bruising effects of the media onslaught and poor results on the pitch were compounded by disquiet in the Ferguson household. His wife, Cathy, and the children were unhappy, eldest son Mark telling his father, 'Dad, it's not working.' Even answering the phone was freighted with anxiety as the chances were it might be another abusive caller.

The FA Cup, so often a consolation for United in recent times, now represented Ferguson's last hope of silverware that season. Going into the tie, United had injury concerns to add to the manager's woes; Webb, Gibson, Ince, Donaghy and Wallace were all missing and, worst of all, so was their captain and talisman, Bryan Robson.

Even today, the third round of the Cup is a special date in the football calendar. In 1990, when live TV on a Sunday afternoon was a relative novelty, viewers eagerly awaited the drama, and the denouement of the Ferguson experiment. They were ready for the axe to fall. The City Ground crackled with tension. But Fergie's boys held their nerve. Roared on by a vociferous travelling support, United showed resolve. In the 53rd minute, two of Fergie's fledglings, 21-year-old Lee Martin and 20-year-old Mark Robins, aided by academy graduate Mark Hughes, combined to produce the winner.

It was a stay of execution. It has since been argued that the manager's position was never in jeopardy. Chairman Martin Edwards had privately assured Ferguson before the game that his job was safe; he hadn't wished to voice his confidence in public for fear of inducing the predictable press speculation. Sir Bobby Charlton, who along with Edwards and Sir Matt Busby was one of the keepers of the United flame, always had faith in Ferguson: 'During that time we never, ever discussed Ferguson's position, because we knew what he was doing was right.'

What Charlton and other insiders could see was the transformation of the club from the bottom up. The disruptive elements within the club had been moved on. The youth system had been revamped, and Ferguson was starting to bring young players through the ranks. Brian Kidd was brought in to overhaul and expand the scouting system and to prioritise the recruitment of local talent from the North West.

The cup run wasn't good for the fans' blood pressure. United scraped past lowly Hereford, and the winning margins were never greater than a single goal; both the semi-final and final were six-goal thrillers which had to be replayed. The two fledglings who had helped win the tie at the City Ground at the start of the run would make telling contributions at the end. Robins came off the bench to score the winner in extra time in the semi-final replay against Oldham. In the FA Cup final replay, it was Lee Martin who wrote himself into United history with the only goal of the game to beat Crystal Palace.

The relief was palpable. Ferguson, writing in his autobiography, said that 'winning the 1990 FA Cup allowed us breathing space and deepened my sense that this was a wonderful club with which to win trophies. To win the FA Cup at Wembley made the good times roll.'

Was his job in danger? It's easy to dismiss the idea in hindsight and in the glow of the two glittering decades of success he enjoyed after his first win. Had Robins not scored on that January afternoon it could well have been a very different story. And even after the Wembley triumph, Ferguson was still on notice. Ferguson never forgot the headline in one newspaper, on the morning after the victory, which declared: 'OK, you've proved you can win the FA Cup, now go back to Scotland.'

To win over the doubters and earn a full reprieve there would have to be more trophies, and he would never rest easy until he won the prize that the fans craved most: the league title.

VITAL SPARK

'The best big-game player I have ever known'
– Sir Alex Ferguson

Leslie Mark Hughes had joined United from school in 1978 as a 15-year-old, serving a long apprenticeship before he made his debut in the League Cup in November 1983. It took him just 12 minutes to make an impact, scoring United's only goal in a 1–1 draw against Oxford United, and he scored again in his first league start the following March.

Ron Atkinson wasn't short of strikers; the established pairing of Frank Stapleton and the boy wonder Norman Whiteside – actually two years younger than Hughes – was supplemented by the signing of Alan Brazil in the summer of 1984. Nevertheless, 1984/85 was Hughes' breakthrough season – he made 55 appearances and was the club's top scorer, netting 24 times. His performances caught the eye of his fellow professionals, who chose him as the PFA Young Player of the Year.

Soft-spoken and mild-mannered off the pitch, this young Welshman was transformed into a Celtic warrior once the referee's whistle was blown. 'Sparky', as he was popularly known, was fiery, fast, physically strong, tigerish in the tackle and always up for the fight – he was no stranger to the referee's book, being sent off on five occasions during his two spells at Old Trafford. He was also capable of the most spectacular strikes – first-time volleys, bullet headers, overhead kicks, bicycle kicks and long-range rockets that Kim Jong-un would have been proud of.

Hughes lit the spark for United's blistering start to the 1985/86 season when they won their first ten league games and were nine points clear at the top of the table. Of course, it didn't last. While Robson's injury lay-off was a major blow, the uncertainty surrounding Hughes' future at the club was another factor in United's slump in form.

Halfway through the season, a deal was struck that would take Hughes to Terry Venables' Barcelona in the summer. United's hand had been forced. Hughes, unusually for the time, had a buy-out clause in his contract, and the chairman, Martin Edwards, felt he had no choice but to sell, albeit for a juicy £1.8 million, thereby helping United's shaky finances. For Hughes, the prospect of European competition, denied to English clubs following the ban imposed after Heysel,* and the tenfold increase in wages was irresistible.

However, it was no Nirvana. An unhappy 12 months at the Camp Nou was followed by a loan spell at Bayern Munich. United's new manager, Alex Ferguson, was keen to bring back the prodigal son, but tax reasons delayed his return until the summer of 1988.

The second coming was greeted enthusiastically by the Old Trafford faithful. He formed a productive partnership with Brian McClair, the pair netting 136 times in four seasons before

---

* The Heysel disaster, on 29 May 1985, occurred before the start of the European Cup final between Juventus and Liverpool at the Heysel Stadium in Brussels, Belgium. Liverpool fans breached a fence into the Juventus section, and the Juventus fans retreated from the terraces towards a concrete wall, where many were crushed. The wall eventually collapsed, allowing fans to escape, but not before 39 people were killed (32 Italians, four Belgians, two from France and one from Northern Ireland) and 600 injured in the confrontation. The tragedy resulted in all English football clubs being placed under an indefinite ban from all European competitions by UEFA, which wasn't lifted until 1990/91.

McClair dropped back into a midfield role after the arrival of Eric Cantona.

But Hughes came into his own in the big games, and in the 1980s and early 1990s the big games usually involved cup competition. In the FA Cup, he scored the winner in the titanic clash with Liverpool in the semi-final replay in 1985; in the 1990 final, it was a brace in the memorable 3–3 draw against Palace; a goal in the 1994 final; and, in 1995, a brilliant extra-time volley to defeat Oldham in the semi-final replay.

The *pièce de résistance* came in the final of the European Cup Winners' Cup in 1991 against Barcelona. Much was riding on the game. For Sparky, there was a point to prove against his old employers. For his boss, Alex Ferguson, it held out the prospect of adding a second trophy to his threadbare United CV. For fans of English football, it was the first chance of European glory since the ban on English clubs had been lifted.

The Feyenoord Stadium was ablaze with red flares; the place was jumping with young Madchester devotees, thrilled to be back on the European stage and singing James' 'Sit Down'. After a goalless first half, Hughes followed up a Steve Bruce header to tap the ball over the goal line. One–nil. Five minutes later, he found himself racing through on the Barca goal, with only the keeper Carles Busquets (Sergio's father) to beat. Busquets forced him wide to the edge of the penalty area to a seemingly impossible angle; it looked as though the chance was gone. But Hughes, with consummate technique, smashed the ball from fully 20 yards with enough pace to beat the defenders racing back and enough accuracy to find the corner of the net. A late Koeman free kick could not deny the Reds a hard-earned but well-deserved win.

The victory in Rotterdam was to prove the spark for the rebirth of United as a serious force in football. Ferguson, whose sole success at Old Trafford had been a domestic cup, could now point to a European triumph, besting Barcelona into the bargain. Finally, the fans were off his back and now believed the manager's big plan might just work.

In addition to the Cup Winners' Cup, Hughes had won two league titles, the double in 1993/94, a League Cup and three FA Cups before moving on to Chelsea in 1995. That night in Rotterdam capped a great year for Sparky; the fans voted him the Sir Matt Busby Player of the Year in 1991 and he also picked up the PFA Player of the Year Award. To quote another Spark – Muriel – he was the crème de la crème.

DAVID BECKHAM'S SCHOOLDAYS

The quarter-final defeat at Guadalajara on 14 June 1970 was hard to take for Bobby Charlton. The hero of '66, substituted in the second half, could only watch on as West Germany came from behind to end England's chances of retaining the World Cup. After the match, Charlton informed Sir Alf Ramsey of his retirement from international football.

The match was also the last that England would play in the World Cup finals for 12 years. Charlton, exasperated at England's failure to qualify for the tournaments held in West Germany and Argentina, decided something had to be done to improve the standard of English football. In 1978, he established the Bobby Charlton Soccer School, offering residential football-based courses for youngsters as young as eight in the summer holidays.

In 1985, one football-mad schoolboy was thrilled to attend the summer camp. Ted Beckham, a Londoner United fan, cheerfully drove his young son up the motorway to drop off the ten-year-old at the Wilmslow camp. And happily did so the following year when young David came top of the class of '86, winning himself a trip to Barcelona. Charlton recognised a special talent – the best he had coached since the school began. As Beckham later recalled in 2017, 'That was when Sir Bobby contacted Manchester United and said, "Maybe you should have a look out for this young kid."' Full of admiration for the

United legend, he added, 'So I owe everything to Sir Bobby because, if not, maybe I wouldn't have had the chance of living my dream of playing for the club that I'd supported for so many years and the club my dad supported.

'He has always been about being successful, but even more so about helping other people. That's what's so special about him – he's respected on the field, but even more so off the field.'

Beckham signed schoolboy terms with United and, if ever United were in London, would rendezvous with the squad, often at the West Lodge Park Hotel in Cockfosters. He was made their mascot for the October 1987 trip to West Ham. Beckham warmed up with Bryan Robson and Gordon Strachan before he managed to sneak onto the row behind the United bench. As the *Match of the Day* cameras zoomed in on the United bench for a second-half substitution, Beckham could be seen sitting behind an animated Ferguson who, as usual, was barking out instructions.

Even as a kid, Beckham was savvy and knew how to win friends and influence people. He modelled his hair on Gordon Strachan's and gave the Scot a tub of hair gel as a present. Beckham's mother then gift-wrapped a pen for Beckham to present to the United manager. 'I'll sign you for Manchester United using this pen,' Ferguson remembered. He was as good as his word.

On finishing school, Beckham moved to Manchester, signing a YTS contract in 1991. He would team up with Giggs, Scholes, Butt and the Neville brothers to form the nucleus of the famous class of '92 and the bedrock of the United team that would dominate English football for more than a decade thereafter. Sir Bobby would surely have been proud that his project produced a star pupil who not only shone for the club he loved but would also go on to captain England in two World Cup finals tournaments. He was a class act.

THE CLASS OF '92

United are rightfully proud of the young talent that has flowed from its academy since the 1930s. The Busby Babes were a spectacular flowering, but thereafter young players continued to graduate through the ranks to the first team on a regular basis. Even under Ron Atkinson, who concentrated most of his energies on the senior squad, stars of the quality of Mark Hughes, Norman Whiteside and Clayton Blackmore made their debuts as teenagers.

Alex Ferguson, however, was shocked with the state of the youth set-up that he found on arrival from Aberdeen in 1986. His first impression of Old Trafford was that it seemed like a theatre of ghosts where the present was haunted by past glories, and he wanted to put in place a proper youth system that could be, in his words, 'the new spirit of the club'. He gave youth coach Eric Harrison more resources and brought in Wembley hero Brian Kidd to scout the North West for new recruits.

Fergie's early years were a struggle. On New Year's Day 1989, faced with an injury crisis, the Scot turned to the academy and pitched Lee Martin, Russell Beardsmore, Mark Robins and 18-year-old Lee Sharpe (signed the previous year from Torquay) to face reigning champions Liverpool. Beardsmore played a blinder, scoring in an emphatic 3–1 win. Over the coming weeks as more youngsters were blooded, the press took notice, and the phrase 'Fergie's Fledglings' took flight across the back pages.

Ferguson was being both pragmatic and tickling the collective tummy of the Stretford End. The sight of home-grown talent wearing the red shirt made hearts beat faster; that winter and early spring, fans shivered with excitement at the prospect of a better future. But as the first-teamers recovered, the young guns made way and their appearances became lesser spotted. It had been a useful diversion, but ultimately the potential was never fulfilled. Of the fledglings, only Lee Sharpe would make a major contribution in the coming years.

In 1989, Ferguson hired World Cup legend Nobby Stiles to add experience to Harrison's team. The seeds of a revitalised youth team were sown. And it wasn't long before their efforts were rewarded with a bumper crop. In 1992, the boys won the FA Youth Cup for the first time since the Busby era. The side that won the cup included four who would join the pantheon of United's all-time greats: David Beckham, Ryan Giggs, Gary Neville and Nicky Butt. The match day squad also included Robbie Savage and Keith Gillespie, who made their names elsewhere. Others, equally talented, such as Ben Thornley and John O'Kane would have their wings clipped by injury or illness.

The following year, Paul Scholes and Phil Neville appeared in the final but lost to an otherwise anonymous Leeds United. Phil, however, had the pleasure of captaining the victorious 1995 finalists. It may be more accurate to label this group of starlets as the Class of '92½, but thanks to the TV documentary and press coverage, the number 92 has stuck.

There have been other Youth Cup winners since – the 2011 champions could boast Pogba, Lingard and Michael Keane in their ranks – but none had the same impact as their illustrious precursors. The freakishly talented Giggs had debuted in 1991 and was an established first-team regular. The following season, the core of the group came through together: Butt, Beckham and Gary Neville all took their first bows in the autumn of 1992; Paul Scholes appeared in 1994; while Phil Neville was as late to the party as some of his tackles, making his first start in January 1995.

This close-knit unit had been moulded in the United way and in Ferguson's image. Before the last home game of the 1992/93 title-winning season, Fergie had the youth team lined up on the touchline to savour the moment and inhale the sweet smell of success. Apart from their abundant skill and ability, these boys would go on to develop the character and the will to win.

They came of age in the 1995/96 season. Not everyone was convinced about Ferguson's faith in youth. On the opening day of the season, when United fielded four players aged 20 or under with another two on the bench, United crashed 3–1 away to Aston Villa. BBC *Match of the Day*'s Alan Hansen was critical. 'You can't win anything with kids' was his verdict; unless Ferguson invested in the transfer market, they would fail to regain their title. Nine days later, when these same kids turned over reigning champions Blackburn at Ewood Park, the football world sat up and took notice.

To a degree, Hansen was correct. United may have gone on to record another triumphant double that season, but the young bloods had the company of experienced teammates like Bruce, Keane, the returning Cantona, Irwin and others to do the heavy lifting. Nonetheless, they had proved themselves, and the Class of '92 would form the core of the United side for the next seven seasons, winning a further five league titles, the FA Cup and the Champions League to complete a historic treble in 1999.

The class broke up after Beckham departed to Madrid in July 2003. Nicky Butt left six months later to try his luck at Newcastle, and Phil Neville moved to Goodison Park in 2005. However, the bonds endured and the six core members of the class remained friends, with shared business interests and joint ownership of Second Division side Salford City.

The talent still rolls off the academy production line: Solskjær's 2021/22 first-team squad was brimful of alumni: Rashford, Greenwood, McTominay, Pogba, Lingard and more. But 30 years earlier, United's academy produced one of its finest vintages, certainly the best since the great sides of the 1950s. Raise a glass to the Class of '92.

UNITED ARTISTS
On Screens Great and Small

The appeal of Manchester United has proved irresistible to movie-makers, and a number of memorable full-length films have been made about the club and its teams, players and managers. The films fall into two broad categories: documentary and dramatised.

The Documentaries

In a golden age of television when the likes of Sky, Netflix and Amazon poured millions into the production of sports films, a number of fine documentaries have been made about United. *Class of '92* (2013) featured the young stars who became the core of Ferguson's all-conquering sides, as did the BBC's *Class of '92: Out of Their League* (2015), which followed these same players as they embarked upon a new adventure through their ownership of the then non-league Salford City. BT Sport's *Too Good to Go Down* charted United's disastrous relegation in the 1973/74 season. The two great United managers were the subjects of *Sir Alex Ferguson: The Secrets to Success* and the simply named and simply excellent *Busby* (2019). The documentary *Never Give In* (2021), directed by his son Jason, offers a revealing and intimate insight into the life of Sir Alex. *George Best: All By Himself* (2016) is a thoughtful, balanced account of the superstar's flawed genius and troubled personal life.

The most poignant has to be Harry Gregg's return to the scene of the most terrible event in United's history. It was captured in the BBC's *One Life: Munich Air Disaster* and broadcast on 6 February 2008 to mark the 50th anniversary of the crash.

The strangest but also one of the most affecting films is surely the award-winning *My Mate, Manchester United* (2011). It covers the ten-year obsession and struggle of an unemployed labourer who wanted to change his name from Marin Zdravkov Levidzhov to Manchester United Zdravkov Levidzhov. For more on this story see page 371.

The Dramatisations

Such was David Beckham's fame and fan worship that he had a hit movie named in his honour. *Bend It Like Beckham* was released in 2002 at the height of Beckham mania. An original, joyful coming-of-age comedy, it starred Parminder Nagra as Jess, the daughter of traditional Sikhs who fled Uganda for middle-class Hounslow and expect her to marry a nice Indian boy. As Jess's mum says: 'Who'd want a girl who plays football all day but can't make chapattis?' But Jess prefers playing football in the local park and confiding her dreams to the poster of Beckham above her bed. She encounters Juliette (Keira Knightley in her first role) and sport and romance ensue. An irresistible crowd-pleaser!

An earlier and more enduring idol, George Best, was the

subject of the eponymous *Best* (2000); the biopic was the brainchild of husband-and-wife team, writer Mary McGuckian and director John Lynch. Lynch, probably best known for playing ACC Burns in BBC hit, *The Fall*, got to play the man himself. Although not a hit, the cast was interesting, to say the least, with Ian Hart as Nobby Stiles, Jerome Flynn (Bronn from *Game of Thrones*) as Bobby Charlton, Linus Roache (*Homeland*, *Vikings*) playing Denis Law, Roger Daltrey as Rodney Marsh, Patsy Kensit as Angie, and Stephen Fry as Frazer Crane – no, not *Frasier* – the architect of Best's modernist house in Bramall.

Then there was *Believe* (2014), a well-meaning, feelgood movie starring Hollywood star Brian Cox as Matt Busby. Retired from management but still haunted by memories of Munich, he coaches a boys' team to the final of the Manchester Junior Footballing Cup. Not in the starting XI, the young hero of the story, a former petty criminal but talented footballer, only appears in the second half to rescue his team from defeat by scoring a late winner. Sound familiar? One reviewer cruelly described the film as an 'unlikely cross between *Billy Elliot* and *Bend It Like Beckham*', another as 'trifling hooey'.

Altogether more interesting was Ken Loach's 2009 fantasy comedy, *Looking for Eric*. This charming film stars a former guitarist from The Fall, Steve Evets, as Eric Bishop, a down-on-his-luck postie who supports Man Utd, but more importantly it features the acting talents of the King himself, who listens to Eric's woes and dispenses some wise life lessons – with flawless comic timing. Cantona has appeared in more than 20 films in Britain and France (he produced this one), as well as advertisements for Kronenbourg 1664 – although, embarrassingly, one of these had to be pulled from distribution. In the banned advert Eric confidently boasts, 'If you find a better-tasting French beer, we'll eat our berets,' but this incurred a ban from the Advertising Standards Agency for misleading drinkers about the beer's origins – the beer was actually brewed in, er, Manchester!

But arguably the best film about the club was the BBC's 2011 film *United*, described in a *Guardian* review as 'beautifully done – powerful, haunting and very human'. Matt Busby's son, Sandy, took umbrage with the portrayal of his father, but David Tennant owns the part of United's assistant manager Jimmy Murphy, and, with Hollywood stars Jack O'Connell as Bobby Charlton and Sam Claflin as Duncan Edwards also featuring, the film vividly depicts the trauma of Munich and its effects on the survivors, the club and the wider Manchester community.

To end on a lighter note, here's my fantasy film star XI (playing an attacking 4-2-4 system):

Goalkeeper: Ron Howard
Full-backs: Jim Carrey, Gabriel Byrne
Centre-backs: Steve McQueen, Julia Roberts
Midfield: Dame Flora Robson, Mel Gibson
Forwards: Sid James, Jude Law, Louis Jourdan and, of course, Eric Cantona
Sub: Tim Robbins
Manager: Busby Berkeley

BRUCE RISES TO THE CHALLENGE
Manchester United 2 Sheffield Wednesday 1
10 APRIL 1993

It was unbearably tense. It was spring, the business end of the season. United had let slip their lead in the inaugural Premier League table and, going into the match against a very good Sheffield Wednesday side that had already reached the finals of both that season's league and FA cups, the manager had described the game as 'win or bust'.

Despite a bombardment of the visitors' goal, Wednesday had the lead with four minutes left on the clock. Surely history wasn't going to repeat itself? The previous year, United had led the league at the end of March but, after dropping 13 points in six games in April, the title was gifted to Leeds United. The long wait to win their first title since 1967 continued, and once again the fans began to fear the worst.

Then, in the 86th minute, from a corner, Steve Bruce rose to head in from fully 15 yards out. Cue wild celebrations. Bruce, who played over 400 games for United, had a knack for scoring goals, hitting the net 51 times in his nine years at the club. The centre-half, who had formed a rock-solid partnership with Gary Pallister at the heart of the United defence, now shouldered the captaincy duties as Bryan Robson was sidelined through a succession of injuries. Cometh the hour, cometh the man.

Deep into injury time (the referee had added six minutes),

United had a corner. Wednesday cleared as far as Pallister, who was out on the wing of all places. He crossed, and the ball found its way to Bruce, who bulleted in his second, finding the corner of the net from ten yards.

The scenes were emotional. Fergie, who had been shouting the odds from the touchline throughout the second half, leapt off the bench and punched the air; his assistant, Brian Kidd, ran onto the pitch and slid to his knees. The fans went berserk.

But where had all that extra time come from? Was it due to the replacement referee John Hilditch, the linesman who had taken the whistle but not the watch from the injured match official Mike Peck, trusting his own timekeeping instead? Or was it down to the intimidating presence of the United manager, finger glued to his own timepiece, demanding those vital extra minutes? One thing we know for sure is that this was the game that brought the phrase 'Fergie time' into the English language.

The controversy continued after the match, the opposing manager Trevor Francis jokingly complaining, 'You scored your winning goal in the second leg,' while Fergie maintained in his autobiography that the extra minutes were fair: 'That night I watched the video of the second half and used my stopwatch to time all the stoppages for injuries and substitutions. There should, in fact, have been an additional 12 minutes.' Later, Sky Sports did their own check and came up with exactly the six and a half minutes Bruce needed to score the decisive goal.

The match proved to be pivotal. This time, they wouldn't bottle it. United took maximum points from their next five games to run away with the title, ten points clear of an Aston Villa side that faded in the closing weeks. The team that Ferguson had put together now had iron in its veins. They had come of age.

CANTONA KICKS ASS
25 January 1995, Selhurst Park

From an early age, Eric Cantona attracted controversy. Growing up in Marseille, he quickly became noticeable for not only his exceptional footballing talent but also for his outrageous behaviour. After a series of incidents, he was branded, *'l'enfant terrible'*. He was banned from the French national side for calling the coach, Henri Michel, 'a bag of shit'; he punched and threw boots at teammates; in a friendly game, he tore off his shirt and kicked the ball into the crowd after being substituted; and, in 1991, he was sent off after throwing the ball at the referee. His response to receiving a month's suspension after the ball-throwing incident was to walk up to each member of the French FA's disciplinary panel and call them idiots; the length of his ban was promptly doubled. And that's when he retired from football – for the first time – in December 1991.

He might as well have worn the T-shirt that professes 'Better to kick ass than kiss ass'. But Cantona had his psychoanalyst to console him and he also had his admirers, none more influential than footballing legend Michel Platini. Platini sought an escape route for Eric, away from his travails in France. He approached Graeme Souness, then at Liverpool, but the timing was wrong. Souness recalled: 'He [Platini] said he had a player – a problem boy but a proper player. Cantona. I said the last thing I needed was another problem player.'

Cantona did make the Channel crossing, landing at Leeds United via a bizarre trial at Sheffield Wednesday. He was vital to the Leeds 1992 title push, laying on assists for Lee Chapman and adding that bit of *je ne sais quoi* required to make Wilkinson's side champions.

English football had seen nothing like Cantona. English clubs had been banned from playing European football after the Heysel disaster, and there were few continentals playing in the league – certainly none with Eric's presence. This Eurostar liked philosophy. He admired the early poetry of Rimbaud, which prompted some fans to send him videos of early Sylvester Stallone movies. He saw himself as an artist, a warrior poet, who once described playing as a mission to interpret Mozart's *The Magic Flute* every Saturday.

Leeds fans adored him, but the manager was wary. Distrustful of Cantona's individuality, Wilkinson commented that 'Eric likes to do what he likes when he likes – and then f**ks off. We'd all want a bit of that.' So when, in a chance call between the chairmen of Leeds and United, Martin Edwards enquired about Eric's availability, he was surprised to learn that Leeds were willing to sell.

Edwards had been tipped off by his friend Irving Scholar, the former Spurs chairman, who lived in Monaco. Scholar raved about Cantona and told Edwards he could see all the attributes to make him a United player.

United were in the market for a striker. In early November, they lay tenth in the table, having only managed to hit the net 14 times in as many games. They had missed out on Shearer, and their second choice, Dion Dublin, had broken his leg less than three weeks into the season. Hearing that Cantona was available, Ferguson didn't hesitate. On 26 November, the Frenchman became a Red.

Finally, Cantona had found his spiritual home. Eric connected with the city, the club and its fans. He enjoyed going to the

Hacienda club to tap into the music scene; in his words, 'I liked to absorb the city, its soul. Growing up in Marseille I felt free. In Manchester I felt that freedom again.' More importantly, he had a great rapport with the manager; Ferguson gave Cantona the freedom to perform on the pitch and allowed him to be himself off it. Other players testified to how Fergie's strict disciplinary rules were not applied to Eric. As Paul Parker remembered, 'He was the boss's favourite by a country mile.'

His arrival at Old Trafford was the catalyst that United needed. His style of play was both electrifying and innovative. His strike partner Mark Hughes later wrote: 'Eric Cantona was the first forward I played with who would drift into spaces. Predominantly, during my playing career, teams played 4-4-2. One striker came short and the other went long, and you just played off each other. But not Eric. He was constantly looking for spaces where he felt he could have an impact – and if he did get the ball in those spaces between the lines, as we call it now, he could be very dangerous.'

When he received the ball, he had the vision to bring others into play with a flick or an incisive pass. His teammates responded to him as an orchestra to a maestro. United didn't look back; they stormed up the table and went on to win the title, their first for 26 years.

Cantona now took centre stage, and made an even greater contribution the following year. In his first full season at the club, he top-scored with 25 goals as United powered to a second successive league title and completed an historic double as the Frenchman scored twice in a 4–0 win over Chelsea in the FA Cup final.

Ferguson admired the spikiness in his make-up: 'He had a devil in him [like Denis Law]. Forwards need it.' Opposing sides resorted to negative tactics to unsettle United's mainspring and provoke a reaction. As the marking got tighter and the fouls more frequent, Cantona lost his cool; his disciplinary record deteriorated, and he received three red cards in quick time. He was banned after spitting at Leeds fans on his return to Elland Road. In the eyes of English referees, he was now a marked man.

Then, in 1995, on a chill January evening at Selhurst Park, Cantona's frustration boiled over. Palace's Richard Shaw had marshalled the Frenchman in the first half, through fair means and foul. Ferguson complained to the referee at half-time about the treatment being dished out, ordering the official to 'do your f**king job'.

Three minutes into the second half, Cantona, hounded by Shaw, kicked his marker and was sent off. As he walked along the touchline, Palace supporter Matthew Simmons raced down 11 flights of stairs to hurl abuse, and Cantona snapped. He launched into Simmons with an acrobatic kung fu kick to the astonishment of Simmons and the wider watching world.

An act of will? An act of madness? It was certainly one that caused a public outcry. Bitter Leeds fans sneered that it was a case of the 'shit hitting the fan'. The *Sun* ran 13 pages on 'The Shame of Cantona'. However, Richard Williams in the *Independent* defended the player, saying that 'Eric Cantona's only mistake was to stop hitting him. The more we discovered about Mr Simmons, the more Cantona's assault looked like the instinctive expression of a flawless moral judgement.' Ian Wright confessed later that he felt 'jealous'. There were, of course, calls for Eric to be thrown out of the game. Instead, he received an eight-month ban and a prison sentence, later suspended.

Cantona fled to France, where he would have stayed had Ferguson not persuaded him to return. Ferguson knew how important Eric was to his team; without him they were pipped by Blackburn to the title. Once his ban was served, he was made captain, and his goals were decisive in no fewer than 13 games as United regained their league title and his crunching volley to beat Liverpool in the cup final sealed their second double.

No longer the scourge of English football, Cantona was recognised as a precious gift, the Premier League's national treasure. The sportswriters voted him their player of the year. *Le roi* reigned supreme.

LES BONS MOTS DU ROI
Quote Unquote

You were never likely to hear Eric Cantona utter platitudes about a particular away venue being a tough place to come to or the advisability of taking one game at a time. When he spoke, people paid attention, waiting for a Delphic pronouncement or a juicy soundbite. His thoughts might be cryptic, poetic, scathing, profound or plain bonkers – or all of the above. Most of all, he is eminently quotable.

On United legends

'After his first training session in heaven, George Best, from his favourite right wing, turned the head of God who was filling in at left-back. I would love for him to save me a place in his team – George Best that is, not God.'

'You may find another Beckham or Ronaldo, but never ever will you find another Sir Alex Ferguson.'

The number 7 shirt

'I have a personal message for Zlatan [Ibrahimović]. You decided to

go red, it is the best choice you ever made. There can only be one king in Manchester. You can be the prince if you want to and the number 7 shirt is yours, if you are interested.'
(Zlatan wisely chose number 9.)

Leeds United's manager, Howard Wilkinson

'The salmon that idles its way downstream will never leap the waterfall.'

Manchester United

'United is life. The rest are mere details. When I think football, I think Manchester United. I still support United and always will. I will die with them in my heart.'

'To understand United is to understand the fundamental aspect of the human mosaic. What thrills us, what scares us, what makes us feel alive.'
(These were the closing remarks in the 2021 documentary, *The United Way*.)

The fans

'I am so proud the fans still sing my name, but I fear tomorrow they will stop. I fear it because I love it. And everything you love, you fear you will lose.'

Playing

'The ball is like a woman; she loves to be caressed.'

'A good goal is one that is important and beautiful.'

'I play with passion and fire. I have to accept that sometimes this fire does harm.'

'Without spontaneity in any sport you can't succeed.'

A life less ordinary

'Become a legend? But I am one already.'

'I am not a man, I am Cantona.'
(From Ken Loach's 2009 film, *Looking for Eric*)

'Anyone who is different from the ordinary is considered crazy. I am happy to be considered so. And proud.'

'I see the world become so uniform; everybody has to be the same. I like people who are different.'

'You need a particular talent only to want to please. I don't have this talent.'

Racism

'Arguing with racist people is like playing chess with a pigeon: it

doesn't matter how good you are! The pigeon is going to knock all the pieces down and shit on the board and parade around like he's won.'

Retirement

'I gave up early because I don't want to do anything without passion. For me that is part of the emptiness. When I felt I had lost the passion I couldn't do it any more. I had to stop.'

Ageing

'"As flies to wanton boys, are we to the gods; they kill us for their sport." [King Lear]. Soon the science will not only be able to slow down the ageing of the cells, soon the science will fix the cells to the state and so we will become eternal. Only accidents, crimes, wars, will still kill us but unfortunately, crimes, wars, will multiply. I love football. Thank you.'

(Cantona's acceptance speech on receiving the UEFA President's award in 2019.)

Seagulls

'When the seagulls follow the trawler it's because they think sardines will be thrown into the sea.'

(Cantona's withering comment on the media made at the press conference following the reduction on appeal of his prison sentence given after the kung fu incident.)

Best moment

'I have a lot of good moments but the one I prefer is the one when I kicked the hooligan.'

Biggest regret

'I would have liked to have kicked him harder.'

What they said about him . . .

'If ever there was one player, anywhere in the world, that was made for Manchester United, it was Cantona. He swaggered in, stuck his chest out, raised his head and surveyed everything as though he were asking: "I'm Cantona. How big are you? Are you big enough for me?"' – Sir Alex Ferguson

'Collar up, back straight, chest stuck out, he glided into the arena as if he owned the f**king place. Any arena, but nowhere more effectively than Old Trafford. This was his stage. He loved it, the crowd loved him.' – Roy Keane

'He gets in my all-time Manchester United side . . . not only because of that extraordinary ability but because he was an absolute inspiration to every young player who came into the team.' – Sir Bobby Charlton

'He was the only player I saw who the manager never had a go at. We all went to a film premiere and were told to wear black ties. Eric

turned up in a cream lemon suit with Nike trainers. The manager told him that he looked fantastic!' – Andy Cole

'In my eyes, he was responsible for the Premier League developing as quickly as it did. Everyone took to him, controversy or not. He oozed charisma and genius in equal measure, and is by far and away the best ever in the Premier League. It was an honour to have played with him.' – Peter Schmeichel

'Eric Cantona brought an extra dimension. Plenty of things he tried didn't come off, but you remember the ones that did – the flicks, the outrageous lobs. He made things look easy that weren't easy at all. Before him, we struggled to score as a team, but as soon as he arrived the goals flowed.' – Ryan Giggs

'He could score, he could pass, he could see a pass that no one else did, he had the charisma. Eric was just unbelievable.' – Ole Gunnar Solskjær

'He stood there as if to say, I am the king. I loved his arrogance and if you're that good, I think you can be arrogant and get away with it.' – Matt Le Tissier

MIND GAMES
Manchester United 1 Leeds United 0
17 APRIL 1996

The 1995/96 title race seemed to be a foregone conclusion in January – Newcastle United were romping away from the rest of the field with a 12-point lead – but then up steps Eric Cantona to score the only goal in a crunch game against the Magpies at St James' Park at the beginning of March. The lead was now one point. Game on.

Since mid-January, the Reds had been on fire, progressing in the FA Cup and winning 11 out of 12 in the league before losing to Southampton at the Dell. Now, in the closing weeks of the season, it was a two-horse race. Like an expert angler, Alex Ferguson was reeling in his fish. He would probably have preferred a racing analogy: United as Red Rum chasing down Crisp in the 1973 Grand National.

By mid-April the teams were neck and neck, both on 73 points. Both were due to play Leeds and Nottingham Forest in their three remaining fixtures.

In itself, the hard-fought win over Leeds doesn't deserve to go down as one of the more memorable games in the annals of the Premier League – apart from being Steve Bruce's last United appearance at Old Trafford. After being reduced to ten men when keeper Mark Beeney was sent off in the 17th minute, with centre-back Lucas Radebe going in goal, the visitors put up fierce resistance, United only winning through a late Roy Keane goal. But it was the post-match comments made by Alex Ferguson that would start a chain reaction that ended in an almighty explosion 12 days later.

Many sides up their game when they play United. It might be historic rivalry, or a chance to test themselves against the biggest team in England, or the live TV audience or, in Leeds' case, all three. Fergie was well aware of these factors and he was also irked by the groundswell of support in the country for Kevin Keegan's team. Newcastle were an attractive side – Sky Sports dubbed them 'The Entertainers' – serving up football that was pleasing on the eye. Geordies everywhere, including a few at Southampton, as a smarting Fergie noted, were to be found on the back pages cheering on the Magpies: 'We'll do it for Kevin.'

In his post-match interview, Fergie decried the Leeds players, claiming that if they reproduced that form and spirit every week, they wouldn't be near the foot of the table – they would be a top six club. They were cheating their manager in his view, adding, 'If they had played like that all season, they'd be near the top. They raised their game because they were playing Manchester United. It was pathetic. I think we can accept any club coming here and trying their hardest so long as they do it every week.' Leeds' next game? Newcastle United.

But before Newcastle played Leeds, United thrashed Forest 5–0 to open up a six-point lead.

Fergie had also kept a keen eye on Forest's match against Newcastle. Newcastle had previously arranged to play Forest for Stuart Pearce's testimonial in May, something that had not escaped the notice of the United boss. Later, Pearce recalled, 'I think he sort of mentioned that [because of the testimonial game] we wouldn't be trying and we'd prefer Newcastle to win.'

Come the end of April, Newcastle, without playing well, ground out a 1–0 win over Leeds in a match covered by Sky's *Monday Night Football*. There were now only three points in it and Newcastle had a game in hand.

There was tension in the air . . . and on air.

After the match Kevin Keegan popped on the headphones to take questions from *Monday Night Football* host Richard Keys. Asked why his side struggled on the night, the dam finally burst. Calling to mind Katherine's words from *The Taming of the Shrew*, 'My tongue will tell the anger of my heart, or else my heart, concealing it, will break', an emotional Keegan let rip: 'A lot of things have been said over the last few days . . . I think you've got to send Alex Ferguson a tape of this game, haven't you? Isn't that what he asked for?

'And we're playing Notts Forest on Thursday, and he objected to that. Now, that [the testimonial game] was fixed up four months ago, we were supposed to play Notts Forest. I mean that sort of stuff, we're bigger than that.'

The blue touchpaper had been lit, and when Keys then put it to Keegan that Fergie's comments were just part of the psychological battle of a title run-in, the Newcastle manager exploded: 'No, no, when you do that with footballers, like he said about Leeds – and when you do things like that about a man like Stuart Pearce . . . I've kept really quiet but I'll tell you something, he went down in my estimation when he said that. We have not resorted to that.

'You can tell him now, we're still fighting for this title, and he's got to go to Middlesbrough and get something – and I'll tell you, honestly, I will love it if we beat them. Love it.

'It really has got to me. I've voiced it live, not in front of the press or anywhere. I'm not even going to the press conference, but the battle is still on and Man United have not won this yet.'

Had Kevin summoned his inner Shakespeare, he might have heeded King Lear's counsel to his daughter Cordelia: 'Mend your speech a little, lest you may mar your fortunes.'

Indeed, Ferguson wouldn't have long to wait. The pressure took its toll on Newcastle, and they could only draw their last two games against Forest and Spurs, while United's victory away to Middlesbrough on the final day of the season saw them over the line. Fergie had seen off the challenge from the North East and secured his third Premier League title in four years.

THE SUPER-SUB SURFACES
Ole Gunnar Solskjær

Sir Alex Ferguson observed of Ole Gunnar Solskjær that he had a great ability to assess the changing dynamic of a game. Over the years Solskjær had plenty of opportunities to practise this skill as he sat on the bench as a back-up striker to the likes of Cantona, Cole and Yorke.

A surprise buy in the summer of 1996, costing £1.5 million, Solskjær was signed after Ferguson had failed a second time to lure Alan Shearer to Old Trafford. But the baby-faced assassin who looked younger than his shirt number proved to be an instant hit. Appropriately, Solskjær scored the first of his 126 goals for the Reds eight minutes after coming on as substitute against Blackburn Rovers. He ended the season as the club's top scorer, with 19 goals in all competitions.

The fans took to him and sang his praises as someone who kept them happy when skies were grey and was 'cheaper than f**king Shearer'. Injury kept Solskjær sidelined for much of the following season, and by the start of the 1998/99 season he was one of four strikers Ferguson had to fit into a front two. With larger egos to keep happy, the slender Solskjær was often the one to miss out, but the good-natured Norwegian was happy to play a secondary role. He had offers to move to other clubs, including Tottenham (an offer United were prepared to accept), but he was happy at Old Trafford.

Sitting on the subs' bench as he did for 150 of his 366 appearances, Solskjær took the chance to observe opponents at close quarters. In 2012, he told the *Observer* that 'I had to think about myself, how can I do the most damage for [sic] the opposition when I come on. I sat and I studied those games . . . I would pay attention to what the defenders and full-backs were doing wrong.'

His observational and analytical abilities made him deadly in front of goal. His manager was appreciative: 'His thought processes underpinned his skills. He had that analytical mind. As soon as he arrived in a shooting position, he had it all sized up. He had mental pictures everywhere.'

His mind must have had more images than the Whitworth Gallery when he came on as a 71st-minute substitute for Roy Keane at the City Ground against Forest in February 1999. United were cruising with a 4–1 lead, but Solskjær produced a clinical display of forward play as he rattled in four of his own to double the Reds' score, helping United to their biggest-ever away win.

On the day of the 1999 Champions League final, Solskjær possessed not just his usual presence of mind but an uncanny prescience. Before the match against Bayern Munich in Barcelona, he called Norway to speak to his friend, Erik, and told him he had a good feeling about the game. Erik said he'd be watching but had to work straight after the game to which Solskjær replied, 'You have to stay for the whole game. I think I'll come on and do something special.' As the team went through their final pre-match preparation in the dressing room, reserve coach Jimmy Ryan spoke to each of the subs to drum in some tactical points and noted Solskjær's self-possession. Ryan recalled him saying, 'I'm ready all right. I know something big is going to happen to me tonight.' When the super-sub scored the winner in the 93rd minute, Ryan recalled, 'I thought I was in a science-fiction movie.'

Barcelona was no fluke; he was often a decisive factor in matches. Of his 126 goals, 50 came in the last 30 minutes of games, and, of those, 33 were in the last 15 minutes. In all, he scored an amazing 28 as a substitute, a record for the club.

Injuries eventually caught up with him, and, in 2007, he finished his league career nearly exactly how he had started it: scoring six minutes after coming off the bench against Blackburn.

His final bow as a player came the following year at Old Trafford when a record 68,000 spectators paid to see United take on Espanyol and to cheer as, on 68 minutes, Ole Gunnar Solskjær came off the bench one last time.

GIGGS' WONDER GOAL
FA Cup Semi-final Replay
14 APRIL 1999, VILLA PARK

As the 20th century drew to a close, in the years before Russian and Emirates oil money flooded the Premier League, two heavyweights ruled the English football world. In the previous six years, United had won the league four times including two double-winning seasons, while Arsenal, under the tutelage of Arsène Wenger, were a rising force, winning the double themselves in 1997/98.

By mid-April 1999, both sides were vying for more silverware: United were a point ahead of Arsenal in the league as the teams squared up in the semi-final of the FA Cup. Arsenal were in imperious form; they hadn't lost a competitive match all year, the famous defensive back five of Seaman, Dixon, Winterburn, Keown and Adams conceding a miserly 12 goals in 17 games. Arsenal had laid down a marker against United by thumping them 3–0 at Highbury in the autumn and holding them to a draw at Old Trafford in February.

After the semi-final ended in a goalless stalemate, the combatants came out of their corners for the replay. If the first game disappointed, the second lived up to and beyond expectations. In a pulsating tie, United dominated the first 70 minutes, taking the lead in the 17th minute with a 25-yard Beckham screamer after a typically clever lay-off from Sheringham. Arsenal were fortunate to level with a deflected long-range effort from Bergkamp before the game turned on its head after Keane's dismissal for a second yellow card; the captain, the heartbeat and inspiration of the team, would miss the final.

Now United were hanging on and Arsenal were rampant. In the last minute of normal time there was yet more drama. Phil Neville's foul on Parlour gave Bergkamp the chance to win the tie from the penalty spot. Bergkamp had missed three of a previous five spot kicks and opted for accuracy in placing the ball to Schmeichel's left but at a comfortable height for the United keeper, who had guessed correctly and made the save.

After three and a half hours, the teams couldn't be separated, and so to extra time in the last-ever FA Cup semi-final replay. Bergkamp almost made amends, but Schmeichel again denied the Dutchman with a flying save. United were on the ropes, their best chance seemingly to take the game to penalties when cometh the hour, cometh the man. On as a second-half substitute, Giggs had fresh legs, and, boy, did they come in handy. Vieira gave away possession with a tired cross-field pass on the halfway line and Giggs, from the left of the centre circle, burst upfield. No footballer in England could match Giggs' ability to keep the ball under close control while running at pace, but the winger had the entire Arsenal back four between him and Seaman in the Arsenal goal with only a distant Dwight Yorke for company. Slaloming left and right, beating first Dixon then Vieira, then squeezing between Keown and Dixon again before avoiding Adams' late despairing lunge, the Welshman drove the ball high into the net from six yards out.

In its own right Giggs' goal was one of the greatest in FA Cup history. But given the context – the rivalry against Arsenal, the team being reduced to ten men, the hopes of a historic treble hanging by a thread – the goal is simply the best, the GOAT. And the heroic celebration, the shirt removed to reveal Giggs' manly chest hair, the garment then twirled joyously in the air as he ran down the pitch side to embrace his teammates was surely the greatest goal celebration ever.

It remains one of the defining moments of the most successful season for the club and in the career of one of its all-time greats. Ferguson eloquently paid tribute to the achievement and the player in his post-match comments: 'The ultimate expression of the incredible natural gifts he has always had since he came to us as a 13-year-old.' That was half a lifetime ago, before he scored the goal of his life.

'FOOTBALL, BLOODY HELL!'
The 1998/99 UEFA Champions League final
26 MAY 1999, CAMP NOU, BARCELONA

By the end of May 1999, Alex Ferguson had been in charge of United for 12½ years. After a difficult start, the Scot had made the Reds preeminent in English football, winning his fifth Premier League title as well as his fourth FA Cup. The challenge that now awaited in Barcelona's Camp Nou stadium was to win the ultimate club prize: the UEFA Champions League and a historic treble. Three decades earlier, Matt Busby's side made history by becoming the first English team to lift the European Cup. Standing in United's way were Bayern Munich, a team with its own illustrious European pedigree, who also had a chance of winning a treble.

Like Sir Matt Busby before him, Alex Ferguson regarded success in the Champions League as the holy grail. 'No matter how much I tried to play down the Champions League final in Barcelona, as far as I was concerned Europe had become a personal crusade,' Ferguson wrote. 'I knew I would never be judged a great manager until I won the European Cup.'

The path to glory was impeded by embarrassing early stumbles as Fergie's Reds took their first faltering baby steps on the European stage. The first campaign in 1993 ended abruptly when United failed to dispose of Turkish champions Galatasaray. There were red faces the following season when United failed to qualify from their group after being tripped up again in Istanbul by those annoying Turks and Barcelona gave them a footballing lesson at the Camp Nou, cruising to a 4–0 win.

But gradually Ferguson's side got into their stride. In 1997, they were unlucky to lose to Borussia Dortmund at the semi-final stage. In 1998, they reached the quarters but lost out on the away-goals rule to Monaco.

In the summer of 1998, Ferguson made two important signings. He bought Dwight Yorke to sharpen up his forward line and also looked to strengthen his defence by buying the man-mountain, Jaap Stam. When Ferguson first met the Dutchman he said, 'Jaap, I want you to play for Manchester United. I want you to command our back line and help us take that extra step and win the European Cup.' No pressure.

In the group phase of the 1998/99 tournament, United had been given a tough draw against the giants Bayern Munich and Barcelona as well as Peter Schmeichel's old club Brøndby. Tough draws were to follow as United matched Barcelona and Bayern home and away while taking full advantage of the Danes. Yorke contributed a quarter of United's 20 goals as they won ten hard-earned points to pip the Catalans and reach the quarter-final.

Things weren't to get any easier as United next faced Italian opposition in the form of Inter Milan. Dwight Yorke was once again on the scoresheet as he hit two past the Italians at Old Trafford, and in the return leg at a hostile San Siro, the Reds stood up to the intimidation of the *Nerazurri* who left them black and blue as they slugged out a 1–1 draw, thanks to a late Paul Scholes equaliser.

In the semi-final, United faced the mighty Juventus, winners in 1996 and finalists in the following two years. After a 1–1 draw at Old Trafford, United faced an uphill task in Turin as their hosts took a two-goal lead after 11 minutes through their goal-poaching maestro, Filippo Inzaghi. A difficult mission had become near impossible considering United had never won on Italian soil and Juventus had twice beaten United at the Stadio delle Alpi in the previous three seasons – the Alps that loomed next to Turin an appropriate symbol for the scale of the task ahead of the Reds.

*

It took a bravura display from captain Roy Keane and nerveless bravery from his teammates to haul themselves back into the game; Keane scored in the 24th minute with a brilliant glancing header before Dwight Yorke was on the scoresheet – again – 11 minutes later. United now had the away-goals advantage, but Andy Cole sealed a historic victory six minutes from time. A glorious night was only clouded by the yellow cards awarded against Keane and Scholes, which meant both were suspended for the final.

At the beginning of May, at the start of that frenetic and season-defining month, there were seven games to go, three trophies up for grabs and 26 days in which to play them. The manager wrote in the May Day matchday programme: 'This is a special season. No matter what happens on the last lap, you should enjoy it because you might never see the like again.' Once more, the manager had called it right. By the 26th day, United had won the league, and goals from Scholes and Sheringham had been enough to see off Newcastle in the FA Cup final just four days earlier. Now the biggest test of all awaited.

The Champions League final was unforgettable and is still spoken of to this day as the apogee of the Ferguson era. The United fans had come from all over the globe to see if their team could lift the premier European trophy for the first time since that famous Wembley night in 1968. A crowd of 92,000 were entertained by a full set from Mancunian tenor Russell Watson and then a rendition of 'Barcelona' by Montserrat Caballé, pitchside, and the ghost of Freddie Mercury on the big screen. As kick-off approached, the atmosphere built and the crowd warmed up; the mercury was rising.

Without its fulcrum of Keane and Scholes, the United midfield had a makeshift look about it with Beckham central and Giggs moving to the right of midfield to accommodate Blomqvist on the left. The Germans took an early lead through a Basler free kick, and the two teams sparred for the next hour before it really kicked off. Schmeichel stretched to save from Effenberg. A chip from Mehmet Scholl hit the upright. Ferguson used his subs: first Sheringham and then, in the 81st minute, Solskjær, whose first touch forced Kahn to make a diving stop. Then a Jancker overhead hit the crossbar with Schmeichel helpless before the two United subs combined to create another chance. Bayern could have been three goals to the good, but Ferguson's tactical changes had lifted United. In commentary, former United manager Ron Atkinson observed that the Reds were 'now creating chances for fun. If they can equalise, they can win it.'

Not in normal time ,they couldn't. The three minutes added on by referee Collina will go down in football history until the end of time. From a Beckham corner, Giggs' scuffed right-foot shot was turned into the Bayern net by Sheringham from the six-yard line to make it 1–1. Extra time and the golden goal lottery beckoned. Then Solskjær won another corner after some neat wing play. Beckham's inswinger was met by Sheringham at the near post, whose glancing header found Solskjær free three yards from goal to slam the ball into the roof of the net. Cue wild celebrations amongst the United supporters.

United had come back from the dead, and benighted Bayern were dead on their feet, some of them flat on the ground while Samuel Kuffour banged his fist on the turf at the perceived injustice of it all. At the final whistle, the soon-to-be-knighted Alex Ferguson looked as if he'd inhaled a cylinder of nitrous oxide. Grinning from ear to ear as he is interviewed immediately after the game, he is ecstatic. 'I can't believe it. I can't believe it. Football, bloody hell.' Then, finding a deeper truth, he added, 'But they never give in and that's what won it.' That character and belief drummed into the players by Ferguson through the years had seen United ultimately triumph. In the words of Clive Tyldesley's breathless television commentary, 'Manchester United have reached the promised land.'

The United Starting XI

Peter Schmeichel, Gary Neville, Ronny Johnsen, Jaap Stam, Denis Irwin, Ryan Giggs, David Beckham, Nicky Butt, Jesper Blomqvist, Dwight Yorke, Andy Cole.

AND THE AWARD GOES TO ...

Here is a roll call of the honours and awards bestowed by royalty, or voted for by the football world and the viewing public to Manchester United players and managers.

The achievements of United both on and off the pitch have been recognised in the Queen's official honours lists.

Knights of the Realm

1968 Matt Busby becomes the first club manager to receive a knighthood. Four years later, he was also made Knight Commander of the Order of St Gregory the Great (KCSG).

1978 Walter Winterbottom, former England manager, received his knighthood. Winterbottom played as a half-back for United in the 1930s before a promising career was cut short following a diagnosis of ankylosing spondylitis.

1994 Bobby Charlton received a knighthood following the awards of an OBE in 1969 and CBE in 1974.

1999 Alex Ferguson became Sir Alex following an OBE in 1985 and a CBE in 1995.

Overseas knights

2008 Ole Gunnar Solskjær: First Class Knighthood of the Royal Norwegian Order of St Olav

2019 Paul Pogba: Chevalier de la Légion d'honneur

Other honours, listed in ranking order, by date are:

Commander of the Order of the British Empire
2016 Denis Law, former 'King' of the Stretford End, was happy to accept the award from a future king, The Duke of Cambridge.

Officers of the British Empire
1990 Bryan Robson
2003 David Beckham
2004 Mark Hughes (following an MBE in 1998)
2007 Ryan Giggs
2019 Harry Gregg (following an MBE in 1995)

Members of the British Empire
1993 Ray Wilkins
2000 Nobby Stiles
2001 (honorary) Peter Schmeichel
2007 Teddy Sheringham
2020 Marcus Rashford

Honourable mentions
Finally, the honours given to those who have spent part of their careers at Old Trafford: Gordon Strachan OBE, Henrik Larsson OBE (honorary), Jim Leighton MBE, David Healy MBE and Casey Stoney MBE.

The sporting world has its own way of recognising excellence.

UEFA Ballon d'Or winners
1964 Denis Law
1966 Bobby Charlton
1968 George Best
2008 Cristiano Ronaldo

Football Writers' Association Player of the Year
1948/49 Johnny Carey
1965/66 Bobby Charlton
1967/68 George Best
1995/96 Eric Cantona
1999/2000 Roy Keane
2000/01 Teddy Sheringham
2006/07 Cristiano Ronaldo
2007/08 Cristiano Ronaldo
2009/10 Wayne Rooney

PFA Players' Player of the Year

The football writers may have favoured Liverpool in their choice of their players of the year, but the professional footballers most often gave their award to United players. The first PFA award was made in 1974.

1988/89 Mark Hughes
1990/91 Mark Hughes
1991/92 Gary Pallister
1993/94 Eric Cantona

1999/2000 Roy Keane
2000/01 Teddy Sheringham
2001/02 Ruud van Nistelrooy
2006/07 Cristiano Ronaldo
2007/08 Cristiano Ronaldo
2008/09 Ryan Giggs
2009/10 Wayne Rooney

BBC Sports Personality of the Year

The BBC's annual jamboree, the Sports Personality of the Year award (affectionately known as SPOTY), recognises excellence across all sporting disciplines. Established in 1954 to honour the sportsperson 'whose actions have most captured the public's imagination', viewers were invited to cast their votes from a shortlist compiled by the broadcaster. The Team of the Year award was created six years later and the Lifetime Achievement award first appeared in 1996.

That United personalities have featured so often should come as no surprise, and it is the usual suspects, one literally from left field, who grace the roll of honour.

Sports Personality of the Year

David Beckham (2001): following the ignominy and public vilification of Becks after his sending-off in the World Cup tie against Argentina in 1998, United's charismatic number 7 had successfully rehabilitated himself and become the darling of fans and the tabloid press. His efforts for club and country since the dark night of Saint-Étienne and his high-profile marriage to Posh Spice had made him an A-list celebrity.

Ryan Giggs (2009): to the amazement of many commentators and the award winner himself, Ryan Giggs won the viewers' vote. In Ryan's own words, 'This is a shock.' Some cynics blamed the Man Utd fanbase for rigging the public vote – Giggs polled 152,842 votes, nearly 30% of the total, proving that, if nothing else, United have a lot of supporters.

Lifetime Achievement Awards

The first United great to win the award was Sir Alex Ferguson in 2001. Fergie had enjoyed an incredible run of success at the turn of the millennium: the 1999 treble, a knighthood in that same year and winning the Premier League three years in a row from 1999 to 2001.

The Busby greats, George Best and Sir Bobby Charlton, were honoured in 2002 and 2008 respectively, and David Beckham returned in 2010 to receive his award.

United won the Team of the Year awards in 1968 and 1999, following their successes in the premier European competitions.

PETER THE GREAT
Peter Schmeichel, United's Number 1, 1991–1999

Size matters when it comes to goalkeepers, and few come bigger than the Great Dane, Peter Schmeichel. A great shot stopper, a big game player, a big personality and, at 6 foot 3 inches and over 15½ stones, really, er, big. The kit makers Umbro had to fit him with a specially made XXXL shirt. Manchester United have been blessed with many great keepers from Harry Gregg to Edwin van der Sar and David de Gea, but none can quite match the impact that Schmeichel made at United.

Growing up in Denmark, opportunities to play full-time football were limited. Schmeichel took various jobs including one as a manager for the World Wildlife Fund before he made a breakthrough by joining Brøndby, aged 23, with whom he won four Danish First Division titles in five years.

Sir Alex Ferguson was on the lookout for a keeper. He brought his old Aberdeen number 1, Jim Leighton, to Old Trafford for a record fee in 1988 to fill the position, but after a poor display in the 1990 FA Cup final, Ferguson decided that Leighton's confidence was shot. Apprehensive about bringing a foreign keeper to the English game with its physicality and aerial bombardment, Ferguson scouted the Dane on six occasions before finally offering Brøndby a transfer fee of £505,000 in

August 1991. The Scot would later call the signing the 'bargain of the century':

To begin with, opposing teams took advantage of the Dane's culture shock as high ball after high ball rained down from the skies, but as he soon adjusted, he settled in well to form the base of a much-improved United defensive unit. Even though United let the title slip through their grasp in 1991/92, they had the best defensive record in the division.

The disappointment Schmeichel felt at losing the title race was tempered by Denmark's success at the Euro '92 Championship. Memorably, the Danish outsiders, who only earned a place in the finals after the disqualification of Yugoslavia, triumphed through defensive organisation in which Schmeichel was a key part. The Danish foreign minister, who was having a hard time from his counterparts in Europe following the Danes' referendum decision to leave the European Community, memorably summed up the team's success by saying, 'If you can't join them, beat them.'

Schmeichel had played a blinder, making the decisive save from Marco van Basten in the semi-final shoot-out; tellingly, he was the only Dane named in the team of the tournament. He was also chosen as the world's best goalkeeper of the year in 1992 by the International Federation of Football History and Statistics, and again the following year.

Schmeichel had a superb aptitude for goalkeeping. He could increase his already imposing size using the star jump technique he first learned playing handball, and his anticipation and reading of the game was masterful. Blessed with sharp reflexes, his shot-stopping ability was helped by his phenomenal reach; and through his bravery and physical presence he commanded his penalty area. Just as important as his defensive qualities was his ability to distribute the ball quickly though devastating long throw-outs which launched so many of United's lethal counter-attacks.

It wasn't all plain sailing. In January 1994, after United drew 3–3 against Liverpool, Ferguson tore strips off Schmeichel in the dressing room after the match. Not for conceding the goals but for wasteful long clearances which ceded possession to their opponents. Schmeichel, who was never shy about voicing, or even barking, his side of the argument on the pitch, let his manager have it with both barrels. Two days later, Ferguson called the Dane into his office to tell him he had no choice but to sack him. This may have been kidology, but Schmeichel couldn't be sure. Contrite, he later offered an apology to his teammates for his behaviour, unaware that the manager was eavesdropping. It won him a reprieve.

Back in favour, Schmeichel became a fixture in the United side. His form seldom dipped below excellent, and, in 1995/96, when United faced a strong title challenge from Newcastle, his heroics ensured that the Reds kept a clean sheet and all three points in a crunch game against the Magpies. Recognising how important Schmeichel was to regaining the Premier League title, his manager said, 'He saves us up to ten or twelve points per season that other keepers are not getting for their clubs.'

The pressures of playing football at the highest level for club and country took their toll on Schmeichel, and in November 1998, at the age of 35, he announced he would retire at the end of the season. He had won just about every prize in the game – only the World Cup and Champions League winners' medals were missing from his collection.

His United career ended not with a whimper but with a three-gun salute. In a thrilling FA Cup semi-final replay, late in the second half, Schmeichel made a vital penalty save from Dennis

Bergkamp to keep United in the game. And the following month, in his last game for the club, in the absence of the suspended Roy Keane, he was given the honour of captaining United in the Champions League final. United had already won the league title and now they stood on the brink of an unprecedented treble.

It must have been nerve-shredding. Bayern Munich dominated most of the game, and Schmeichel's goal was under siege; more than once he had the woodwork to thank for restricting the Germans' lead to a solitary goal. As the clock ran down to the final minute of normal time, Schmeichel bounded up the pitch to the opposing penalty area for a rare United corner. The Great Dane was now a menacing cat amongst terrified pigeons. Amidst the ensuing chaos, United equalised through Teddy Sheringham. Two minutes later, Schmeichel celebrated with a joyous cartwheel as Solskjær completed the comeback.

Peter Schmeichel's last act as a United player was to lift the Champions League trophy. What a way to bow out. In 2001, a Reuters poll of 200,000 participants named him the greatest ever goalkeeper ahead of Lev Yashin and Gordon Banks. To call him the Great Dane seems to belittle his achievements. Peter the GOAT is, frankly, worse. Better to look to history, to someone who came from a far northern land to England as a young man, who became a leader, a saviour and a moderniser: who better than Peter the Great?

KEANE AS MUSTARD

Managers often build their teams from the back. Sir Alex maintained that 'attack wins you games, defence wins you titles'; others say scoring goals is the hardest part of the game and the reason why top strikers are prized so highly. But many wise judges say that whoever wins the midfield battles usually prevails. England fans who watched their World Cup 2018 and Euro 2020 hopes dashed against the ascendant Croatian and Italian midfields would no doubt concede the point (or the tie).

The success of Ferguson's teams was down to many factors, but strengthening his midfield helped turn a good side into a title-winning machine. As Bryan Robson's playing days neared their end, Ferguson broke the British transfer record by spending £3.75 million to beat off competition from Kenny Dalglish's Blackburn to land Roy Keane from relegated Nottingham Forest.

The manager saw potential in the 21-year-old Irishman and was impressed with his box-to-box style, energy, two-footedness and tackling ability. On his league debut, he also revealed a talent for scoring goals, netting twice against Sheffield United. Keane was to be the junior partner in a midfield pairing with Paul Ince – the self-styled 'Guvnor' – who had assumed leadership in the middle of the pitch from the ageing Robson.

Keane made a successful start in his first season, and his absence through injury was sorely felt as United ceded the title to

Blackburn the following year and Ince's form declined. Following Ince's transfer to Inter Milan, United fans looked to Keane to step up. Typically, Keane had no pretensions: 'I don't want to be the new "Guvnor". I just want to do my job. This club is an institution. It will be around a lot longer than any of the players, whoever they are.'

Step up he did. He became the lynchpin of the young United team. Awarded the captaincy after Cantona's retirement in 1997, he sat frustrated on the sidelines as a cruciate ligament injury, incurred when fouling Alf-Inge Haaland, kept him out for virtually the entire season when, once again, United relinquished their title.

On his return, Keane entered a golden period in his United career. He added steel and intensity to his game; he bawled instructions to teammates, screaming at them if they fell short of the high standards he demanded. Nothing exemplified Keane's desire and will to win more than his extraordinary performance to haul United back from a losing position to beat Juventus in Turin in their 1999 Champions League semi-final. The manager said of his captain, 'Pounding over every blade of grass, competing as if he'd rather die of exhaustion than lose, he inspired all around him.' He may have missed the final through suspension, but without his heroics that night United could never have hoped to win the treble.

Keane was now regarded as the best midfielder in world football. In 2000, he picked up both the PFA and Football Writers' Player of the Year awards. As time went on, he became frustrated with some of his colleagues who he thought had become complacent, who 'forgot about the game, lost the hunger that got you the Rolex, the cars and the mansion'. He was also unhappy with the changing, more gentrified fan base – the so-called 'prawn sandwich brigade' – as the sport became ever more commercialised in the Premier League era.

Keane was not one to mince words, as present-day viewers of his TV punditry will know only too well. Sir Alex Ferguson wrote: 'The hardest part of Roy's body is his tongue. He has the most savage tongue you can imagine. He can debilitate the most confident person in the world in seconds with that tongue.'

Here are just a few targets of a Roy Keane tongue-lashing.

The prawn sandwich brigade

'Away from home our fans are fantastic, I'd call them the hardcore fans. But at home they have a few drinks and probably the prawn sandwiches, and they don't realise what's going on out on the pitch. I don't think some of the people who come to Old Trafford can spell "football", never mind understand it.' (After a goalless draw against Dynamo Kiev in September 2000.)

The opponent

'I'd waited long enough. I f**king hit him [Alf-Inge Haaland] hard. The ball was there (I think). Take that, you c**t. And don't ever stand over me sneering about fake injuries.'

(Keane took revenge against the Norwegian in the 2001 Manchester Derby four years after the incident that led to his cruciate injury.)

His international manager

'Mick [McCarthy], you're a liar . . . you're a f**king w**ker. I didn't rate you as a player, I don't rate you as a manager, and I don't rate you as

a person. You're a f**king w**ker and you can stick your World Cup up your arse. The only reason I have any dealings with you is that somehow you are the manager of my country! You can stick it up your bollocks.'

(International teammate Niall Quinn wrote in his autobiography that 'Roy Keane's ten-minute oration was clinical, fierce, earth-shattering to the person on the end of it'.)

His own teammates

In the infamous MUTV interview in 2005, deemed too savage to broadcast, Keane described Kieran Richardson as a 'lazy defender', doubted 'why people in Scotland rave about Darren Fletcher' and said of Rio Ferdinand, 'Just because you're paid £120,000 a week and play well for 20 minutes against Tottenham, you think you're a superstar.'

That interview effectively ended his time at Old Trafford; he never played for the Reds after that. It was an inglorious exit for a man who had captained United for eight years. The four Premier League titles, two FA Cups and the Champions League United won under his leadership make him the most successful captain in United's history.

Roy Keane set the bar high, and those who fell short of its measure felt the wrath of their skipper. There were many others who were only too glad to have United's standard-bearer in their team, the former teammate who later became United's manager, Ole Gunnar Solskjær, for one. As a manager, how he would have loved to have had Keane in his side. When still a player, Solskjær said, 'If I could pick one player in my team, I would always pick Roy Keane in front of other players I played with. Keane had everything: he was a leader, a great player and probably the best I ever played with.'

THE COMEBACK KINGS
Tottenham Hotspur 3 (3)
Manchester United 5 (0)
29 SEPTEMBER 2001

One of the defining characteristics of a Manchester United team under Sir Alex Ferguson was their never-say-die attitude. The game is not over until the final whistle; until then, the Ferguson motto 'Never give in' applies.

There have been many famous comebacks from seemingly hopeless positions: from 2–0 down in Turin, needing three goals to overcome Juventus in the 1999 Champions League semi-final, and then seven weeks later in the final as United trailed Bayern Munich at the end of 90 minutes. Earlier that season, goals from Yorke and Solskjær in the dying moments of the fourth round FA Cup tie against Liverpool secured an unlikely 2–1 victory.

Few United fans who saw it will ever forget Federico Macheda, a raw 17-year-old debutant, scoring against Villa to complete a comeback and seal the 2009 title; or when Paul Pogba's quick-fire double in the second half of the Manchester derby in April 2018 put United on the path to victory at the Etihad. But for sheer entertainment value, the game that stands out more than any other is United's win against Tottenham in September 2001.

Since the early 1950s, when they contested the league title, and again in the 1960s, games between United and Spurs had been highlights of the football calendar – Best, Law and Charlton up against Greaves, Gilzean and Mackay was fantasy football come to life. Both clubs were part of football's aristocracy, whose fans grew up on a diet of attractive attacking football; in their meetings in the 1965/66 season, both sides won their home fixtures 5–1. Even in lean times, the prospect of the United v. Spurs game quickened the pulse.

Whereas United emerged from the doldrums under Sir Alex Ferguson, the manager's office at White Hart Lane had been fitted with a revolving door as the London side struggled for consistency. As the 2001/02 season began, United, seeking a third successive title, enjoyed the upper hand over underachieving Spurs, who were looking to rebuild under the direction of their former star Glenn Hoddle.

For the previous two seasons, United had been motoring, but the mood was punctured by the sudden and unexpected departure of centre-back Jaap Stam (the Dutchman had just taken delivery of a new kitchen when he heard of his surprise transfer to Lazio). Although Sir Alex was able to find a stellar replacement in Laurent Blanc, whom the Scot had long admired, the wheels of the United defence were showing signs of falling off. In their first six league games they had conceded ten goals.

It's an old cliché that losing sides in games face a mountain to climb. As the first half drew to a close Spurs led 2–0 through Dean Richards and Les Ferdinand when, on the stroke of half-time, Christian Ziege scored a third for the home team. What was an uphill struggle for the Reds now looked like an expedition to conquer Mont Blanc.

The United players expected the worst as they slumped on the dressing-room benches at half-time. The manager's tolerance for sub-standard performances was notoriously low to subterranean.

As Fergie approached a large tea pot, the tension mounted; after all, he had previous. In his Aberdeen days, during one half-time rant, he had battled with a Romanian samovar before smashing the crockery in a rage. What would he do this time? The players looked on anxiously as he walked to the pot and then . . . proceeded to pour himself a cup of tea and retire to a small adjoining room. To everyone's consternation, Fergie maintained a stony silence. As assistant manager Jimmy Ryan later recalled, the boss eventually returned: 'He's looking at everybody and he looks like he's boiling, but he drinks his tea, puts it down. Two or three minutes of the break are left now.'

The Scot eventually sat down and calmly said, 'Right, I'll tell you what we're going to do. We're going to score the first goal in this second half and see where it takes us. We get at them right away, and we get the first goal.'

But as the referee's whistle goes for the end of the half-time break and everybody starts to stand up, he fires a parting shot: 'Okay, now get it f**king sorted.'

You can guess what happened next. Primed and ready, United exploded out of their blocks. Within a minute of the restart, Andy Cole's header had reduced the arrears. The comeback was on. Two more headed goals followed: the first from Laurent Blanc in the 58th minute, the second from van Nistelrooy in the 72nd. Now to win it. United were on the rampage, and four minutes later, a beautiful flowing move involving Scholes and Solskjær ended with new boy Verón rifling a low, angled shot from the edge of the area past Sullivan. The comeback was complete. The cheeky grin on the face of the United manager caught by the TV cameras said it all. Three minutes from time, an exquisite volley from Beckham after more clever play from Solskjær put the icing on the cake. Sorted. Spurs were f**ked.

It wasn't so much a case of Tottenham 'Spurs-ing' it, they just couldn't cope with a rampant United who were inspired by their manager's uncomplicated but categorical instruction. When asked by the BBC at full time just what he'd said to inspire his team to their recovery, he replied: 'I'm not saying exactly what I said to them at half-time! Why am I always asked that?' Well, he couldn't really repeat the expletive, could he? Or tell viewers that he had spent most of the break in a silent fury. No, to quote a line from a Ronan Keating song in *Notting Hill*, a film popular at the time: 'You say it best when you say nothing at all.'

CHAMPIONS LEAGUE, YOU'RE HAVING A LAUGH
Photobombing in Munich, April 2001

Two United fans, friends since childhood, shared another passion that would make them minor celebrities and put a smile on the faces of sports fans around the world. Both Karl Power and Tommy Dunn loved a prank. As a teenager, Karl would blag his way into boxing matches holding a bag and a towel, pretending to be a corner man, while Tommy learned to leap over the turnstiles at Old Trafford before he was out of short trousers.

A victim of a horrific knife attack, Karl feared he would never walk again, but with the help of his friend he devised a recovery plan to regain his strength. It involved a madcap scheme that would provide him with a goal, something to get him out of his wheelchair.

In the late 1990s, the two teamed up with a plan to gatecrash a series of high-profile sporting events. The first one was to take place at the San Siro, the venue for the 2001 Champions League final, but a home defeat for United in their quarter-final against Bayern Munich necessitated a change of plan. Tommy and Karl, fearing an early European exit for their beloved United, decided they would have to execute their plan at the return fixture in

Bavaria. And the big idea? Karl was going to photobomb the United team.

Leaving nothing to chance, the boys travelled to Munich with three different replica United kits. If the stunt was to have any chance of working, Karl would have to look the part. Ever resourceful, Tommy Dunn went to the United hotel on the evening before the game to see what he could find out. Pretending he had brought his young son to see the game, he asked United's chief executive which kit the boy should wear for the game, and Peter Kenyon duly obliged. Tommy was comfortable in these settings; for years he'd wandered behind doors marked 'private' into 'secure areas'. His mobile phone, sharp suit and businesslike demeanour gave him, in his words, a cloak of invisibility. Throughout the 1998/99 season he attended United's European post-match press conferences without any accreditation, and was proud of his record of asking Alex Ferguson a question at every single one.

Come the evening of the game, Dunn and Power blagged their way to the pitchside with fake press passes. As the United team shook hands with the Bayern team, Karl stood at the back of the pack of press photographers. Once Andy Cole had shaken the hand of the last Bayern player and moved to join the rest of the United side for the team photo, Karl took off his tracksuit top to reveal his white shirt with the name of his hero, Cantona, and the number 7 on his back. He calmly strolled over to the United group to join the end of the back row, chest puffed out, Cantona-style.

Gary Neville saw that something was wrong. 'Who's that?' he said, pointing at Karl. Quick as a flash, Karl replied, 'Shut it, Gary, you grass. I'm doing it for Cantona.' Stunned into silence, Neville took it no further. Karl was perhaps lucky that he was standing at the opposite end of the row from Roy Keane for, in the photo that made the back pages of every tabloid the following morning, he can be seen looking daggers at the imposter. After the pictures were taken, Karl stepped back into the crowd to enjoy the game and thought little more of it.

Karl woke up to find that he had become an overnight sensation. The *Sun* bought their story, paid for hotel suites for him and Tommy, and then flew them back to England on a private jet.

The two hoaxers continued with their grand tour of the sporting calendar. Karl went out to bat at the Ashes Test at Headingley; the two of them enjoyed a knock-up at Wimbledon's centre court; and Karl, dressed in his Ferrari-red racing overalls, beat Michael Schumacher to the podium at Silverstone and waved to the cheering crowds, accompanied by Tommy who brought a magnum of champagne for authenticity.

The last item on the bucket list was to play football at Old Trafford. Eleven mates, all United fans including our two pranksters, assembled before the big game against Liverpool at Old Trafford on 5 April 2003. With his usual chutzpah, Tommy led the players past two security checks and onto the pitch, losing only one of the party on the way. The remaining ten posed in the centre circle for a photograph, Tommy sporting a long blond wig.

What were they up to? All became clear: the impersonators were going to re-enact Diego Forlán's first goal in United's win at Anfield earlier in the season. Tommy had even lined up a dwarf to play the role of the hapless Liverpool keeper, Jerzy Dudek, but he cried off the night before. But nothing could spoil the enjoyment of scoring in front of the thousands of cheering United fans.

It was Tommy's favourite stunt despite he and his co-conspirators being banned for three years from Old Trafford for their exploit. It had all been worth it. They had achieved what they had set out to do. Karl was back on his feet, they'd hoodwinked the sporting world, made headlines in the papers and, best of all, they were having a laugh.

THE GAME'S AFOOT
Metatarsal Casualties

Historically, April has been an anxious time for World Cup national team managers. Injuries to key players throw their best-laid plans up in the air and induce nerve-shredding tension as they wait to see whether recoveries can be made. For some unknown reason, during that month, fractures to the small bones in the foot known as metatarsals seem to afflict Manchester United's England players more than any other club.

Sven-Göran Eriksson lost Gary Neville (fifth metatarsal) when his first-pick right-back was ruled out of 2002 World Cup selection after suffering the injury in the European Cup semi-final against Bayer Leverkusen. It was a bad loss to England but, apologies Gary, probably not one to keep the imperturbable Swede awake at night.

In 2006, the nation held its breath as Wayne Rooney battled to recover from a break to his fourth metatarsal suffered in the 3–0 defeat to Chelsea at the end of the month – a recurrence of the injury he'd picked up in the Euros two years before. Experts said the injury would need seven weeks to properly heal; the World Cup group stages were six weeks away. Even at 20, Rooney was regarded as irreplaceable, a talisman for the team, and every technique known to medical science would be employed to accelerate his recovery. He did recover in time for the second game of the group stage, but it didn't end well, with Rooney making minimal impact on the tournament before being red-carded against Portugal in the quarter-finals.

Rooney's injury had been big news in the build-up, and the saga had echoes of the drama that played out four years earlier ahead of the tournament held in Japan and Korea. No, it wasn't Gary's misfortune but rather that of his friend, teammate and global celebrity, David Beckham, who had been injured two weeks before in a Champions League tie against Deportivo de la Coruña. In a feisty game in which the Spanish side picked up six yellow and two red cards, Becks was felled by a crunching tackle by the Argentine Aldo Duscher.

Until Beckham suffered his metatarsal (fifth) injury, few outside the medical profession knew what a metatarsal was. Over the next weeks leading up to the World Cup, catching bulletins on the state of Beckham's foot became a national obsession. Not only a media celebrity, he was now England's main player and crucial to the nation's hopes.

Beckham was at the peak of his footballing powers. But four years before, he was the object of ridicule and vilification for his soft dismissal against Argentina in the 1998 World Cup; one headline after England's heroic defeat read: 'Ten Lions and One Stupid Boy'. At the beginning of the new domestic season, crowds booed him and sang obscenities about his girlfriend, Victoria Adams. Ignoring the abuse, he doggedly rebuilt his reputation: acting manager Peter Taylor made him England captain in 2001, and his rehabilitation was complete after an amazing performance in the World Cup qualifier against Greece that October in front of a sell-out Old Trafford stadium.

In a tie where England had to secure at least a draw to be sure of qualifying, they had trailed Greece for most of the game. The captain, playing like a man possessed, seemed to be taking on the Greeks single-handed. He had already laid on one equaliser, but deep into injury time England were again a goal down and in urgent need of a miracle. They were awarded a free kick fully 30 yards out from the Greek goal, and if ever England needed their golden boy to deliver, it was now. Up stepped Beckham to send a swerving right-foot rocket into the top corner. His status as England's hero was sealed. The Old Trafford DJ played 'The Great Escape' over the PA, and England were headed to the finals.

Come June, the nation could finally let out its collective breath as fortunately, with the help of oxygen tents and a surgical boot, the injury healed in time for Becks to take part in the tournament. He later admitted that he wasn't fully match fit but he was able to enjoy his revenge against his Argentine tormentors. Four years on from the disgrace of Saint-Étienne, he stepped up to take a penalty conceded by Mauricio Pochettino. Beckham smashed it past Cavallero to score the only goal of the game. His celebration was cathartic and utterly joyous; the ghosts of the past were finally exorcised. The boot was firmly, painlessly, on the other foot. There can be few better descriptions of Beckham's emotion than the words of Don Pedro in *Much Ado About Nothing*: 'From the crown of his head to the sole of his foot, he is all mirth.'

KING EDWARDS
Martin Edwards, Chairman of
Manchester United, 1980–2002

Before the advent of Premier League and satellite TV rights deals, football clubs were anything but licences to print money. By the end of the 1970s, United's income was falling and annual turnover dipped below £2 million – roughly equivalent in 2022 to Paul Pogba's monthly salary – and a major reason for chairman Louis Edwards planning to raise funds through a rights issue. Edwards' butchery business was also losing money and came under the spotlight during an investigation by Granada TV's *World in Action* accusing him of corruption and bribery both in his business practices and at Manchester United. The scandal shook the United chairman, who died four weeks after the programme aired and before he had a chance to make the case for his defence.

When Martin succeeded to the post of chairman on his father's death in 1980, he saw a club in urgent need of modernisation. Martin had worked in the family's meat-supply firm and wanted to bring a more businesslike approach to club affairs. He introduced financial budgeting to the club, and once an FA rule change allowed one club director to be paid, he drew a salary of £30,000 per annum. Some of his ideas, like copying Barcelona's basketball team, came to little.

Times were hard for the football industry in the 1980s. English clubs were banned from European competition; hooliganism gave the sport an image problem which, combined with the effects of rising unemployment, led to falling attendances. Despite Edwards' efforts, United kept losing money.

He resisted an approach from Robert Maxwell in 1984 to buy United for £10 million, but accepted an offer of £20 million from property developer Michael Knighton in 1989 for his majority shareholding. At the first home game of the 1989/90 season, Knighton enjoyed his 15 minutes of fame by playing keepy-uppy in the centre circle of the pitch as the Tannoy introduced the fans to their new owner. However, the deal fell through as Knighton's financial backers took fright at the contents of United's books. It was hard to know where to go next.

Meanwhile, Edwards had more success with the team's performances on the pitch. The FA Cup was won in 1983 and 1985, and the fans enjoyed the devil-may-care style of Ron Atkinson's side. But by the beginning of November 1986, following a run of poor results, United were in the relegation zone. Edwards replaced Big Ron with Aberdeen's Alex Ferguson, and to his eternal credit, stuck by his manager as the Scot came to grips with the monumental task at hand. Although Ferguson is now the object of veneration, it's hard to recall the abuse thrown his way after his early struggles. The 5–1 defeat to Manchester City in September 1989 prompted shouts of 'Ferguson out' ringing round Maine Road; then, in December, after the home defeat to Crystal Palace, superfan Pete Molyneux unveiled his notorious banner: 'Three Years of Excuses and It's Still Crap, Ta Ra Fergie.'

The 1990s saw a change of fortune on and off the pitch. In 1991, Edwards went public, floating Manchester United plc on the Stock Exchange. Edwards also played a leading role in the formation of the Premier League, bringing new money and attracting new audiences from home and abroad. He embarked on a major programme of modernisation at Old Trafford, starting in 1995 and culminating in a stadium that could hold in excess of 76,000 spectators by 2006. He even sacrificed the view of the pitch from his office window to squeeze in another row of paying seats. He hired Edward Freedman from Spurs to overhaul their marketing and merchandising operation; the United superstore and museum soon followed, generating new revenue streams.

Not everyone was as keen as Edwards on the commercialisation of the club. Ferguson worried that the building of the massive new north stand (now, ironically, named the Sir Alex Ferguson Stand) would rip the soul out of the club. The diehard fans recoiled; Andy Walsh, a founder of FC United, decried Edwards' vision, saying, 'You had to block out the embarrassment and the shit, the shirt changes, the corporate boxes, the money making . . . it was indefensible.' In the foreword to Edwards' autobiography, Peter Schmeichel acknowledged that he was unpopular with some United fans: 'Many disliked him, even hated him over the years.'

However, Edwards' faith in Ferguson began to pay off with cup successes in 1990 and 1991, and Edwards also played a crucial role in luring Eric Cantona from Leeds United, whose move provided the missing piece of the jigsaw to turn United from the nearly team of 1991/92 to the champions of the following season. In a call from Bill Fotherby enquiring about the availability of Denis Irwin, Edwards first insisted that his full-back was not for sale and then – prompted by a scribbled note from Ferguson who was in Edwards' office at the time – asked the Leeds chairman whether he would consider parting with the maverick Frenchman who had hit a hat-trick against United in the 1992 Charity Shield.

The £1.2 million transfer was arguably the best piece of business during Edwards' chairmanship.

It was the dawn of a golden era for United. In the 1990s, the trophy cabinet groaned under the addition of five league titles, four FA Cups, a League Cup, the European Cup Winners' Cup and, best of all, the European Cup in 1999. Manchester United were not just the biggest club in England; they were now on the way to becoming a global brand.

By 1998, the club that was worth £20 million less than ten years before was now valued at £623 million – the offer bid by BSkyB which the United board accepted. But the deal fell through partly due to an effective PR campaign by fan activists, and the takeover was referred to the Monopolies and Mergers Commission, whose recommendation to bar the deal was accepted by the government.

Edwards stepped down as chief executive in 2000 and as chairman two years later, leaving the club in a strong financial position – it was profitable and debt free – but, as a plc, vulnerable to further takeover bids. He did well personally out of his 20 years at the helm, selling the last of his shares in 2002 to Harry Dobson for £20 million; in the 11 years since United had gone public, he had netted close to £100 million.

But as with his father before him, his time at United ended under a cloud. He had survived a number of stories in the tabloids about dalliances with prostitutes, but then, in August 2002, Edwards accepted a police caution following an incident at the Mottram Hall Hotel in Cheshire. In what became known as the 'Peeping Tom scandal', a woman alleged that he had entered the ladies' toilets and spied on her.

He resigned from the Manchester United board soon after news of the caution broke – caught with someone else's pants down.

JUMPING FOR JOY
Goal Celebratons

In the modern game, with as many as 20 TV cameras capturing every move and facial expression, goal celebrations have become part of football's theatre. Some are passionate, some cathartic; many play out an inner narrative for the scorer which onlookers are left to divine. They all add to the colour and the gaiety of the nation.

Before the Big Brother media omnipresence, players' main impulse would be to share their joy with the spectators in the ground. An elegant leap and a fist in the air evolved into more inventive ways to celebrate: the knee-slide, a dance by the corner flag or David Beckham's trademark aeroplane with his arms stretched wide.

Some are memorable because they evoke a key moment or reflect on the character of the scorer, others because they are funny, ingenious or bizarre. The top ten excludes Ronaldo's famous '*Siiuu*' celebration, first performed in 2013 and only seen by United fans on his triumphal return to Old Trafford in September 2021, due to its association with his time away in Spain and Italy.

10. Jumping for joy

You would have thought that someone who had scored over

300 times for club and country would know how to celebrate. Not so *Bobby Charlton*. The United legend was a thoughtful introvert who might give a little hop in the air or raise a hand after scoring but, as often as not, he didn't bother.

In the 53rd minute of the European Cup final in 1968, Charlton broke the deadlock with a glancing header. A header from Bobby was a freak occurrence. His shock was reflected in his celebration. Bobby sprang upright with arms in the air, before quickly bringing his hands back down to his side, thus effecting a sort of bizarre standing long jump. His second goal finished off a fine night's work, allowing Bobby to lift the coveted trophy and take a giant leap for man(United)kind.

9. Naked distraction

Diego Forlán was a firm favourite with the United fans. He was a skilful, tireless forward who gave everything on the pitch. His only problem was he had left his shooting boots back home in Uruguay. In the 36 times he appeared for the Reds before the game at Southampton in November 2002, he only managed to score twice. So, imagine his joy and relief at grabbing a late winner.

Maybe a little out of practice, his goal celebration went awry. Having pulled off his shirt to reveal his toned torso, Diego struggled to put it back on. The game kicked off again and Diego played on with crumpled shirt in hand.

After the incident, FIFA banned the practice of baring naked flesh in goal celebrations, thereafter making the offence punishable with a yellow card. The one and only time those guys *didn't* want to take the shirt off someone's back.

8. The passion play

Footballers, especially those who grew up supporting their club, can be more passionate than the fans. And you don't even have to be the scorer to go ballistic. Picture Brian Kidd on his knees when Steve Bruce scores the injury-time winner against Sheffield Wednesday to put United on the brink of their first title in 26 years.

For sheer Red mistiness look no further than *Gary Neville*. In a top-of-the-table clash against arch-rivals Liverpool in 2006, Rio Ferdinand headed the winner in the final minute. Gary Neville sprinted towards the travelling Liverpool support and let his feelings be known in a primeval, hip-thrusting, badge-flaunting rant uttering words to the effect of, 'Take that, you Scouse *@?*$*s.'

7. Boxing clever

Wayne Rooney loved scoring and showing off to camera – his crucifix pose in the corner flag after his sensational overhead against City in 2011 a sublime moment. But he also had a nicely wicked sense of humour.

In 2015, a leaked video of Wazza and teammate Phil Bardsley boxing went viral. Both men, keen boxers in their youth – Rooney's uncle ran a gym in Croxteth – had indulged in a spot of sparring, both ending up bloodied with facial injuries. The tabloids speculated, wrongly, that Rooney had been knocked out. Shortly after he scored against Spurs he treated the fans to a little shadow boxing and then slowly collapsed backwards onto the turf. Knockout!

6. A merry dance

Dancing celebrations were a feature of the young United side of the 1990s: Ryan Giggs and Lee Sharpe were expert. Their youthful exuberance later made way for the more sinuous moves of the uber-cool Paul Pogba.

One player made the dance floor his own. *Jesse Lingard* had tried various signature celebrations – the twirling shirt at the 2015 FA Cup final, the Pied Piper, the J-L finger salute – but he finally nailed it with his version of Russ's 'Gun Lean' – his shoulders moving left, right, left, right. It made its debut in a 5–1 win over Cardiff when he grabbed the ball off Pogba to take a penalty and many speculated that he did so solely because he was desperate to show off his new moves. Paul just shrugged his shoulders.

5. The gymnast

Footballers in the Premier League are more athletic than the average Division One player of yesteryear – and some can combine this prowess with gymnastic ability. Rooney could execute a decent somersault, and Peter Schmeichel performed an elegant cartwheel after Solskjær's winner in the 1999 European Cup final. There was, however, one Red who surpassed them all. The pocket battleship that was *Nani* went literally head over heels with joy after scoring, celebrating his goals with a range of tumbling routines including a 360-degree backward somersault with a twist. Flipping heck!

4. The storyteller

Players acknowledging their children, born and unborn, following a goal is a familiar sight on grounds around the world, Bruno Fernandes being a prime example at United. Not many fans know the true aim behind *Edinson Cavani's* archer celebration – the Uruguayan, down on one knee, firing off an imaginary arrow. A deeply patriotic and humane individual as well as an ace marksman, Cavani explained: 'When my little daughter, India, was born, her name is just a small reference to our native Uruguayans, the Charrúas. So that arrow that I take out and then fire is a goal celebration that encapsulates all these things: a mix of my daughter's name and the indigenous peoples of my country.' *Ay, caramba!*

3. The salute

Not many players are honoured by their clubs with a statue outside the home stadium. *Denis Law* has two: one outside Old Trafford along with George and Bobby, and another inside the stadium at the Stretford End.

Both statues combine the Lawman's goal celebration: arm pointing straight up, index finger pointing skyward, hand clutching his sleeve of his shirt. It was a sight that fans in the 1960s never tired of seeing. Others copied it – but where George Best would raise his arm with a warm smile and a gentle jog trot, Denis beamed with delight, the triumphant gesture a simple assertion of his striking genius.

2. The late, late show

Late winning goals can often spark off wild celebrations. Picture Nemanja Vidić wheeling away, arms whirling like windmills after a tap-in against Sunderland in 2008, or Michael Owen's best moment in a United shirt when his 96th-minute strike decided a seven-goal thriller in the 2009 Manchester derby, haring off, arms outstretched, behind the goal in front of delirious supporters.

But no one will ever forget the sight of *Ryan Giggs*, scorer of the extra-time wonder goal against Arsenal in the 1999 cup semi-final, running back, bare-chested (apart from a mat of hair), shirt twirling above his head to be mobbed by the entire United bench. It was one of those rare occasions when the celebration matched the quality of the goal.

1. The Royal Command performance

Eric Cantona had presence: a presence of mind and a charismatic bearing that marked him out as a special player.

In December 1996, United faced Sunderland at Old Trafford. In the tunnel before kick-off Cantona approached his compatriot Lionel Pérez, Sunderland's goalkeeper, to say a quick *bonjour* only to be blanked. Pérez would later pay for his *lèse-majesté*. On 80 minutes, the King saw his chance: free at the edge of the penalty area, he looked Pérez straight in the eye before chipping the ball over his head into the net. *Incroyable!*

Cantona's reaction was extraordinary. He stood stock-still, then slowly turned to accept the crowd's adulation and to present his greatness to his subjects. It was if to say to the watching world, 'Look on my works, ye Mighty, and despair.'

SLIDING DOORS MOMENT NUMBER 1
Manchester United v. Porto
CHAMPIONS LEAGUE (ROUND OF 16), 9 MARCH 2004

It should have been a routine European tie for Sir Alex's side. They were regulars in the Champions League for all but one of the previous 11 years and accustomed to progressing to the later stages. Their opponents, the previous year's UEFA Cup winners Porto, held a slender 2–1 lead going into the second leg. But the Reds had the comfort of Quinton Fortune's away goal.

Ferguson had injury and suspension concerns: Louis Saha was not fit to start, and Roy Keane and Rio Ferdinand were suspended. He placed his trust in home-grown talent, fielding the Class of '92 stars – minus the departed David Beckham – and Wes Brown, Darren Fletcher and John O'Shea from the new generation. The selection of Eric Djemba-Djemba (so bad they named him twice, so the cruel joke went) to fill in for Roy Keane raised one or two eyebrows; it was only the Cameroonian's second start in three months.

The young manager of the Portuguese champions, José Mourinho, had crossed swords and cross words with Ferguson after the first-leg dismissal of Roy Keane for a foul on the Porto keeper. A protégé of Bobby Robson's, Mourinho had turned down a managerial position at Newcastle and been approached by Tottenham. But he kept his options open: 'It would be a dream,' he said, 'to be the coach of a Premier League side.'

Everyone remembers Paul Scholes in his pomp as the midfield genius, sliding clever passes to attackers and dictating the tempo of a match. The younger version was a potent scoring threat with his stealthy late runs and deadly finishing earning him the nickname 'Ginger Ninja'. In his first ten seasons he netted 125 times; in his final nine years he managed 30.

It was Scholes' free kick that had led to Fortune's goal in the first leg. In the return, Scholes headed United in front with a deft header from the edge of the six-yard box. United were now ahead in the tie, and a second goal would require Porto to score at least twice to stay in the tournament. On the stroke of half-time, Scholes was again in the right place at the right time to put the ball in the Portuguese net from close range. Game over, surely.

But wait. Gennady Krasyuk, the Russian linesman, had been watching a different game. To everyone's amazement, the official raised his flag for offside. In the days before VAR, the referee was deprived of the replays that millions of fans around Europe could see on TV that showed Scholes and two other teammates clearly onside.

A series of misfortunes befell United in the second half. A young Cristiano Ronaldo came on as a substitute only to leave shortly afterwards after being scythed down by Nuno Valente. Then, in the final minute of normal time, Phil Neville was unlucky to be penalised for a brush on Jankauskas just outside the box. Tim Howard in goal failed to deal with Benni McCarthy's free kick; instead of catching it or turning it behind for a corner, he pushed the ball straight into Costinha's path who duly accepted the gift to score an unlikely equaliser.

That was the cue for Mourinho to sprint 50 yards down the touchline to join the wild celebrations of the Porto players who had fallen on Costinha. The draw was enough to secure victory over United on aggregate.

Had United kept their lead, they would have had a relatively easy route to the final. Lyon, Deportivo de la Coruña and Monaco were not formidable opponents as Porto would later prove. Instead, it was Mourinho who took the plaudits and paraded the Champions League trophy in Gelsenkirchen at the end of the season.

Benni McCarthy, the Reds' tormentor, scorer of Porto's two goals in the first leg and whose free kick set up the equaliser at Old Trafford, accused United of arrogance and showing a lack of respect. Perhaps a team that included Deco, Ricardo Carvalho and Maniche should have been taken more seriously. Or perhaps it was just fate – had Scholes' second 'goal' stood, the Portuguese threat would have evaporated.

If Porto had exited in the round of 16, the team may have broken up, the best players may have been sold on to richer clubs, and José Mourinho may have slipped back to relative obscurity. Roman Abramovich may have turned to Sven-Göran Eriksson to replace Claudio Ranieri as Chelsea's coach later that summer. Instead, the Russian chose the 'Special One' and Mourinho would lord it over the Scottish knight for the next three seasons.

THE BATTLE OF THE BUFFET
Manchester United v. Arsenal
24 OCTOBER 2004

In October 1996, following the sacking of Bruce Rioch, Arsenal appointed Arsène Wenger as their manager. Back then, foreign coaches were a novelty in the English game: Dr Jozef Vengloš lasted a season at Aston Villa, Ossie Ardiles not much longer at Tottenham, while Ruud Gullit's appointment at Chelsea as player-coach was an experiment yet to run its course.

The media marvelled at this latest exotic creature like an artwork loaned to the National Gallery or a panda donated to London Zoo. Dubbed the 'Professor', Wenger introduced new tactics and innovative methods of coaching and dietary conditioning. He could also speak several languages. Alex Ferguson, very much of the old school, scoffed at the admiration being heaped on the Frenchman, pointing out that he had a 15-year-old Ivorian in his academy who could match Wenger's polylingualism.

Over the next eight years, Arsenal and United came to dominate English football. They enjoyed a duopoly with Arsenal winning the Premier League title three times and the FA Cup three times (the double on two occasions) while United won five titles and the FA Cup twice (and one historic treble).

During this period, matches between the two giants took on huge significance. If anything, Wenger had the edge over

Ferguson; in the 16 games played between the two teams from his arrival at Highbury to the game in October 2004, Arsenal had won seven, United four, and five were drawn. Twice the Gunners had secured 1–0 victories at Old Trafford on their way to winning the league. In the 2003/04 season, they were dubbed the 'Invincibles', having gone through the season unbeaten, and the *Guardian*'s Kevin Mitchell was moved to write that Wenger was the most astute manager in the Premier League, and 'probably all of football at the moment'.

It's unlikely that Sir Alex was a *Guardian* reader, but had he been, he would have cancelled his subscription. Still smarting at the events that took place during the 'Battle of Old Trafford' in October the previous year, the Scot was out for revenge. In that earlier acrimonious encounter, van Nistelrooy had been accused of faking injury to have Vieira sent off, and when the Dutchman missed a late penalty, he was immediately surrounded by baying Arsenal players led by Martin Keown, face contorted and veins bulging, refusing to observe any accepted norms of social distancing (even back in 2003).

In the transfer window, Ferguson had moved to buy the hottest property in English football. Two years before, as a 16-year-old, Wayne Rooney had dented Arsenal's title hopes by blasting a howitzer in a 2–1 win for Everton at Goodison Park. Now Rooney was a United player, and at the end of September he instantly won new fans with a hat-trick on debut in the Champions League. Ferguson was assembling a formidable strike force combining the energy and trickery of Rooney and Ronaldo with the deadly finishing of van Nistelrooy.

Against that, Wenger had added to his growing army of technically gifted players from Europe and South America. Going into the game at Old Trafford, Arsenal – fielding seven foreign internationals – had continued their unbeaten league run, which had now extended to 49 matches, and they were clear at the top of the table. United had drawn too many games and now languished 11 points adrift in seventh place. Ferguson knew this was an opportunity to change the course of the campaign; it was time to ruffle some of that exotic Arsenal plumage.

The United players were revved up. Wayne Rooney recalled that 'all week Arsenal had been banging on about how great it would be to make it to 50 games unbeaten at Old Trafford. Big mistake. They fired us up. Fifty games unbeaten? No way. Not at our place.' Phil Neville, who filled in for Roy Keane that day, caught the mood: 'It was a build-up of 12 months because the happenings in the 2003 game were totally out of order with people jumping all over Ruud. But in every game we played back then [against Arsenal] the tension in the air was incredible. It was just so ferocious. It wasn't war, but it was like two heavyweights clashing in a ring. Nobody used to give an inch.'

The match was an even contest; Arsenal shaded possession and territory. Even without Roy Keane, United snapped into their tackles, targeting their opponents' flair players. The Neville brothers both saw yellow – Gary was lucky to stay on the pitch; van Nistelrooy was fortunate that the referee didn't see him rake his studs down Ashley Cole's leg.

In the 73rd minute, United were awarded a penalty after Rooney fell over Sol Campbell's outstretched leg. Van Nistelrooy stepped up to take the kick and this time there was no mistake. To round things off, the new boy Wayne Rooney, on his 19th birthday, celebrated by finishing off a breakaway move to tap in for the second. Given the ill-feeling, there was no swapping of shirts at the end of the game, and, anyway, the Arsenal players would no doubt have been embarrassed had they had to reveal the '50 not out' T-shirts beneath their jerseys.

Instead of a battle on the pitch, the match ended in a war of words in the players' tunnel; a furious Wenger branded van Nistelrooy a cheat and Ferguson stepped in to defend his players. And then the arguments descended into chaos as the Arsenal players weaponised their after-match buffet. The youngest member of the Arsenal squad, 17-year-old Cesc Fàbregas, launched a slice of pizza into the air which landed smack in the face of Sir Alex. There was a collective intake of breath. Ashley Cole captured the moment in his autobiography: 'All eyes turned and all mouths gawped to see this pizza slip off that famous puce face and roll down his nice black suit.'

That brought about an immediate cessation of hostilities. The incident was hushed up as Ferguson quickly changed into a tracksuit for the post-match interviews. In the aftermath, Wenger was fined for criticising referee Mike Riley's decisions, van Nistelrooy was given a three-match ban for his ugly tackle on Cole, and the tabloids had a field day – one headline summed up the events as 'War and Pizza'.

Ironically, for the first time in ten years the Premier League was won by neither Arsenal nor United; that honour belonged to Abramovich's Chelsea. A cold war took hold as relations between Wenger and Ferguson frosted over, neither speaking to each other until the Champions League semi-final in 2009.

Since Pizzagate, Arsenal have failed to win the Premier League although they have enjoyed some success in the FA Cup. United, on the other hand, would win a further five league titles – all under Ferguson's stewardship. The Scot is convinced that United's victory that day was a pivotal moment – he felt that Wenger's management was disorientated by the defeat. The tide of the war between the two footballing titans had turned. Sir Alex may have been a casualty in the Battle of the Buffet but he ended as the winner on points – and points mean prizes. He had taught the Professor a lesson.

WELL RE(A)D
United on the Printed Page

So much has been written about Manchester United and so many writers have built up impressive catalogues of books on the club, it's hard to know where to start.

Honourable mentions must go to the much-loved *Manchester Evening News* sportswriter David Meek who covered United for nearly four decades and wrote or co-authored some 20 books; the prolific Ivan Ponting who penned copious yearbooks as well as ghosting several player autobiographies including Bill Foulkes, Wilf McGuinness and Gary Pallister; and Iain McCartney, author of more than a score of books on the Reds including many excellent works on the early history of the club and the Busby era.

The blockbusters

Books by and about George Best are always incredibly popular. George himself is officially the author of five autobiographies including *Blessed* and the splendidly titled *The Good, the Bad and the Bubbly* with its memorable first line: 'I punched Michael Caine to the floor in Tramp one night.' Gary Neville's *Red* should win a prize for doing what it says on the tin. The wittiest autobiography title has to be the posh-sounding *One* belonging to Peter Schmeichel.

Roy Keane has written two bestsellers, *Roy Keane: The Autobiography* and *The Second Half*, an innovative co-write with the Booker Prize-winning novelist, Roddy Doyle – both of which are as brutally honest as you might expect.

Sir Alex Ferguson literally takes the biscuit though. After signing thousands of copies of his autobiography, hundreds of books had to be rejected as spoils due to chocolate stains on the title page. The great man had worked his way through the biscuit tin during the epic signing session! But there's no doubting the success of *My Autobiography*: nearly 850,000 hardbacks were sold in the UK alone according to the industry sales checker, Nielsen BookScan. Add in paperbacks, eBooks and overseas sales, and it's multi-million seller.

Mention in passing must be made of *I am Zlatan Ibrahimović*. Written before his two-year spell at Old Trafford, the Swede's critically acclaimed, rags-to-riches autobiography stormed up bestseller lists all over the globe. The film adaptation, released in June 2022, was praised by the *Guardian* as a 'sympathetic, realist film . . . a compelling watch'.

Celebrity autobiographies

Unscrupulous publishers are not shy of cashing in on the marketability of the modern football icon and, as a result, some less than literary offerings have been seen in bookshop windows around Christmas over the past 20 or 30 years.

At the tender age of 20, typically quick off the mark, Ryan Giggs published his autobiography. Not to be outdone, the 22-year-old Wayne Rooney topped that by signing a multi-million-pound, five-book deal in 2006. Sadly, Wayne was a late developer as a writer and the books never recouped the advance, but he since became a respected columnist for *The Times*.

David Beckham, stylish as ever, produced a number of autobiographical titles: *My Side*, *Both Feet on the Ground* and *David Beckham*, which featured a lot of nice pictures of, er, David. *My Side* sold an impressive half a million copies.

Classics (apart from those written by Sir Alex Ferguson)

The more discerning United fan has been treated to some very fine books to read. Worthy of mention are: *Sir Matt Busby* by Patrick Barclay; the collectible *Duncan Edwards: The Greatest* by James Leighton; *George Best: An Intimate Biography* by close friend Michael Parkinson; *Manchester United: The Biography* by Jim White; *The Lost Babes and the Forgotten Victims of Munich* by Jeff Connor; Philippe Auclair's excellent biography of Eric Cantona, *The Rebel Who Would Be King*; Juan Mata's intelligent *Suddenly a Footballer*; and capturing the thrill of the epic 1998/99 season, Daniel Harris's linguistically gymnastic *The Promised Land: Manchester United's Historic Treble*.

The controversial

Eamon Dunphy's *A Strange Kind of Glory*, a well-written work, managed to ruffle a few feathers due to its depiction of Old Trafford as an unhappy place riven with cliques and disputes as Busby's era drew to its close.

Jaap Stam caused mayhem with uncharitable comments about the Neville brothers and his raking over the controversy surrounding his transfer from PSV Eindhoven in *Head to Head*. His transfer to Lazio following so soon after the publication of the book aroused suspicion, but Ferguson maintained that the Dutchman's powers were waning and the move was good business – he later regretted his decision.

The most expensive

Manchester United: The Opus, one of a handful of super-exclusive titles published by Kraken, is arguably the biggest book on United. Weighing in at 37 kilos, it's half a metre square, 850 pages long, and, costing £1,500 new, is the most expensive book on United.

Criminal writing

Steve Bruce, despite managing numerous clubs after his playing days, found time to write crime fiction in 1999. Drawing on his experience in football and an over-active imagination, he penned a bizarre murder mystery trilogy – *Striker!*, *Sweeper!* and *Defender!* – based around a football manager called Steve Barnes. They featured amongst other things war criminals, terrorists and Nazi hunters, and caused merriment and bewilderment in equal measure. Although much derided, the books have since acquired the status of minor cult classics. As Seamas O'Reilly said in his Balls online review: 'Harper Lee has famously only published one novel in her lifetime. Well, she can eat s**t because Steve Bruce has published three.'

(Former Chelsea star Frank Lampard has penned an impressive 18, but he needn't concern us here.)

Children's books

In November 2020, Macmillan Children's Books announced a major initiative, the Marcus Rashford Book Club, which would donate books to help promote reading and literacy amongst poorer communities. Rashford's first novel, *The Breakfast Club Adventures*, was published in May 2022 – an exciting, fun-filled adventure for 6- to 8-year-olds.

Literary XI

Here's my fantasy football team packed with international literary giants, again based on the 4-2-4 system.

Goalkeeper: Roland Barthez
Full-backs: Peter Carey, George Bernard Shaw
Centre-backs: John Buchan, James Hogg
Midfield: Molly Keane, Hans Christian Andersen
Wingers: P.D. James, Tom Sharpe
Forwards: Sally Rooney, Ted Hughes
Sub: Dylan Thomas
Manager: Maggie O'Farrell

THE UNITED STAKES
The Glazers Take Control
of Manchester United plc

It has been said that when a butterfly flaps its wings in the Amazonian jungle, subsequently a storm ravages half of Europe. An illustration of chaos theory or, at least, a simplistic, popularised version of it. The theory might also be applied to the battle for ownership of Manchester United in the early years of the current century. In this instance, it wasn't a butterfly but a racehorse, and for the jungle read Arlington Park, Chicago, for Europe, Manchester United plc.

The star of the 2002 domestic racing season was the stallion Rock of Gibraltar, winner of seven consecutive group one races. The horse ran in Sir Alex Ferguson's colours – red silk with white-starred sleeves – and the United manager must have felt on top of the world. Ferguson was passionate about horses; in the late 1990s, going to the races was a thrilling distraction from the pressures of club management. In 1998, after Arsenal had romped away with the league, United's chairman Martin Edwards and Ferguson had a bust-up after Edwards accused his manager of losing his focus on United because of his liking for the turf.

Ferguson co-owned Rock of Gibraltar with Susan Magnier, wife of John Magnier, who, jointly with business partner J.P. McManus, had just increased their shareholding in Manchester

United plc to 8.65%. The two Irishmen – who owned the hugely successful Coolmore Stud and its racing arm, Ballydoyle – had become friends with Sir Alex through their mutual love of racing, and it was thought that their growing shareholder influence would strengthen the Scot's position within the club. The club's board was undergoing upheaval; long-serving Martin Edwards had stepped down as executive chairman in 2000 and resigned from the board in November 2002 following a tabloid exposé into his private life.

In October 2002, after the Breeders' Cup Mile in Chicago, Rock of Gibraltar's racing days came to an end and he was put out to stud. That's when the trouble started. Sir Alex and John Magnier's definitions of ownership were at odds – would Sir Alex have to be content with half the prize money (over £1 million) or would he also expect to have a stake in the even more lucrative stud earnings? The friends fell out, and, in late 2003, Sir Alex began legal proceedings against John Magnier to secure his share of the breeding rights. Much was at stake as estimates of potential earnings were as much as £200 million.

Then things got ugly. Magnier and McManus increased their stake in United to 23%, buying up BSkyB's shares which were no longer of interest to the broadcaster once their own takeover bid had been blocked by the government in 1999. A private detective was hired to investigate the business affairs of one of Ferguson's sons; in early 2004, a list of 99 questions was tabled by Cubic Expression, the shareholding vehicle used by Mangier and McManus, to the board of Manchester United seeking clarifications on finance and transfer dealings. Sir Alex was feeling the heat. Fans were impatient at the turn of events. In support of the beleaguered manager, the self-styled Manchester Education Committee staged a protest at Hereford racecourse that brought proceedings to a halt; the offices of the private detective agency were picketed; the Coolmore Stud's server was targeted and their staff bombarded with hostile emails. At one stage, a demonstration was planned for the showcase event of the jump racing year, the Cheltenham Festival.

Ferguson's position was now under threat. Club captain Roy Keane advised him to drop the legal action; in his view, Ferguson couldn't win against the Coolmore duo and the club's reputation was suffering collateral damage. The United board were rattled by the developing power struggle and decided to seek out new investors to dilute the influence of Magnier and McManus. A pebble had been dropped into the pond, and on the other side of it, the ripples caught the eye of Avram Glazer, son of Malcolm Glazer, owner of the Tampa Bay Buccaneers NFL franchise.

The Glazers first dipped their toes in the share market in March 2003 with a 2.9% stake building up to 16% by November. Coolmore still had a formidable lead but they stopped short of the 30% marker which would have forced them to make a formal offer to buy out other shareholders. In October, the Glazers were coming up fast on the rails, their stake now up to 28%.

Ferguson and Magnier may have settled their differences by the end of 2004, but by then the nature of United's ownership had changed. Although other dragons had been circling – Dutch TV magnate John de Mol Jr amongst them – there were two main frontrunners with a sizeable number of shares: one held by Coolmore, whose main interest was in horse racing and who had fallen out with the club's manager; and one held by the owner of a major sports franchise with a history of aggressive empire-building – the Glazers – who had tried unsuccessfully to buy the LA Dodgers baseball team the previous year.

The Coolmore boys cashed in their winnings and made a tidy profit by selling their shares to the Glazers in May 2005. Within a month, the Glazers were able to delist the company from the Stock Exchange.

The takeover was complete. The race was run.

FROM SHOW PONY TO THOROUGHBRED
The Stellar Rise of Cristiano Ronaldo

August 2003. United had just played a pre-season friendly against Sporting Lisbon. John O'Shea was exhausted after an afternoon being tormented by Sporting's winger, an 18-year-old by the name of Cristiano Ronaldo. As he and the other United players waited in the coach for over an hour after the game, Rio Ferdinand wondered what was causing the delay. Inside the stadium, Sir Alex Ferguson and Peter Kenyon were hammering out a deal to bring the teen sensation to Manchester. They wouldn't leave until they had their man (or even boy).

The players only had themselves to blame for the wait. At half-time during the match, they had raved about the young Portuguese and implored the manager to sign him up. But in truth, United had been tracking Ronaldo's progress for a couple of years. Seeing his talent close up, their minds were made up, and, following David Beckham's departure to Real Madrid in the summer, there was a vacancy to fill. United had just missed out on Ronaldinho – the Brazilian had had a late change of mind and chosen Barcelona over Manchester. So, a fee of £12.5 million was agreed, a transfer record for a teenager in English football.

Cristiano got off to a flyer in his first outing. George Best described it as 'undoubtedly the most exciting debut I have ever seen'. Yet, in that first season, he had his doubters. The excessive stepovers, his scrawny physique and his frequent diving led some to think him a prima donna, a show pony. He was more concerned with his dribbling skills than putting the ball into the penalty area. Alan Hansen on *Match of the Day* wondered if you'd want to play with him in your side or against him, concluding: 'The jury's still out.'

Ronaldo was nothing if not driven. His ambition was to be the best footballer in the world, and he sought help to improve his physical strength, and stayed late at the training ground to hone his skills. Rio Ferdinand recognised that desire, declaring, 'I don't know a stronger, more determined, obsessed player that I've shared a dressing room with.'

If Euro 2004 saw Ronaldo emerge as a star, then the 2006 World Cup painted him as a villain. In their quarter-final against England, many were convinced that he helped to get Wayne Rooney sent off by bending the referee's ear, suspicions seemingly confirmed by the knowing wink caught by the TV cameras after his United teammate was shown a red.

He could be annoying. Ruud van Nistelrooy, tired of making pointless runs into the box for crosses that never came, tore strips off Ronaldo, once reducing him to tears. Van Nistelrooy had come to the conclusion that Rooney and Ronaldo were too immature and if he was to achieve his ambition of winning the Champions League he had to quit United for Real Madrid.

Facing the ignominy of a hostile media and the abuse of fans following the World Cup, a lesser character might have faltered. Any thoughts of leaving England were countered by Ferguson and his Portuguese assistant, Carlos Queiroz, offering him their support; it helped that Rooney bore no ill will. Like Beckham eight years before, Ronaldo rode out the storm and developed into one of the world's greatest all-round players. Not only could he dribble, but his pace made him deadly on the counter-attack; his decision-making in the final third had improved beyond measure; he could score with either foot; and with his height and athletic physique he was now the best header of a ball in England. His tireless training-ground practice perfected new techniques at free kicks – striking the ball on the valve – with spectacular results; his effort against Arsenal, from 35 yards, in the 2008 Champions League semi-final, was out of this world.

In his last three seasons at United, he scored 91 goals in 155 appearances, won three consecutive Premier League titles, two League Cups and, best of all, the Champions League, scoring a header in the final.

Since childhood Cristiano Ronaldo had pushed himself relentlessly to improve, to get fitter – not just physically but mentally. In 2008, he won his first Ballon d'Or. In 2009, after a year's hiatus he got his wish to join Real Madrid. In 2008, Ferguson had fought off advances from the Spaniards, refusing to be bullied into selling his star player. He told Ronaldo he was staying put, saying that had he sold him, then all honour would be gone. 'I'd rather shoot you than sell you to that guy now.'

Ferguson knew he wouldn't be able to keep him; playing for Madrid or Barcelona was the apogee for Iberian footballers. Ronaldo stuck it out for another season, winning his fourth Premier League title and reaching another European final. Honour was satisfied, and he was allowed to leave for a world record fee of £80 million. The United management were philosophical. Carlos Queiroz had predicted that 'if you get five years out of him, you've struck gold. There's no precedent for a Portuguese player going to another country and staying five years.' Getting a sixth was a bonus.

He joined Madrid as the finished article. Now a *Galactico*, his longevity and further achievements – four more Champions Leagues, four more Ballons d'Or, three more Golden Boots – are testimony to an exceptional athlete dedicated to being the best he could be. His social media presence and his CR7 brand added to his superstar status, helping to make him the first footballer to earn more than $1 billion during his sporting career. Madeira renamed their airport in his honour complete with a bust that looked more like a demented Geoffrey Boycott than the island's most famous son. Yet he never lost his love for United and often spoke of his affection and gratitude to Sir Alex Ferguson for helping him on the path to greatness. It was that special affinity that eventually drew him back to Old Trafford in dramatic style in August 2021.

For such a stellar talent it was fitting that in 2015 the *Galactico* had a galaxy named after him. The galaxy Cosmos Redshift 7, or CR7, made it official: Cristiano was truly out of this world.

THE MAGNIFICENT SEVENS
Seven Greats Who Have
Worn the Number 7 Shirt

The number 7 shirt possesses a special mystique in the imaginations of United fans and, indeed, players. More than any other shirt number, it is an object of reverence – its wearer the spark or talisman to whom all eyes turn. Some, like David Beckham, swell with pride when told that they are to be allocated the number; others shrink when burdened with the extra responsibility.

In a cold historical analysis, it's not clear why players wearing 7 should be regarded with any more veneration than other numbers. The number 11 has been worn by legends such as Charlie Mitten, David Pegg, Ryan Giggs and, yes, George Best; the number 10 by Mark Hughes, Denis Law and Wayne Rooney; and 9 by Bobby Charlton, Tommy Taylor and Jack Rowley.

The reasons are twofold. For over three decades – from 1977 to 2009 – United were fortunate to have some of the most talented and charismatic figures in their history wearing the shirt in an unbroken sequence. And this period coincided with the expansion of television coverage and the greater exposure of the sport.

In choosing the magnificent seven, some detective work – nay, guesswork – is needed when looking into history before the modern era. Until 1939, United players didn't wear shirt numbers, and from 1946 to the Premier League era, numbers weren't designated to specific squad players but rather to players on the pitch – until 1993 the FA required the numbers 1 to 11 to be worn on the field. And because of injuries, suspensions or loss of form, shirt numbers would be swapped between the players. Hence George Best, who many count as one of the greatest, actually played more often as number 11 (246 times as 11 to 141 wearing 7 in a total of 470 appearances).

Johnny Berry

The choice in the Busby era comes down to picking either Jimmy Delaney or Johnny Berry. Many questioned Busby's decision to bring the crocked, 30-something Delaney from Celtic, but the Scot was a key part of that first great post-war team, featuring in the famous 1948 FA Cup final win. Berry edges it through his consistent wing play, which helped United to win three league titles before the injuries he sustained in the Munich air disaster ended his career.

George Best

Okay, any excuse to sing the praises of the most naturally gifted player to wear the number 7 shirt. In the classic match in Lisbon in 1966, George wore it as he scored twice in a 5–1 win against Benfica, making him a global star in the process. He then rubbed salt into Portuguese wounds two years later when he scored the second goal in the European Cup final. Two-footed, he could play on either wing; after the arrival of Willie Morgan from Burnley in 1968, the Scottish wingman became the regular number 7.

Steve Coppell

When it comes to consistency, no one could beat Steve Coppell. Forming an effective wing partnership with the more mercurial Gordon Hill, the brainy Scouser was integral to Docherty's attacking side of the 1970s. Appearing in three FA Cup finals and receiving a winners' medal in 1977, Coppell went on a remarkable unbroken run of 206 games from 1977 to 1981. Sadly, a knee injury incurred on England duty cut short his career at the tender age of 28.

Bryan Robson

No stranger to the treatment room himself, 'Captain Marvel' was a mainstay of the 1980s for both club and country. On his day he was unstoppable. Had he not been sidelined by injury in the middle of the 1985/86 season, United may have kept up their momentum and won the league title. His longevity ensured that he won two league championship winners' medals and lifted the FA Cup on three occasions as well as the European Cup Winners' Cup in 1991.

Eric Cantona

When squad numbers were made mandatory at the start of the 1993/94 campaign by the Premier League, Cantona was handed the shirt. In his debut season, he had been the difference between Ferguson's team being nearly men and champions. The Frenchman dazzled the United faithful in a short but eventful career and was instrumental in United winning four titles and two FA Cups, scoring the winner against Liverpool in the 1996 final, when he had also been named captain.

David Beckham

In 1996, when David Beckham first made fans sit up when he chipped the Wimbledon goalkeeper from the halfway line, he was proudly wearing the number 10. Hearing that Teddy Sheringham – signed to replace the retired Cantona – would be given the shirt number, Becks was aggrieved. But shortly after Ferguson contacted him to say he'd be wearing the number Cantona relinquished, Becks remarked, 'United fans grow up with famous 7s. I went from being upset to one of the happiest people.' In the next six seasons, he played 294 games as number 7, adding five more titles and a Champions League victory to his impressive medal collection.

Cristiano Ronaldo

Last but not least, as a young teenager Ronaldo took over the shirt once Becks departed for Real Madrid in 2003. He served his footballing apprenticeship at United, maturing into a match-winner before the eyes of adoring United fans. Becks may have been a hard act to follow, but Ronaldo ended up topping the bill.

In the intervening years between his departure in 2009 and his return 12 years later, the number 7 had been something of a millstone. Michael Owen's powers were in decline, Antonio Valencia was Mr Dependable without ever threatening to lift fans off their seats. Things worsened after Ferguson's retirement: Ángel Di María, Memphis Depay and Alexis Sánchez all disappointed. While Edinson Cavani performed a brilliant cameo under Solskjær, Ronaldo's reclaiming of the shirt prevented any chance of the Uruguayan from taking his place alongside the great 7s from the past.

A tagline on a poster promoting the 1960 Hollywood movie, *The Magnificent Seven*, read: 'Once you've met them, you'll never forget them.' For anyone who has encountered any of these seven magnificent United stars, they will live long in the memory.

CROWNING GLORIES
United Hairstyles Through the Years

Plenty of young men in their late teens and early 20s are only too willing to parade their peacock tendencies, and footballers are no different – apart from having considerably more disposable income available to splash on their appearance. Given that they have to wear their school uniform on matchdays, one of the few ways to express their individuality is through their hair.

Back in the day, when football was a working-class sport for spectators and players alike, hairstyles were utterly conventional. The occasional dandy like Billy Meredith would sport a moustache. In the 1930s, a lick of Brylcreem might be smoothed on. In the 1950s, a few tried a more daring look: Dennis Viollet, a bit of a ladies' man with a penchant for sharp Italian-cut suits, had his hair slicked back and quiffed. That was about it – all very understated. But that was all about to change . . .

In the Swinging Sixties, George Best – who else? – was the trendsetter. Sporting a mop top, he was dubbed 'El Beatle' by the press after his virtuoso display in the 5–1 demolition of Benfica in March 1966. As the decade progressed the hair grew longer, then sideburns appeared and then a beard; he was turning into half-man, half-werewolf. Restoring nature's equilibrium, as George's hair grew, so Bobby Charlton's receded. The England legend's combover, one of the most famous hairstyles in all sport, was voted the worst footballer's haircut in a recent international poll conducted by Head and Shoulders shampoo (little to be lost by annoying that particular customer). Charlton won a whopping 49% of the vote, with Rio Ferdinand's kinky afro coming in a distant third (Peter Beardsley's pudding bowl was second).

In the 1970s, men's hair grew longer still – inspired by bands like Led Zeppelin, T. Rex and Status Quo. At United it was no different; Willie Morgan had the most luxuriant hair, the blond Gordon McQueen the prettiest. United fans would have to wait until Bryan Robson's arrival in 1981 for the first decent perm; it was gorgeous – Deirdre Barlow without the glasses.

Robson had the good sense to ditch the perm, but his teammates were quick to adopt another 1980s atrocity: the mullet. Mark Hughes, in his first spell at Old Trafford, opted to combine his mullet with a perm and quiff. Legend. Before long the place was teeming with them: Duxbury, Whiteside (whose nickname 'Shankhill skinhead' owed more to his aggressive play than his coiffure), Olsen and Nicholl to name a few. The reddest of all mullets belonged to Gordon Strachan whose cut featured curtains, surely the inspiration for the early Beckham barnet.

The combover wasn't completely abandoned. Ron Atkinson, United's ebullient, bejewelled manager somehow managed to get away with his – a perma-tan and a ready smile certainly helped. More Terry Wogan than Donald Trump in construction, Big Ron's hair seemed to fit his personality – a triumph of style over substance.

In the modern Premier League era, styles became increasingly diverse, with Rio Ferdinand managing to champion several.

He arrived at Old Trafford with a blond Sisqó (named after the rapper), moved on to corn rows, then the ill-advised afro, then dreadlocks, before reverting to a neat crop.

The buzz cut – the antithesis of the Best look – enjoyed popularity around the turn of the century. Cantona wore his imperiously; it made Roy Keane look even more menacing; and Jaap Stam looked like a scary elderly Orc from *Lord of the Rings*. Needless to say, Beckham could make any style look good – except the cornrows, which he confessed were done while on holiday after 'a glass of wine or two'.

Some of the Latin Americans – Cavani, Tévez and Heinze – liked the Aerosmith tribute band look pioneered by Kempes, Caniggia and Pochettino. Zlatan Ibrahimović had his man bun and, unusually, facial hair – a feature mostly shunned by players with the exceptions of Mike Phelan's military moustache and Barthez's pencil beard.

Like Charlton before him and Rooney after, Barthez was follically challenged. His solution to the problem was to opt for the boiled-egg look and shave his head. Rooney opted for hair transplants, first in 2011 and again two years later, at the cost of around £30,000 – small change for Wazza. It would have taken the 20-something Bobby Charlton – who finally ditched the combover in the 1990s – five years to have earned that amount.

In the post-Ferguson era, fans loved Marouane Fellaini's exuberant frizz; the popular Fellaini afro wigs at least kept the fans dry in the leaky Old Trafford stadium. Wan-Bissaka's tasteful spider dreadlocks were greatly admired by *GQ* magazine. Most controversial of all were the elaborate and ever-changing designs that adorned Paul Pogba's head. Pogba used his hair as a canvas on which his barber, Ahmed Alsanawi, creates fabulous colour and imagery – zigzag flashes, neon stars, Chinese calligraphy, you name it. Although toned down since his leopard-spotted Mohawk in his early Juventus career, his hair stuck in the craw of media critics such as Stan Collymore and Graeme Souness (he's one to talk – remember his abundant 1970s tache?). Like ancient Druids of old studying the runes, Pogba's new haircuts are scrutinised for hidden meanings – or as Souness might grumble, 'That boy needs his head examined.' The notorious blue streak he wore in the 2018 derby match incurred the displeasure of Gary Neville; even scoring twice to win the match was not enough to win over some of his detractors.

Would Sir Alex have stood for Pogba's tonsorial artworks? There's a clue in his treatment of David Beckham. Beckham carried off different styles with brio (*Men's Hairstyles* magazine recently listed the top 25): the teenage curtains, the man bun, the buzz cut, long hair with headband, the pompadour and the *Peaky Blinders* undercut. In 2000, ahead of the showpiece Charity Shield game against Chelsea, Becks hatched a plan. He was going to unveil his new Mohawk at the kick-off. The day before the game, Becks was careful to keep the new style under wraps or, more accurately, under the beanie which he wore in training and at the hotel breakfast table. An hour before kick-off, an irritated Ferguson told Becks to take off his stupid hat. The terrible secret was laid bare. Despite Becks' protestations, Fergie ordered him to shave it off or he wouldn't be playing. Reluctantly, Beckham gave in and removed the offending bristles, thereby creating yet another new, if unwanted, style.

It may have been small consolation, but at least Becks was spared the hairdryer treatment that day.

BEST OF BRITISH
Paul Scholes, Midfield Genius

During the 20-year hegemony of Sir Alex Ferguson's all-conquering United, the teams he fielded brimmed with world-class talent, big personalities and controversy. David Beckham, Roy Keane, Ryan Giggs, Cristiano Ronaldo, Eric Cantona and Wayne Rooney all dominated the pages of the tabloids – front and back.

Fans might argue about who was the greatest or who was their favourite. But the international football world was in no doubt: that honour went to Paul Scholes. When Barcelona manager Pep Guardiola was asked which of United's players he would have in his team he was unequivocal: 'Out of everyone at Manchester United I would pick Paul Scholes. He is the best midfielder of his generation.' Zinedine Zidane, no mean player himself, was also an admirer. 'I never tire of watching him play. You rarely come across the complete footballer, but Scholes is as close to it as you can get.'

He was not quite in at the beginning of the Ferguson era; had he been a few years older, no doubt United would have won yet more silverware. As a late graduate of the Class of '92, he was part of the revolution that transformed a very good side into one of the greatest English football had ever seen. The 19-year-old made an instant impact on his introduction to first-team football. On his first outing, a League Cup tie against Port Vale in 1994, he scored twice; on his league debut three days later, he found the net against

Ipswich. Despite *Match of the Day's* Alan Hansen asserting that 'you win nothing with kids', United did just that by winning the Premier League. And then a double and then a treble.

One regret Scholes must have had would have been missing out on the third part of the historic 1999 treble. Suspended for the Champions League final, he and Roy Keane had to watch the drama from the sidelines. But four days earlier at Wembley, Scholes had made a telling contribution to winning the second part of the treble. Scholes slid in substitute Teddy Sheringham to give United the lead against Newcastle before Sheringham returned the compliment with a cute lay-off to the edge of the area where Scholes arrived with his customary, impeccable timing to fire in a second to win the FA Cup.

While Scholes was ever-present in United's first-choice XI throughout his 19 seasons, his England career suffered from selection blight. His breakthrough came at Le Tournoi, the 1997 curtain-raiser for the '98 World Cup. In a 2–0 defeat of Italy (yes, really, that's not a misprint), Scholes showcased his range of talents by first chipping a 50-yard pass for Ian Wright to run onto and score, and then Scholes himself made one of his trademark late runs to slam home the second from the edge of the penalty area. He had taken apart a defence that included Cannavaro and Costacurta, and the *Azzurri* had to bring on Nesta in the second half to stop the rot.

With successive England managers never quite working out their best midfield permutation, the United man was too often sacrificed to make way for Lampard and Gerrard, or given the graveyard shift on the left of a 4-4-2 set-up. In 2004, Scholes, aged only 29, gave up his international career to the bemusement of any foreign judges. In Andrea Pirlo's view, 'the only great English midfielder in my career was Paul Scholes. He had elegance in him. Others were pretenders.'

Luís Figo neatly summed up Scholes' footballing genius and self-effacing personality: 'I'm star-struck when I see Paul Scholes because you never see him. On the pitch you can't catch him. Off the pitch he disappears.'

European club competition offered Scholes the chance to shine on the international stage. By the late 2000s, Ferguson had assembled another great side, one capable of winning the Champions League. Arguably his most balanced squad, they possessed a blend of experience, energy, defensive nous and attacking flair. They also had the genius of Paul Scholes, now playing in a deep-lying position and able to use his vision and passing accuracy to devastating effect.

Barcelona presented the final obstacle on the path to the Champions League final in Moscow. Over two legs it was a tight affair; it finished goalless at the Camp Nou. Shortly after kick-off at Old Trafford, there was a nice cameo as one of Scholes' famous 'mistimed' tackles stopped the precocious Lionel Messi in his tracks. Just one goal settled the tie. Not just any goal – it took a 25-yard wonder strike, hit with power and swerve from Scholes, to beat Victor Valdés and end the Catalans' resistance. United were on their way to a famous night in Moscow, and, this time, Scholes would be there to be a part of United's triumph.

That would be the last time United landed a glove on Barcelona. Under the management of Pep Guardiola, Barca brushed the Reds aside in finals at Rome in 2009 and at Wembley in 2011. It began to feel like the end of an era. After the Wembley final, Scholes took his first leave before being dragooned by the boss, six months later, to shore up an injury-hit midfield. Along with his manager, Scholes retired at the end of the 2012/13 season having made his 713th appearance for the club and collected his eleventh Premier League medal.

So how good was he? Thierry Henry was unreserved in his praise: 'Without any doubt the best player in the Premier League has to be Scholes. He knows how to do everything and he is the one who directs how the team plays. On top of that, he has indestructible mental strength and he is a genuine competitor.' In Sir Alex Ferguson's opinion, Scholes, along with Ronaldo, Giggs and Cantona, was one of four truly world-class players he had had the privilege to manage.

Let's leave the last word with Zidane. When he was asked what it felt like to be the best footballer in the world, the Frenchman replied, 'I don't know, ask Paul Scholes.'

THE FINAL STRAW
Champions League 2008–2011

For any other club, playing three Champions League finals in the space of three years would be a stellar achievement, a cause for celebration and the defining moments in the careers of players and coaches. And yet, United's experience in the premier European competition was ultimately humbling.

Sir Alex Ferguson, like Busby before him, regarded success on the European stage as the pinnacle of footballing accomplishment – a benchmark by which their teams were to be judged. By 2008, United were back on top of English football. The January 2006 acquisitions of Vidić and Evra strengthened the defence; the arrival of Carrick and Hargreaves had filled the void left in midfield by Roy Keane; and the maturing partnership of Rooney and Ronaldo was supplemented by the wily Carlos Tévez. Ferguson could also call on the experience and guile of two survivors from the Class of '92, Ryan Giggs and Paul Scholes.

It was Scholes' long-distance strike in the Champions League semi-final against Barcelona that separated two evenly matched sides over the two legs. Rather than attacking flair, it was an impressive defensive display against the Catalans, who dominated possession, that earned the Reds their passage through to the final in Moscow.

Before kick-off, Sir Alex spoke movingly to his players about personal achievement. Patrice Evra remembered the speech as the greatest he had ever heard. Sir Alex talked about Evra's upbringing as one of a family of 24 children in Senegal; of Rooney's childhood in Croxteth; and Tévez's start in life amidst the crime-ridden district of Fuerte Apache in Buenos Aires. Their success in overcoming disadvantage to be on this stage was his victory. He told them, 'We have already won the Champions League. Enjoy the game.'

In a closely contested and bad-tempered match that went to penalties, van der Sar's save from Anelka proved to be the decisive moment. United, winning the trophy for a third time, were once more kings of Europe.

Sir Alex would later say that he felt his teams should have won more Champions League trophies. It must annoy him greatly that Liverpool have a better record in the competition than United, the one perch from which he was unable to dislodge the club's greatest rivals. In the following three seasons, United created opportunities to add to their European total. In 2009, after clinching a third successive Premier League title, they were in the Champions League final again. Could they be the first team to retain European football's top prize since AC Milan won in 1990? En route they had impressively dispatched Arsenal with an emphatic 3–1 win at the Emirates in the semi-final, Ronaldo scoring twice in a virtuoso performance; the first a free kick from over 30 yards, the second to finish a devastating counter-attack started by an audacious flick from the number 7 deep in his own half.

Standing in the way of a fourth European triumph was the team they had beaten in the semi-final the year before. But this time the Catalans had a new manager and a new system – Pep Guardiola and tiki-taka. Guardiola didn't invent tiki-taka but he did develop it to a new intensity. For the method to succeed, his team would have to have players of great skill and the bravery to think on their feet. Fortunately for him, Barcelona had Xavi, Iniesta, Busquets, Touré and, above all, their 21-year-old superstar, Lionel Messi.

Despite a strong start by United, with Ronaldo looking dangerous, an early goal by Samuel Eto'o calmed Barcelona's early nerves and they began to take control of the match. Messi was brilliant, but it was Iniesta who won the biggest plaudits; after the game Rooney acclaimed the Spaniard as the 'best player in the world'. Ferguson warned before the game that Barca would try to put their opponents on a carousel, and by the time Messi scored a second, United heads were spinning. The attacking threat of Rooney and Ronaldo was effectively neutralised by starving them of the ball.

A depleted midfield shorn of Hargreaves through injury and Fletcher through suspension couldn't cope. Michael Carrick, usually so influential in midfield, was chasing shadows; Anderson was subbed off at half-time. Not so much the anticipated merry-go-round as the run-around.

The following year, United were tripped up at the quarter-final stage by Bayern Munich as Raphael was shown red and a special strike from Arjen Robben put Bayern through on away goals. However, in 2011, United made it to the final once again, to Wembley, the site of their first European triumph, for a rematch with Barcelona.

Ferguson wanted to take the game to Barca by pressing high and attacking. But any thoughts of turning the tables on Barcelona were quickly dispelled as Pedro gave the Catalans an early lead. Although Rooney drew the scores level with an equaliser against the run of play, Barcelona dominated the game. It was fitting that Messi, who gave the man-of-the-match display, should score as Barca cruised to a 3–1 lead. An exhausted United team couldn't recover; in the 81st minute Rooney reportedly told Xavi, 'That's enough. You've won. You can stop playing the ball around now.' It was curtains. Rooney also doubted whether United had adopted the right tactics: 'We lost two finals going to-to-toe with Guardiola's Barcelona by trying to press high and get round them, which was suicidal.'

Ferguson's dream of European glory had been dashed by the brilliance of Guardiola's team who were at the peak of their powers. In Messi they faced, in his manager's words, the best player he had ever seen. In his post-match comments, a deflated Sir Alex was honest enough to admit: 'Nobody's given us a hiding like that, but they deserve it.' He added, 'In my time as manager it's the best team I've faced.'

Ferguson had been defeated in his attempts to conquer peak Barcelona. There was to be no curtain call for Ferguson's team; instead, the final curtain had fallen on his dream of being European champion one last time.

TALLEST, OLDEST, LONGEST
Edwin van der Sar, Record-breaker

Edwin van der Sar could have joined United in 1999 as Peter Schmeichel's replacement if Sir Alex had had his way, but Martin Edwards had already shaken hands on a deal to bring Mark Bosnich back to Old Trafford on a free, a price that always appealed to the chairman. It would be another six years before the giant Dutchman would become United's number 1.

An outstanding goalkeeper, he stood out for more than just the obvious reason.

Tallest

When he joined United in the summer of 2005, van der Sar became the tallest player to appear for the club. At 1.97 metres (or 6 foot 5 inches), he was an inch taller than centre-backs Harry Maguire and Gary Pallister. Big Jim Holton was a fraction smaller than the 6 foot 2 inches fans liked to claim.

Height is a useful attribute in goalkeepers, but it doesn't always intimidate opponents: in the 1998 World Cup, playing for the Netherlands against Argentina, he was headbutted by the diminutive Daniel Ortega, all 1.7 metres (5 foot 7 inches) of him – Ortega came up to his chin.

Oldest

When van der Sar hung up his gloves on 28 May 2011, at 40 years and 211 days he was the oldest male player to play in the European Cup in the Champions League era. Six days previously, he also set the record as the oldest player to win a Premier League champions' medal.

Longest period without conceding

After conceding in the 48th minute to Samir Nasri on 8 November 2008, van der Sar began a record-breaking sequence which only came to an end on 4 March, nearly four months later. In that time he kept a clean sheet in 14 consecutive Premier League matches, a record. In total, van der Sar went 1,311 minutes unbeaten, a British record. In 266 appearances for the club he managed 135 clean sheets, averaging better than one every two games.

Although not the most successful keeper in terms of medals – no one would ever be able to match Peter Schmeichel – in his six years at United van der Sar did all right, winning four league titles and two League Cups, and appearing in three Champions League finals, winning one by saving Nicolas Anelka's penalty in the 2008 shoot-out. He was voted UEFA's Goalkeeper of the Year for a second time in 2009, 14 years after his first award when he was a key part of van Gaal's European Cup-winning Ajax side.

CULT HEROES XI

Where do you draw the line between a club legend and a cult hero? There are players who have racked up hundreds of games for United and yet never got the media plaudits they deserved but who have won the hearts of supporters. And there are those who stay for a couple of years or maybe only ever make a handful of appearances but who, by force of character or through a moment of inspiration, earn themselves a piece of sporting immortality and the lasting love of the fans.

It's impossible to measure the status of players from bygone eras where no folk memories remain and there's scarcely any video footage to look at. Let's leave aside the Busby Babes; they've collectively achieved hero status as the club's band of brothers. So, my personal selection has to be made from the modern (colour) televised era.

In the era of Best, Law and Charlton, the names of Nobby Stiles, Paddy Crerand, Alex Stepney and the versatile David Sadler may have been eclipsed by the famous Trinity, but their contributions were no less vital to the club's domestic and European successes.

In the relatively fallow years between the Busby and Ferguson eras, there were plenty of stars blazing across the Old Trafford firmament to thrill the crowds. Here are three of the best.

Jim Holton

'Six foot two, eyes of blue, big Jim Holton's after you' pretty much says it all about the tough, no-nonsense Scottish centre-half who played in the early 1970s. The fact that his eyes were brown shouldn't spoil a good rhyme. Big Jim's career was sadly blighted by injury and his career was limited to 69 appearances.

Gordon Hill

Together with club legend Steve Coppell, Hill formed the exciting wing partnership that was the hallmark of Tommy Docherty's newly promoted side. Hill memorably scored twice to win the 1976 FA Cup semi-final and was part of the cup-winning side the following year. Scoring 39 times in a mere 101 appearances, his career at United was ended shortly after the arrival of Docherty's successor, Dave Sexton, and he left on a transfer to Derby County.

Norman Whiteside

He might easily be considered a legend but for the fact that he was sold after injury problems and a drinking habit started taking its toll. A teenage prodigy, he became the youngest-ever United goal scorer aged just 16, and netted in the 1983 and 1985 FA Cup finals. His lack of speed saw him move back into midfield where he excelled as a fierce competitor.

As we move into the Premier League era our roll call expands.

Jaap Stam

In 1998, Stam became the most expensive footballer in Dutch football history when he moved to Old Trafford. Integral to the side that won the treble, Stam was the bedrock of United's defence. He left under a cloud after the publication of his book, *Head to Head*, which, amongst other controversies, included unflattering remarks about teammates. Ferguson later regretted selling Stam, admitting it was his single biggest managerial mistake.

Philip Neville

From the Class of '92, Phil never quite matched the achievements of his older brother. He was a prime example of the fan on the pitch giving everything for the United cause in 386 appearances. Often filling in as left-back or partnering Seba Verón in midfield in an injury-ravaged United team in 2002/03, Philip was happy to play wherever the manager wanted. He left reluctantly in 2005 for Everton, playing for a further eight years in a distinguished spell at Goodison, where he ended up captaining the side.

Lee Sharpe

A teenage prodigy bought from lowly Torquay United in 1988, he made his debut aged 17. A forward who could play on either wing, a hat-trick in the famous 6–2 League Cup win over Arsenal at Highbury in 1990 was an indication of early promise and a marker that Fergie's United were on the march. Good-looking, with a big personality on the pitch and a nice line in mic-synching celebrations at the corner flag after scoring, Sharpe was a firm fan favourite. His United career was affected by illness and then finished by stellar competition from the likes of Giggs, Kanchelskis and Beckham.

Denis Irwin

Roy Keane's mate was regarded by his fellow countryman as 'the first name on the team sheet'. Mr Consistency joined United in 1990, playing as a full-back mostly on the left side. Deadly from the penalty spot and free kicks, Denis bagged 33 goals in 529 appearances in his 12 years at Old Trafford.

John O'Shea

Quiet and unassuming, the likeable Irishman was the ultimate utility player who could play anywhere along the back line or midfield – once even taking the goalkeeper's jersey against Spurs after van der Saar had to leave the field. He's fondly remembered for nutmegging Luís Figo in a tie against Real Madrid and for scoring a late winner against Liverpool in front of the Kop.

Scoring against Liverpool elevates most players to cult status, but two in particular stand out.

Diego Forlán

The Uruguayan, a big-ticket purchase in 2002, was signed to score goals: a skill that came easily to him later in Spain and at the 2010 World Cup, but too often eluded him in the Premier League. However, the fans took to him after he scored two goals in three minutes at Anfield in a 2–1 win, the feat immortalised in song: 'Diego, oh-oh-oh, he came from Uruguay, he made the Scousers cry.'

Dimitar Berbatov

The ultra-cool, stylish centre-forward's love of conserving energy infuriated many fans, but there was so much to admire in his elegant touch and ability in front of goal. Technically gifted, Berbatov was also capable of the spectacular, including an overhead kick in a hat-trick at Anfield in September 2010 – the first against Liverpool by a United player for 64 years. Two months later, he managed five against Blackburn and a further treble followed against Birmingham in January 2011.

Park Ji-sung

The popular Korean had bags of energy and stamina, which earned him the nickname, 'Three-lung Park'.

The manager liked to pick him for the big games, often to

man-mark key opponents, and trusted Park implicitly to follow team orders. One of his scalps, the talismanic Andrea Pirlo, said of him, 'They'd programmed him to stop me. His devotion to the task was almost touching. Even though he was a famous player, he consented to being used as a guard dog.'

So, that's my XI. There are many other candidates who came close to selection: Chicharito, Ander Herrera, Marouane Fellaini (possibly too Marmite) and Lee Martin for his 1990 Cup-winning goal, but there's room for one substitute and, no, it's not Ole Gunnar Solskjær – the once cult hero has now moved to a more exalted status.

Federico Macheda

In April 2009, Liverpool had overtaken United at the top of the table and the Red Devils were losing at home against Aston Villa. Rooney was suspended, Berbatov injured, so, with half an hour to go, the manager subbed on a 17-year-old Italian striker to make his debut. He only went on to score the injury-time winner!

After that minor miracle, United regained their momentum and pipped Liverpool to the top spot, equalling their rivals' record of 18 championship titles.

Cult XI

O'Shea (GK); Irwin, Stam, Holton, Neville; Sharpe, Park, Whiteside, Hill; Berbatov, Forlan.

WAYNE'S WORLDIE
Manchester United 2 Manchester City 1
12 FEBRUARY 2011

Manchester United have been blessed with fantastic goal scorers over the years: Rowley and Spence in the first great Busby side; Tommy Taylor and Dennis Viollet fronting the Busby Babes; Best, Law and Charlton in the 1960s; then Cantona, Cole and Yorke in the 1990s; and van Nistelrooy in the new century as Ferguson's United dominated the Premier League. But topping them all in the scoring charts is Wayne Rooney.

Rooney was a teenage sensation. Seven days before his 17th birthday, he announced his arrival to the football world with a spectacular winner for Everton against Arsenal in March 2002, ending the champions' 30-game unbeaten run and helping Manchester United reclaim the title from the Gunners.

Rooney had been on Ferguson's radar for a while; indeed, United had previously tried to sign him as a schoolboy before finally succeeding in 2004, beating off competition from Newcastle and paying a world record fee for a teenager of £27 million at the end of the August transfer window. Ferguson waited for Rooney to regain full fitness before unleashing the new boy in a Champions League home tie against Fenerbahçe at the end of September. And what an entrance! Rooney fired a hat-trick in a 6–2 demolition of the Turkish champions.

His early impact for both United and England quickly earned

him the nickname of Wazza, a jokey homage to Paul Gascoigne. Comparisons didn't stop there: he was hailed as the 'White Pelé' by banners in the stands and in the classic fan chant 'I Saw My Mate the Other Day'. Even Ferguson conceded there were similarities between the Brazilian and United number 10s. 'Is he like a Brazilian? Look at Pelé. He was a very aggressive attacker as well who could look after himself. So can Rooney.'

In an interview prior to a Champions League tie against Benfica in 2011, Ferguson expanded on the qualities that made Rooney such a special player but placed him in the British tradition, comparing him to 'players like Paul Gascoigne, George Best, Bobby Charlton and Denis Law. The similarities are that the boy has great courage. He wants to play all the time. He has incredible stamina. These are added extras to the talent he has. There are similarities that way in strength and speed, determination.'

Rooney also had character. He needed it to cope with the tabloid stories about his private life, to deal with metatarsal and other injuries, and the legal actions and constant attention of an often hostile mainstream and social media. He was big news: a football superstar, with a huge online following. Advertising deals with Nike and Coca-Cola and being the face of EA's FIFA video games all added to his ever-growing profile. In 2011, his replica shirt was the bestselling sports product under the Premier League's auspices.

There were tensions too, though, when Rooney sought a move away from United in 2010, citing a lack of ambition on the club's part; there were fears that he might 'do a Tévez' and move to the newly rich Manchester City. At one point, 40 figures in balaclavas appeared outside Rooney's house warning him not to 'pass into darkness'. Three years later, there was more speculation of a move abroad to Real Madrid or possibly Chelsea, who put in a £20 million offer that July.

These issues unsettled the United fans, but in truth Rooney remained loyal to United. He stayed with them for 13 years, making 559 appearances. He managed to score a club record of 253 goals, winning 16 major trophies and becoming the only English player, alongside teammate Michael Carrick, to win the Premier League (which Rooney won five times), FA Cup, Champions League, League Cup, Europa League and FIFA Club World Cup.

He won countless player awards on a monthly and annual basis. He also won the BBC *Match of the Day* Goal of the Season on three occasions – in 2005, 2007 and in 2011 – more than any other player. It was the third of these that has become Rooney's defining moment. It came on a pivotal day in the title race as United lined up for the derby on 12 February 2011, when so much was at stake in the game against the reigning champions.

Rooney was not having the best of seasons. The long-running transfer dispute and injury had kept him out of the team, and he didn't score from open play until January. The game was evenly poised until Rooney's decisive intervention in the 78th minute. The goal, which has been rated as the best in Premier League history, was dramatic, spectacular and technically brilliant. As Nani's cross came into the penalty area, it took a slight deflection, wrong-footing the City defence and giving Rooney a glimmer of a possibility. In an act of supreme athleticism, balance and imagination, Rooney executed an unstoppable overhead kick that flew into the corner of the net. His celebration was one of pure elation as he ran to the corner flag, arms stretched wide, and lifted his head heavenward to proclaim his genius and accept the crowd's adulation.

'The deflection [from Nani's cross] actually helped me, because it slowed the ball down and gave me time to adjust myself, turn my body.' Modestly, he added, 'To be honest, I just thought I'll go for it. I wasn't having the best game, and thankfully it's gone into the top corner.' Not everyone was impressed; City keeper Joe Hart's churlish complaint that the shot came off Rooney's shinpad was quickly batted aside. 'I always say to him it's a harder skill to score off your shin than your foot!'

Sir Alex said it was the best he had ever seen at Old Trafford. To Rooney it was his most important. To football fans everywhere it was a moment of sheer magic, a feeling that Terry Venables memorably put into words in a voiceover for Richard Swarbrick's animated short film which became a Sky advertisement for its Premier League coverage: 'It was one of those times when you really do get goosebumps . . . With a flash like a strike of lightning, he changed direction, his body's up in the air. It was like a right foot with an explosion but with timing and the beauty of a dance.'

RED CARPET REDS
United's Celebrity Fans

Watford have Sir Elton, Celtic have Rod Stewart, Manchester City have the warring Gallagher brothers, and Hibernian have The Proclaimers casting eternal sunshine on Leith. Teams who play in claret and blue enjoy the support of former prime minister David Cameron, Prince William narrowed it down to Aston Villa, and Liverpool have 007 himself, Daniel Craig, cheering for them (although Bond legend Roger Moore happily donned a Man Utd shirt during a UNICEF benefit match in 2002).

However, no team can match the army of celebs who follow United. The Pride of Manchester website lists over 400 famous names who support the Red Devils, from Hollywood to Bollywood, and Pyongyang to the Punjab. Here are just a few.

Hollywood

Julia Roberts is the mother of three children – twins Hazel and Phinnaeus, and Henry – who all support United and played at Old Trafford with Wayne Rooney's children after a match against West Ham in 2016. Roberts starred in *Erin Brockovich* alongside Albert Finney – also a diehard Red.

Megan Fox took a shine to the Reds in general and to Chicharito in particular, sporting a Manchester United

T-shirt emblazoned with Javier Hernández – who had a huge following in Fox's native LA.

Football-crazy Channing Tatum has also been known to step out in a United strip on the streets of West Hollywood.

Bollywood

Through sheer audience size alone, Shah Rukh Khan – aka 'King of Bollywood' – is one of the most successful film stars on the planet. Star of more than 80 films, he is also a philanthropist who champions children's education and women's rights. He would love his son to play for Manchester United and has hung out with Rio Ferdinand.

Head of state

North Korea's little Rocket Man, Kim Jong-un, is rumoured to have enquired about buying the club from the Glazers. While studying in Switzerland, he regularly attended matches at the San Siro in Milan. His favourite player is Wayne Rooney.

Economist

Baron O'Neill of Gatley, better known as Jim, all-round economic guru is a Red.

Broadcasters

Eamonn Holmes, breakfast TV host, led George Best's funeral procession to the parliament buildings in Belfast in 2005.

Nick Robinson, BBC radio presenter, and Mark Chapman, presenter of *5 Live Sport* and *Match of the Day 2*.

Springwatcher and Goodie, Bill Oddie, and *Countdown*'s Rachel Riley can be counted amongst the faithful.

Film and TV

Lovejoy star Ian McShane is the son of Harry McShane who played more than 50 times for United in the 1950s.

Brendan Coyle, grand-nephew of Sir Matt Busby, played Lord Grantham's valet, Bates, in *Downton Abbey*.

Steve Coogan, comedian and actor, aka Alan Partridge, cast his lager-loving layabout character of Paul Calf, star of *Get Calf*, as a Manchester City supporter.

Michael Parkinson, friend of George Best and author of numerous books on the United legend.

Lifelong fan James Nesbitt presented Cristiano Ronaldo with his award at the 2015 Ballon d'Or ceremony and had the chutzpah to ask him to come back to Old Trafford.

Jamie Dornan, *Fifty Shades of Grey* heart-throb, is a United season-ticket-holder.

And, finally, a Hobbit! Merry Brandybuck from *The Lord of the Rings* – aka Dominic Monaghan – regularly strolls around Beverly Hills in a Man U shirt and opines on football matters.

Actual lords of the ring

Floyd Mayweather wore a United shirt in a weigh-in in 2007, and Manny Pacquiao, Tyson Fury and Conor McGregor all support the Red Devils.

Rey Mysterio, the Mexican-American wrestler, met the Manchester United squad in 2018 during the club's pre-season tour of the United States. He also received a shirt with the number '619' on it. The number alludes to the name given to his famous finishing move in wrestling.

Musicians

Rihanna: *'I'm into football in a big way. Manchester United are my team. Those guys are so talented and crazy.'*

Justin Timberlake: *'As soon as you get into football, you start liking Manchester United. But it wasn't David Beckham. I met Alan Smith and he invited me to a match and I fell in love with the whole experience. I can't think of a faithful as strong as the Manchester United fans.'*

Gary Lightbody of Snow Patrol tells a nice story of how, when he was at school, his mum and dad bid in an auction for him to play snooker with his hero, Norman Whiteside.

'They knew how big a fan I was and they ended up winning the auction. I couldn't believe it. I came in my Sunday best with a tie and everything. I was so excited! I remember being ushered in to the snooker hall and meeting Norman, which was amazing. I broke and made a hash of it and he then made a break of something like 68 and the game was over!'

Lu Han, Chinese singer and social media star, is a passionate Reds fan. His 'Ten Years a Fan, Lifelong a Red Devil!' post from September 2015 received more than 100 million comments and broke the Guinness World Record for the most comments on a Weibo post. He visited Old Trafford in 2019, meeting Ole Gunnar Solskjær and the squad, and watched Man Utd beat Brighton & Hove Albion 2–1.

Roger Taylor of Queen donated £10,000 to the supporters' campaign to defeat the Murdoch bid in 1998.

The ensemble of music fans extends to Stormzy (who famously namechecked David Moyes – but not in a good way – during his 2019 Glastonbury set), Snoop Dogg (who had a kickabout with Rio Ferdinand in 2010 during a visit to a Salford community centre), Duran Duran front man Simon Le Bon, Ian Brown and Mani of The Stone Roses, Goldie, Richard Ashcroft of The Verve, Thom Yorke of Radiohead, Smiths bassist Andy Rourke, New Order's Bernard Sumner and Peter Hook, Mick Hucknall and, of course, the fabulous Harry Styles.

Bass-baritone Bryn Terfel and the 'people's tenor', Russell Watson, who sang 'O Sole Mio' and 'Barcelona' before 92,000 spectators at the 1999 European Cup final, represent the world of opera.

Cricket

Fans include former England captains, Michael Atherton and Michael Vaughan, batting legend Geoffrey Boycott, T20 captain Eoin Morgan, World Cup hero Jofra Archer and West Indian opener, Chris Gayle.

Indian cricketer Yuvraj Singh often sports the club's jerseys and has been part of podcasts and interviews with United fans. He participated in a fireside chat with Marcus Rashford in 2020.

Sourav Ganguly, the swashbuckling left-hander, began his love affair with the club when he played county cricket for Lancashire.

MS Dhoni is often the face of promotional campaigns for the partnership between Manchester United and sponsor Gulf Oil.

Olympians

Swimmer Adrian Moorhouse, long-jumper Greg Rutherford and sprinter Darren Campbell from Team GB, and, famously, Jamaica's Usain Bolt are all supporters. Bolt, who used to give sprinting tips to the players, would have gladly swapped the Caribbean sunshine for soggy Manchester if only Sir Alex had taken one of the many hints he dropped about becoming a United player.

Sportsmen

Reds from the world of rugby include England fly-half Owen Farrell, league legend Martin Offiah and, from across the Irish Sea, Brian O'Driscoll, Johnny Sexton and Keith Wood.

Golf ace Rory McIlroy may not be a relation of Sammy's, but hails from the same part of the province.

KEEPING UP APPEARANCES
Ryan Giggs, United's Duracell Bunny

In the modern era, it is rare indeed to find a player who commits their entire career to one club. Sir Alex Ferguson was fortunate to have had three youngsters who turned out to be both loyal servants and major talents who gave their all in the United cause – Gary Neville, Paul Scholes and Ryan Giggs. Maybe in time Marcus Rashford and others will add their names to that list, but they have a way to go; between them, the three Class of '92 veterans amassed 2,283 appearances in competitive matches.

Of the trio of legends, one stands as the *primus inter pares*, the one voted by United fans in 2011 as the club's greatest ever player: Ryan Giggs. As much as they liked him, he is not unlike Shakespeare's player in *As You Like It*: 'All the world's a stage, and all the men and women merely players; they have their exits and their entrances; and one man in his time plays many parts, his acts being seven ages.' Giggs' stage was the Theatre of Dreams and he played his part in many a drama – usually in the role of hero.

From his father – Danny Wilson, a Welsh rugby league international – he inherited some of his African heritage and athleticism; from his mother, her love and family name. As a schoolboy, racist bullies made his life a misery, but Ryan Wilson found release through sport where his boots could do the talking. After the family moved to England, Ryan became a member of Manchester City's School of Excellence and was capped for England Schoolboys. But that was all about to change.

Alex Ferguson, newly appointed to the managerial post at United, first witnessed the 13-year-old Wilson score a hat-trick playing for Salford Boys as he terrorised United's Under-15 side at the Cliff. Ferguson, keen to add fresh talent to United's youth set-up, wasted no time, offering him a traineeship on his 14th birthday. In a few short years, as Ryan Giggs, he made his debut against Everton aged 17, and the following season he became a regular in the first team, while still captaining the side that would win the Youth Cup and later become known as the Class of '92.

His older teammates were excited by the teenager. Steve Bruce said, 'When Ryan ran, he ran like the wind. You couldn't hear him he was that light on his feet.' His ability to run at lightning speed with the ball under control was exceptional; beautifully balanced, he could dribble, feint and dummy to the torment of right-backs throughout the land.

He wasn't the automatic pick for United's left-wing berth straightaway. He and Lee Sharpe vied for the position; Sharpe was the PFA's Young Player of the Year in 1991 and Giggs took the prize the following season.

Giggs' career achieved lift-off with the start of the Premier League. He was now adding goals to his game, scoring 11 in 1992/93 and 17 the following season as United won back-to-back league titles. His absence through injury towards the end of the 1994/95 season, combined with Cantona's lengthy suspension, dented United hopes of seeing off Blackburn's title challenge.

Giggs was at his quicksilver best in the 1990s, as United dominated the English scene and gradually found their feet on the European stage. Juventus legend Alessandro Del Piero, who witnessed Giggs race through and smash in a goal against his team, was a fan: 'I cried twice in my life watching a football player; the first one was Roberto Baggio, the second was Ryan Giggs.' In 1999, he scored the greatest goal in FA Cup history in the semi-final win over Arsenal (see page 206) en route to claiming the treble. And, of course, in the 1999 Champions League final he could claim an assist for Sheringham's late equaliser. Assists were a speciality. In the history of the Premier League no one comes close to Giggs as a provider of goals. He has been credited with 162 assists, over 50 more than second-placed Cesc Fàbregas.

As the years passed, Giggs' fortunes fluctuated as he suffered injuries and occasional lapses in form. There was talk in 2003 of the winger, now approaching 30, being 'moved on'. But Ferguson and, to his credit, Giggs were having none of it. The Scot, who had been so protective of Giggs as a young man, knew that he couldn't afford to lose such an important player. His assistant, Carlos Queiroz, was of like mind, marvelling at his skilfulness: '[Giggs] could play football in a phone box and would always find the door, no matter how many players you put in there with him.'

That skill and his footballing intelligence allowed him to adapt his game as advancing age blunted his speed. He moved into a midfield role where his precision passing created chance upon chance. Later, fed up with injuries, he turned to yoga and a better diet, and then retired from international football, thereby extending his playing career into his 40s. And whereas his contemporary, David Beckham, embraced showbiz and celebrity, Giggs guarded his privacy; instead, he focused his energies on his playing for United. In all, he played a record 962 times for the Reds, scoring 168 goals, which places him eighth in the list of the club's top scorers.

He signed for United nearly a year after Sir Alex arrived at Old Trafford and retired from playing a year after the Scot relinquished his managerial post; he played his last game aged nearly 40½, over 23 years since making his debut. He even enjoyed four games in Fergie's old seat once David Moyes was dismissed. Arguably the greatest manager and, arguably, the greatest player's exits and entrances coincided and, for what seemed like an age, United were the kings of English football. For the United fan, it was just as they liked it.

DREAM VOLLEY: ROBIN VAN PERSIE'S GOAL OF THE SEASON
Manchester United v. Aston Villa
22 APRIL 2013

Something had to be done. At the end of the 2011/12 season, Sir Alex Ferguson and his team had suffered the agony of seeing their title taken by their noisy neighbours in added time on the final day to a goal by 'Aguer-r-r-o-o-o-h'.

Entering his twenty-sixth season in charge, Ferguson wanted to reassert the natural order and win the league which he regarded as rightful United property. He was happy enough with his squad but wanted to add an X factor, another 'Cantona', to give the team a cutting edge. In the summer transfer window, he tried to sign Robert Lewandowski from Borussia Dortmund, but the Germans wouldn't part with the Pole. Ferguson had other options; he had been aware for some time that Robin van Persie, whose contract with Arsenal was nearing its end, might become available.

Van Persie was pure pedigree and at the peak of his considerable powers. He had been a star in the Arsenal side, scoring 30 league goals in the 2011/12 season and winning the Premier League's golden boot. He had been at Arsenal for eight years and was looking for another challenge – a shot at winning a league title. He would have been well remunerated in Italy, and his manager would have preferred him not to play for an English rival, but, in the end, he got in touch with his inner child. 'I always listen to the little boy inside of me in these situations – when you have to make the harder decisions in life. What does he want? That boy was screaming for Man United.' He joined for a fee of £22.5 million, with an additional bonus if United won the title or the Champions League.

To begin with United players weren't quite on his radar. They didn't fully appreciate his clever movement or the timing of his runs; as Wenger had predicted, 'You don't realise what a good player you're getting.' But it didn't take long for things to click: he scored against his old club in a 2–1 victory and hit the winner in a close Manchester derby, ending City's long unbeaten run.

The season was unfolding beautifully, and as United lined up against Aston Villa at Old Trafford on 22 April 2013, there was a sense of occasion amongst the crowd who were all too aware that victory would secure the twentieth title. The manager had already decided it was his last season and he had wanted to go out on a high. Van Persie stepped up to deliver the crowning glory, the *coup de grace* and, jeez, was it graceful.

The Dutchman eased any nerves by scoring the opener in the second minute. His second was a thing of beauty: running onto a long through ball from Rooney, van Persie peeled off his marker, watched the ball drop over his shoulder, and volleyed a rocket first-time from 20 yards past Guzan. The athleticism, the concentration, the technique – his head still over the dropping ball – was sensational. Not surprisingly it was *Match of the Day's* goal of the season. Van Persie completed a first-half hat-trick and finished the season with a total of 30 goals in all competitions.

Van Persie had achieved what he had come to do, and Ferguson ended his reign by wresting the Premiership back from City and clinching his thirteenth Premier League title. For both the inner child of van Persie and the veteran warrior, their dreams really had come true.

SIR ALEX FERGUSON
Quote Unquote

There's no apology for this being a long entry. Sir Alex was never shy about offering an opinion, and they were always good value and worth repeating.

Management and leadership

'You start with what you believe in. I believe in building a football club rather than building a football team.'

'You can have the best collection of footballers ever, but if there is no one driving the bus, you'll not get there.'

'I always said to the directors the minute a player becomes more powerful than the manager of Manchester United you have lost control of the whole club. So, I always made sure I was in control. They always knew who the manager was.'

'Distinguish between power and control. Delegate. Be decisive – and remember people's first names.'

'Don't ever think you're above a challenge. It's not right. Arrogance is

not a quality, it's a hindrance to success.'

'Attack wins you games, defence wins you titles.'

Sir Matt Busby

'There have been some outstanding managers in this country, but, without doubt, he is the greatest there has ever been.'

The players

Eric Cantona
'If ever there was one player, anywhere in the world, that was made for Manchester United, it was Cantona. He swaggered in, stuck his chest out, raised his head and surveyed everything as though he were asking: "I'm Cantona. How big are you? Are you big enough for me?"'

'Of all the many qualities a good team must possess, the supreme essential for me is penetration. And Eric brought the can-opener.'

Ryan Giggs
'I remember the first time I saw him. He was 13 and just floated over the ground like a cocker spaniel chasing a piece of silver paper in the wind.'

Cristiano Ronaldo
'Courage in football, as in life, comes in many forms. The courage to continue, no matter how many times he is going to be kicked, identifies Ronaldo.'

'Ronaldo could play for Millwall, QPR or Doncaster Rovers and still score a hat-trick. I'm not sure Messi could do it.'

David Beckham
'The finest striker of a football, not because of a God-given talent but he practises with a relentless application that the vast majority of less gifted players would never contemplate.'

Gary Neville
'If he was an inch taller, he'd be the best centre-half in Britain. His father is 6ft 2in – I'd check the milkman.'

Roy Keane
'It was the most emphatic display of selflessness I have seen on a football field. Pounding over every blade of grass, competing as if he would rather die of exhaustion than lose, he inspired all around him. I felt such an honour to be associated with such a player.'

(On Roy Keane's performance in the semi-final of the UEFA Champions League against Juventus in 1999.)

Paul Scholes
'I think Paul Scholes is the best player in England. He has the best skills, the best brain. No one can match him. There isn't a player of his mould anywhere in the world.'

Wayne Rooney
'Wayne is truly blessed. He doesn't just have ability, he has a fire inside him.'

The dressing room

'I've got a temper if I need it. Nothing wrong with losing your temper if it's for the right reasons.'

'Myths grow all the time. If I was to listen to the number of times I've thrown teacups then we've gone through some crockery in this place. It's completely exaggerated, but I don't like people arguing back at me.'

'I came in, there was the big urn and I went to smash it – and I'm not kidding you, I nearly broke my arm. I kicked the tray so hard the cups went up over the wall. Archie Knox, my assistant, was sitting there with tea running down the back of his tracksuit.'

'It was a freakish incident. If I tried it a hundred or a million times, it couldn't happen again. If I could, I would have carried on playing!'
(After the boot kicked in anger connected with David Beckham's head in 2003.)

The boot could sometimes be on the other foot. Fergie recalled a disagreement with Peter Schmeichel: 'He was towering over me and the other players were almost covering their eyes. I'm looking up and thinking if he does hit me, I'm dead.'

As to the famous hairdryer incident, it's not possible to produce a transcript of one of his tirades, but, with the help of this account by Rio Ferdinand, one can imagine being on the end of one: 'We played Benfica away and I think we got beat. We didn't play well and he was shouting at me and I thought I was one of the best players on the day. So I was going back at him. And the problem is, which I failed to learn quickly, is that the more you shout at him, the louder he gets, and the more aggressive he gets, and the closer he gets to you.'

The rivals

Liverpool
'My greatest challenge is not what's happening at the moment, my greatest challenge was knocking Liverpool right off their f**king perch. And you can print that.'
(After winning the 2002/03 title.)

Manchester City
'It's City, isn't it? They are a small club, with a small mentality. All they can talk about is Manchester United, that's all they've done and they can't get away from it.'
(Commenting on the infamous 'Welcome to Manchester' poster following Carlos Tévez's transfer.)

'Sometimes you have a noisy neighbour. You cannot do anything about that. They will always be noisy. You just have to get on with your life, put your television on and turn it up a bit louder.'

Arsène Wenger
'He has no experience of English football. He's come from Japan and now he's into English football and he is now telling everybody in England how to organise their football. I think he should keep his mouth shut. Firmly shut.'
(A warm welcome from Fergie to Arsenal's newly appointed manager.)

Real Madrid

'Do you think I would enter into a contract with that mob? Absolutely no chance. I would not sell them a virus. That is a "No" by the way. There is no agreement whatsoever between the clubs.'

(Fergie dismisses speculation in 2008 that Ronaldo is heading to the Bernabéu.)

The press

'On you go. I'm no f**king talking to you. He's a f**king great player. Yous are f**king idiots.'

(On media criticism of Juan Sebastián Verón.)

'You've no right to ask me that question, John. You're out of order . . . you know full well my ruling on that. Right, that's the interview finished . . . I'm going to cancel that interview, the whole f**king lot of it. Cancel it, right? F**king make sure that does not go out, John.'

(The BBC's John Motson gets short shrift in 1995.)

Football as a rollercoaster ride

'It's getting tickly now – squeaky-bum time, I call it.'
(As the 2003 title race built to a climax.)

'I can't believe it. I can't believe it. Football. Bloody hell.'
(His immediate reaction to 1999 Champions League triumph.)

The will to win

'I've never played for a draw in my life.'

'For me, drive means a combination of a willingness to work hard, emotional fortitude, enormous powers of concentration and a refusal to admit defeat.'

'The way to win battles, wars and games is by attacking and overrunning the opposing side.'

'Very often our victories were squeaked out in the last few minutes after we had drained the life from our opponents. Games – like life – are all about waiting for chances and then pouncing on them.'

'This isn't just a job to me, it's a mission. I am deadly serious about it. Some people reckon too serious. We will get there, believe me. And when it happens, life will change for Liverpool and everyone else, dramatically.'

(Prophetic words spoken in 1988.)

BUSBY V. FERGUSON
Who Is United's Greatest Manager?

Who is the greatest? You can make a case for Mangnall as the manager who put United on the footballing map but he didn't stay long enough to make a lasting imprint; worse than that, he quit to join local rivals, Manchester City. In reality, there are only two serious contenders. Picking between the two long-serving Scottish knights, Sir Matt and Sir Alex, requires the wisdom of Solomon or perhaps the judgement of boxing impresario, Jack Solomons. Let's go 12 rounds with Sir Matt and Sir Alex.

Round 1: Vision

For such a young man, Matt Busby was incredibly bold. He was clear when he took the job that he wanted complete control over team affairs and transfers, needed five years to achieve success and wanted to promote young players into the first team. Having such a free rein was a radical new approach to management. In Ferguson's case, he placed a similar trust in youth but most of all, he wanted to win trophies and knock Liverpool off their perch.

Scorecard: even

Round 2: Coaching and tactics

Busby was an innovator as football's first tracksuit manager in contrast to the suit-and-trilby brigade that were typical of the day. He wasn't overly fussed with tactics; he preferred to pick players with 'skill, flair and character', and simply asked them to 'just go out and play'. He was fortunate that he could call on the coaching genius of his assistant, Jimmy Murphy, whom Busby had hand-picked from his army days.

Fergie may have been more tactically minded but, like Busby, he delegated the finer details to his assistants. By the turn of the century, Sir Alex enjoyed the benefits of a bigger coaching set-up compared to the skeleton staff afforded to Sir Matt.

Sir Alex built his success from back to front. As quoted earlier, he said, 'Attack wins you games, defence wins you titles.' Sir Matt just wanted his boys to outscore the opposition.

Scorecard: Ferguson win

Round 3: Making an impact

It is hard to overstate the impact Matt Busby made on United's fortunes. The legacy of the pre-war side was of serial underperformance in front of sparse crowds. The stadium was a bomb-damaged ruin, with no running water and nowhere to train. Well within the five years he had allowed himself, he won the FA Cup in 1948 and his first league title in 1951/52 after four runners-up placings. The crowds came back too: 81,962 turned up to see United play Arsenal in January 1948.

It took Fergie longer to get motoring. He cleared out the Augean stables (no, not a pub in Royston Vasey), revamped the youth system and eventually stamped his authority on the squad. While he enjoyed some early cup success, it would take him six and a half years before his stated ambition of winning the title was realised.

Scorecard: narrow win for Busby

Round 4: Football philosophy

Matt Busby believed it was his players' duty to entertain. He would say, 'Give that man [the shopfloor worker] something he can't do himself, something exciting. That's why Manchester United always play attacking football.' Born in a North Lanarkshire mining village, the Scot felt a deep solidarity with United's blue-collar support. It was for these men (mostly) that he set his teams to play the 'United Way'.

Ferguson shared similar values, but he felt the best way to win supporters' hearts was to win, whatever it took. His philosophy was to attack the opposing side and never, *ever* give in. So many games were won in the last quarter or in 'Fergie time' because his teams would lay siege to their opponents and grind them into submission by sheer force of their manager's personality.

Scorecard: Busby win

Round 5: Youth development

Both managers have an impressive history of bringing young talent into the side. The term 'Busby Babes' still has significance seven decades after it was coined.

Even after the trauma of Munich destroyed the flowering young side, Busby could still introduce starlets of the calibre of

Johnny Giles, George Best, John Aston Jr and Brian Kidd into the first team.

Sir Alex made youth development a priority and, particularly in his early years at the club, looked to young players to add energy to his squad. While Fergie's Fledglings may not have lived up to expectations, the Class of '92 surpassed them; the classmates formed the core of the first team for the next decade and more. But although he continued to look to the academy for new talent, either the quality was lacking or the better youngsters – Pogba and Piqué – left to join clubs that offered more first-team opportunities.

Scorecard: narrow win for Busby

Round 6: Pastoral care

Again, it's hard to put a cigarette paper between them. Busby was a paternal figure who looked after his players and their families. But Busby didn't much care for those who didn't toe the line or anyone who asked for a pay rise; Charlie Mitten, Giles and Viollet all left the club when they had much more to offer. However, Sir Matt struggled to deal with the impact of popular culture and the waywardness of George Best in particular; at times the kindness he felt for Bestie tipped over into unhelpful indulgence.

Sir Alex had the benefit of Busby's experience in dealing with young players who had suddenly become the focus of media attention. He put a protective arm around Ryan Giggs and other young players; he even prowled Manchester's bars and nightclubs to round up any stray sheep.

Fergie's strict regime did incur casualties, notably David Beckham, and his intolerance of criticism accounted for Stam and

Keane. But for the manager, be it Sir Alex or Sir Matt, no one, but no one, was ever bigger than the club. Ever.

Scorecard: even

Round 7: Transfer market

Both managers were canny in the transfer market; they liked value for money but would spend big when they had to. Busby bought Delaney and Taylor in his early years and later Herd, Law (for a record fee) and Crerand as part of his third great team. Ferguson can count Cantona, Keane and Schmeichel as fantastic additions but others – Milne, Wallace and Kléberson – fell short of expectations.

Busby could go for years without bringing anyone to Old Trafford whereas Ferguson liked to freshen up his squad with two or three signings every summer. When Harry Gregg joined in December 1957 he considered it a huge honour saying that 'of the 40 players who had played for Busby since the war only four had been brought in'.

Although Ferguson had more money at his disposal than Busby could ever dream of, particularly in his later years, he could still boast that his net spending in the market had averaged £5 million a year during his time in charge.

Scorecard: even

Round 8: Team building

What's remarkable about the two managers is the way they created multiple title-winning sides. Busby blended experience with youth to win in 1952, who then made way for the Busby

Babes and finally the 1960s side and its United Trinity. Fergie also gave youth its head after winning his first title before he bought in a steely defence and lethal strike force to continue success well into the new century.

Scorecard: even

Round 9: Results

On paper this has to be a walkover for Sir Alex. However, it has to be remembered that Busby suffered the catastrophic loss of most of his best team, and the opportunities in Europe – United were only eligible in seven seasons – and in the League Cup were fewer than those enjoyed by Ferguson. That said, it's impossible to argue against Fergie's incredible record.

Scorecard: Ferguson win

Round 10: Europe

A huge admirer of the trail-blazing Hungarian national side, Busby was keen to learn from European football and to pit his young side against the best the continent could offer. In the teeth of fierce opposition and obstruction from the Football League, United became England's pioneers in the European Cup in 1956/57 when they reached the semi-finals. Tragedy killed the hopes of the Busby Babes, but the conquest of Europe was the spur that drove Busby in the aftermath of the disaster to finally take United's place among Europe's elite.

Ferguson also saw Europe as the pinnacle of club football competition, and after a few missteps, he got the hang of it. Four finals and two victories in the Champions League were maybe less than his sides deserved but still rank as colossal achievements.

Scorecard: even

Round 11: Leadership

Busby had an aura, a gravitas, that had his players in awe – no one dared to question his authority, but after Munich he was a more remote figure. Sir Alex was more proactive: the inspirational team talks, the mind games, the animated touchline body language, the contrived 'them against us' battle cries, even the hairdryer – every trick in the book was employed in pursuit of success. And where Busby was perhaps overly loyal to some of his older players, Ferguson could be ruthless in benching underperforming stars, be it Jim Leighton or even Wayne Rooney.

Scorecard: Ferguson win

Final Round: Legacy

Both men cast lengthy shadows over their successors, who shrank by comparison. Busby's long service on the United board after retirement added moral authority to the club but also complicated the management of team affairs. Ferguson got a say in the choice of his successor, and while keeping his distance – and his own personal parking space at Old Trafford – he has remained an influential figure behind the scenes.

Neither man left their playing squads in the best shape, and the managers who followed ended up having to panic-buy in heavily inflated transfer markets.

Busby invented the United brand of entertaining, attacking football based on young talent and playing 'the right way'. But Ferguson picked up Busby's torch and added a steely winning mentality. Busby had to face heart-breaking adversity after the Munich disaster robbed United of a great crop of young stars; Ferguson had the Liverpool Goliath to fell, and oil barons and oligarchs to slay.

Scorecard: even

It will come as no surprise that this judge has scored the contest a draw. Evenly matched, both men were up for the challenges they faced and the ones they set themselves; they were equally magnificent.

SONGS OF PRAISE

British football is known for its fans and for their exuberance. This devotion can, sadly, find expression in drink-fuelled verbal and physical aggression at times, but it more frequently finds its voice in celebratory songs and chants.

The Red Devils are the most serenaded team in the world. According to the Fan Chants website, Manchester United lead the way with, at the time of writing, 551 songs and chants. They can also boast the only club songs to have made it to the top of the UK Chart with Status Quo's 'Come On You Reds' reaching number 1 by the weekend of the 1994 FA Cup final – it also reached number 1 in Peter Schmeichel's homeland and number 2 in Roy Keane's.

The Quo classic does exactly what you'd expect and gets the crowd rocking at Old Trafford to this day. It was one of a number of records released by the club to celebrate United making it to the FA Cup final. In the days before the Premier League became the main domestic football prize, the FA Cup final was the showpiece occasion – *the* biggest day in the football calendar – and clubs would cash in on their cup runs by selling souvenir T-shirts, memorabilia and releasing a cup song – often sung by the players themselves.

Most of these songs are instantly forgettable, but one or two have become classics. 'Glory, Glory, Man United' (sung to the tune of the 'Battle Hymn of the Republic') was released for the 1983 final and later recorded by the World Red Army. The song title is also commemorated in the abbreviated signature adopted by fans everywhere: GGMU. The B-side of the 1976 single, 'Manchester United' is an oddity: 'Old Trafford Blues' maybe tapped into the 1970s vibe and, sung by the team captain Martin Buchan, its lyric takes aim at his teammates, goalkeeper Alex Stepney having played since 1917 and full-back Alex Forsyth being 'the ball boy's friend, his crosses landing in the Stretford End'.

The original and best is, of course, 'The Manchester United Calypso', released after a 16-year-old sent it into a newspaper song competition and Caribbean singer Edric Connor recorded it in 1957. It is the perfect ode to the Busby Babes, Connor summing up the free-flowing and attacking football United played with his swagger and the endearing lyrics: 'Now, football is a pleasant game, Played in the sun, played in the rain, And the team that gets me excited, Is Manchester United.'

*

Football sides are famous for their entrance songs: Everton have the *Z Cars* theme, West Ham, 'Forever Blowing Bubbles' and Liverpool, 'You'll Never Walk Alone'. At the beginning of the 21st century United's players entered the arena to Ewan MacColl's 'Dirty Old Town'. Written in 1949, the song is a ballad that speaks of Salford's industrial past and has been covered many times by the likes of Rod Stewart, Simple Minds and, of course, The Pogues.

The new millennium called for a new tune. At Gary Neville's prompting, one of his favourite songs, 'This Is the One' by the Stone Roses, was adopted as United's entrance song. Much to the delight of Ian Brown, the band's front man, who is a lifelong Red.

There's another song that is sung by United fans that is altogether more solemn. 'The Flowers of Manchester', a lament written a month after the Munich disaster, was first heard in the Princess Louise pub in Holborn. It tells the story of the crash and its victims, and it is the centrepiece of the two memorials that take place in February every year below the memorial plaque at Old Trafford.

*

The chants and corrupted pop songs that have echoed round Old Trafford are a festival of wit and ingenuity. Many of them are insulting and just plain rude, with Liverpool and Manchester City fans bearing the brunt of the abuse; one or two of these will make my list, but only because it would be bizarre not to make any mention of them at all.

United fans draw their inspiration from songs the world over. 'We Are the Pride of All Europe' sung to the tune of 'One of Those Songs You Hear Now and Then' by Jimmy Durante is a firm favourite, as is 'Take Me Home, Country Road', the John Denver classic. 'We'll Never Die', to the tune of 'The Red Flag', remembers Munich; 'Banks of the Irwell to Sicily' to the tune of the US Marine Corps anthem: 'The Halls of Montezuma', and 'Stretford End Arising' to the tune of the Creedence Clearwater Revival hit are some of the other classics supporters love to sing.

But the wittiest ones are sung in tribute to individual players with the occasional dig at rivals.

Eric Cantona could have an entire album of chants if he wanted – the pick of the bunch being 'Ooh ah Cantona', which can be sung to the tune of '*La Marseillaise*' or to the groovier 'Oops Up Side Your Head' by The Gap Band. And then there's 'We'll drink a drink, a drink, a drink to Eric the king, the king, the king – he's the leader of our football team' to the tune of The Scaffold's 'Lily The Pink'. 'Twelve Cantonas' echoes 'The Twelve Days of Christmas', the gift on each day an ever-diminishing number of the French legend, pausing deliciously on the five *Cantonaaaaas*.

Ryan Giggs has two hits sung in his name: 'Ryan Giggs, Ryan Giggs, Running Down the Wing' to the tune of the 1950s Robin Hood TV theme and 'Giggs Will Tear You Apart Again' courtesy of Joy Division.

Ole Gunnar Solskjær's tributes span his time as a player and as a manager: 'You are my Solskjær, my Ole Solskjær' includes a nice reference to his arrival at Old Trafford shortly after the failure to sign Alan Shearer from Blackburn: 'You are my Solskjær, my Ole Solskjær, You make me happy when skies are grey, Oh, Alan Shearer was f**king dearer, So please don't take my Solskjær away.'

'Ole's at the Wheel' neatly adapts The Stone Roses' 'Waterfall' to his time driving the United team in the managerial seat. 'Ole's at the wheel, Tell me how does it feel, We've got Sancho, Paul Pogba and Fred, Marcus Rashford a Manc born and bred, Du du, du, du, du . . .'

The late, great George Best is fondly remembered in a version of Norman Greenbaum's 1969 hit 'Spirit in the Sky':

'Going on up to the spirit in the sky, It's where I'm gonna go when I die, When I die and they lay me to rest, I'm gonna go on the p*** with Georgie Best.'

George's fellow scorer in the 1968 European Cup final win over Benfica will have enjoyed this clever chant – 'Eu-se-bi-o, and I say Kidd-o' – to the tune of The Beatles' 'Hello, Goodbye'.

'Tom Hark' was originally an instrumental by a South African kwela band before becoming a big hit for The Piranhas in the 1980s. It has spawned any number of fans' versions since. The United fans like the 'White Pelé' tribute: 'I saw my mate the other day, He said to me he saw the white Pelé, So I asked, who is he? He goes by the name of Wayne Rooney, Wayne Rooney, Wayne Rooney, He goes by the name of Wayne Rooney . . .' And so it goes on.

A more macho version has United fans expressing a clear preference when it comes to warring with opposing fans: 'We fought in France, we fought in Spain, We fought in the sun and we fought in the rain, We took the Kop and Chelsea too, But what we like most is kicking a blue, Kicking a blue, kicking a blue, But what we like most is kicking a blue, kicking a blue . . .' That's the City fans name-checked.

Here are some other gems.

The 1958 Italian Eurovision song contest entry, 'Nel blu, dipinto di blu', popularly known as 'Volare', is a go-to tune for supporters. Not least to salute Diego Forlán, whose double in a 2–0 victory at Anfield is immortalised by 'Diego, who-oh, Diegwhowoh-oh-oh-oh . . . He came from Uruguay, he made the Scousers cry.' Liverpool, tick.

It took an African-American spiritual, 'Kum Ba Yah', to pay homage to the great Paul Scholes: 'He scores goals galore, He scores goals, He scores goals galore, He scores goals, He scores goals galore, He scores goals, Paul Scholes, He scores goals.' Get the picture?

And Scholes receives an indirect compliment in this chant about Michael Carrick (sung to 'It's Magic' by Pilot): 'It's CARRICK you know, It's hard to believe it's not Scholes, It's CARRICK you know, It's hard to believe it's not Scholes.' And repeat . . .

Nemanja Vidić: 'Nemanja wo-oh, Nemanja wo-oh-oh-oh, He comes from Serbia, He'll f**king murder ya.' (You guessed it: 'Volare' again.)

The Brazilian midfielder Anderson made a great start to his United career and his chant also touches on his disappointing compatriot. Sung to the tune of 'Agadoo', it goes: 'Anderson-son-son, he's much better than Kléberson, Anderson-son-son, he's our midfield magician.'

Fan-favourite Ander Herrera's heritage earned this amusing and factually accurate tribute, sung to the tune of 'Bad Moon Rising': 'Ole, ole, Ander Herrera, Ole, ole, ole, ola, Drinks Estrella by the cask, He's not Spanish, he is Basque, Ole, ole, ole, ola.'

And I have to include this one honouring my namesake. While no longer current, it is fun to recall, and the last line is inspired. Sung to the tune of Bowie's 'Rebel, Rebel': 'Neville, Neville, your future's immense, Neville, Neville, you play in defence, Neville, Neville, like Jacko you're bad, Neville, Neville, is the name of your dad.'

Bruno Fernandes is serenaded to the tune of Scott Joplin's

'Ragtime' in: 'Bruno, Bruno, Bruno, he's our Portuguese Magnifico.'

Last but not least, is another magnifico who delighted fans on his 2021 return to Old Trafford and was treated to a noisy rendition of 'Viva Ronaldo' on his first day back. 'Viva Ronaldo, viva Ronaldoooo, Running down the wing, Hear United sing, Viva Ronaldoooo.'

THE CRUELLEST MONTH
David Moyes' Dismissal, April 2014

At the end of the 2012/13 season, Sir Alex Ferguson, having reclaimed the Premier League title from the noisy neighbours by a whopping 11 points, decided the time was right to step down from the managerial hot seat. In his 26½ years at Old Trafford, his achievements had made him the most successful manager in English football history – indeed British history if his time at Aberdeen is counted – and he could leave on a high.

He was the hardest of acts to follow. The squad was a mixture of emerging talent (the likes of Smalling, Welbeck, Januzaj and Cleverley) and ageing veterans (Ferdinand, Vidić, Carrick and Evra), and then there was Wayne Rooney, once again agitating for a move away. It was a team in transition that needed careful management and investment in the transfer market.

Making life harder yet for Ferguson's successor was the decision, that same year, of David Gill to relinquish his role as the club's chief executive. In post for the previous ten years, he had proved to be an extremely capable executive who had overseen the growth of the club as a business, forged good working relationships with both the new owners and Sir Alex, and was a shrewd operator in the transfer market.

Unusually in club football, the outgoing manager was allowed to nominate his successor. In recommending fellow Glaswegian

David Moyes, Ferguson showed admiration for Moyes' record of 11 years of over-achievement at Everton, his appetite for hard work and his integrity. But would Moyes' character of the scrapping underdog who had never won any silverware in his managerial career fit in to the culture of swagger and entitlement that had developed at Old Trafford over the previous two decades? Would this deeply committed Christian command the respect of the Rooneys, the van Persies and Vidić? How would David cope with this Goliath of a club?

Moyes was out shopping with his wife when he received the call from Sir Alex asking him to come to a meeting at Ferguson's home. Perhaps betraying a deference to the top dog, Moyes went home to change out of his jeans into a suit before going to the audience. He left duly anointed.

The start didn't do him any favours. First, the transfer business over the summer was one cock-up after another. He passed on the chance to buy Thiago Alcântara, a move Ferguson had lined up earlier that year; the pursuit of Ander Herrera of Athletic Bilbao ended in farce with United accusing three lawyers of hijacking the deal on deadline day; worst of all was the long-running transfer saga involving Marouane Fellaini, which ended with United paying £5 million more than his buy-out clause.

Not confidence-inspiring. And his decision to dispense with Ferguson's backroom staff, René Meulensteen and Mike Phelan in favour of his Everton coaching team was understandable but not a move that would sit easily with the players. However, Moyes did take care of the Rooney issue: old hatchets were buried, talk of an exit to Chelsea laid to rest, and United's talisman was put on a fitness programme to shed the pounds and restore his sharpness.

If Moyes had any nerves as the opening of the new season approached, they would not have been soothed by the sight of the fixture list. In the first five games United would face Mourinho's Chelsea, Liverpool away and Manchester City away. The fans offered their support; up on the Stretford End a banner appeared with the words 'The Chosen One' alongside a giant picture of the new man. It was an image that would later come to haunt Moyes.

The season started badly – a crushing 4–1 loss to Manchester City stung – and results were inconsistent throughout the season; a streak of three wins in succession would be followed by a poor run of form. The new signing Fellaini – probably trying too hard to impress – looked out of sorts, out of place and couldn't buy a goal. It didn't help that United flopped against their adversaries: both City and Liverpool did the double over United that season while Moyes' old employers also inflicted defeats.

More damaging still was the fearfulness now infecting the team. Opponents who might have been beaten before setting foot on the pitch against a Ferguson team now came to Old Trafford with fresh confidence; the fear factor had gone. Lowly West Bromwich, a team that had never beaten United in the Premier League, recorded their first victory at Old Trafford in September. Moyes horrified United fans when he declared Liverpool favourites in advance of a home game against their old rivals. The 3–0 defeat left United trailing leaders Chelsea by 18 points and 12 points short of fourth spot, effectively putting qualification for the Champions League out of reach. A 3–0 home defeat to City shortly after prompted one disgruntled fan to stage a protest during the next home game by flying a banner over Old Trafford emblazoned with the blunt verdict: 'WRONG ONE – MOYES OUT.' Ouch!

The Champions League had offered some crumbs of comfort to the embattled Moyes. They topped their group in style, thumping Bayer 04 Leverkusen 9–2 over two legs, and advanced to the quarter-finals to meet Bayern Munich. Freed from the anxieties of the Premier League grind, United saved some of their best performances for the European stage. United and Bayern had drawn 1–1 at Old Trafford, and in the return leg on 9 April the sides shared a goalless first half. On 57 minutes, a thumping volley from Patrice Evra put United ahead. For a fleeting moment, or 72 seconds to be exact, Moyes could dare to dream of glory: a path to the semi-finals, the final and the trophy itself. But hope very quickly turned to despair as an average Bayern side equalised and then proceeded to dispatch the Reds 3–1. United were out of Europe for the first time in a generation.

The fatal blow to Moyes' short tenure was dealt 13 days later, in a brutal irony, at Goodison Park. Mocked and jeered by the home support and by many of the travelling United fans, Moyes watched his old team record a 2–0 victory and a rare double over the reigning league champions. It was a cruel blow, a twist of the knife.

From Ferguson's promised land he had taken the club to a wasteland, one from which they have not yet emerged. The United board came to the conclusion that he was indeed the wrong man and, on 22 April, he was out. That may have been an unfair judgement; Sir Alex was an impossible act to follow. Moyes has since restored his managerial reputation by making West Ham a top-six side, but at United – who had never finished lower than third in the previous two decades before Moyes' appointment – fans demanded and expected much, much more.

SLIDING DOORS MOMENT NUMBER 2
Leicester City 5 Manchester United 3
21 SEPTEMBER 2014

The experiment with David Moyes, the 'Chosen One', had not lasted long, and United looked to the Dutch master, Louis van Gaal, to restore their fortunes. The new campaign had yet to click into gear, but United hoped to kick-start their season with a trip away to newly promoted Leicester City.

All was going well as United took a 3–1 lead in the 57th minute when Ander Herrera deflected a Di María shot past Kasper Schmeichel. The Argentine winger, a record signing in the summer, had produced an exquisite chip in the first half to score his second Premier League goal, and it looked like normal service had been resumed for the Red Devils.

But fortune was fickle that day. Leicester's first goal had had an element of luck; the cross for Ulloa's header seemed to have been struck after the ball had crossed the goal line. The second goal, which gave Leicester hope and momentum, came after Rafael fouled Vardy in the penalty box although the Leicester striker's barge on the full-back seconds before seemed a more blatant foul.

United's defence was brittle. That summer three celebrated defenders – Ferdinand, Vidić and Evra – had left the club, and the new back line was still bedding in. To make matter worse on the day, in the 30th minute Jonny Evans was stretchered off.

What should have been a good away win turned into a disaster. With the crafty Cambiasso in their midfield and new boy Jamie Vardy scoring his debut Premier League goal, Leicester showed the first glimpse of the dynamic style that would take them to title-winning glory the following season.

For United and Di María it was a different story. His early good form flattered to deceive, and a combination of culture shock, the arrival in a team stuttering through transition and the trauma of an attempted break-in at his Cheshire home severely dented his confidence. The player whose performance in the 2014 European Champions League final had inspired Real Madrid to victory would depart the following summer for Paris Saint-Germain where his rediscovered form helped PSG to win four Ligue 1 titles.

Van Gaal's two years at Old Trafford were tough on him and tough also for the fans. His management style was highly technical, strict and regimented; he installed overhead cameras at United's training ground to monitor players' movements in minute detail. Although the Dutchman had his admirers – Rooney later claimed that van Gaal was the best coach he ever played under – he wasn't always to the fans' liking; 'Attack, attack, attack' had given way to slow possession football. A final cruel twist came the day after he won his first and only trophy – the FA Cup victory over Crystal Palace in 2016 – when he was sacked.

Jamie Vardy went on to score his 100th Premier League goal against Crystal Palace in June 2020 while Di María managed just one more in top-flight English football. But it might have all been so different had United's luck held that Sunday afternoon.

ROOKIE REWRITES THE RECORD BOOKS
Marcus Rashford's Amazing Debut Season

Say what you like about Louis van Gaal, but he was a manager who was never afraid to bring young blood into his teams. While most of his tyros were pitched in to fill holes in United's creaking defence, it was an attacker plucked from the Under-19s who made the football world sit up and take notice. In the course of three short months in 2016, the 18-year-old Marcus Rashford announced his arrival in spectacular style, ripping up record books and quickening the pulses of United's supporters who had had precious little to cheer since the departure of Sir Alex Ferguson.

The local boy from Wythenshawe made his first-team debut in the Europa League against Midtjylland on 25 February. Chosen to make up the numbers in an injury-depleted squad, Rashford was thrust into first-team action when Anthony Martial pulled out during the pre-match warm-up. In scoring two of United's goals in an emphatic 5–1 win, Rashford became the club's youngest-ever scorer in European competition, beating George Best's record (it has since been broken by Mason Greenwood).

But Marcus was just warming up. Three days later, he made his Premier League debut against Arsenal. Once again, he scored a double and also added an assist in a 3–2 win over the title-chasing Gunners. Three weeks later, it was his first Manchester derby, and he skinned Demichelis before sliding the game's only goal past Joe Hart at the Etihad and becoming the youngest scorer in the fixture in the Premier League era, this time pinching Wayne Rooney's record.

So that was three notches on his belt. Could he make it four? United were drawn against West Ham in the sixth round of the FA Cup. West Ham had celebrated their last league game at their old Boleyn Ground at the end of the previous season with an epic 3–2 win over United and in the process bucketed on United's parade, depriving them of the precious fourth spot in the table and their last hope of qualifying for the Champions League. Time for revenge. Although Rashford failed to score in the match at Old Trafford, he got the opener in the replay, thereby bagging a goal in his debut FA Cup tie.

United were on their way to Wembley.

In total Rashford managed eight goals in 18 appearances in the 2015/16 season, picked up an FA Cup winners' medal and was given the Jimmy Murphy Young Player of the Year Award.

Rashford's bursting onto the scene had caused a sensation, and there was soon a clamour for an England call-up. Just four months after his United debut he was called into the England Euro 2016 squad. And, to the surprise of no one, he scored on debut in a warm-up game against Australia. In so doing he became the youngest player to score on debut since Tommy Lawton and the third youngest in history. In the tournament itself he came on as a 73rd-minute substitute in England's 2–1 win over Wales; his debut came at the age of 18 years and 229 days. Thus he became England's youngest-ever player at a European Championship, breaking Wayne Rooney's Euro 2004 record by four days. And that was only the start . . .

THE SPECIAL ONE
Time for José Mourinho, Manager, 2016–2018

José Mourinho was a great admirer of Sir Alex Ferguson and Manchester United and, according to one Spanish journalist's account, the Portuguese, eager to escape his ordeal at the Bernabéu, was devastated when he wasn't made Sir Alex's successor in 2013.

Mourinho thought he enjoyed a friendship with the Scot and had earned his respect through his achievements (often at United's expense). At Porto he masterminded a Champions League victory over United in 2004, then at Chelsea he challenged United's ascendancy as he led the Blues to successive titles, and, in the Champions League once more, in Ferguson's final season, his tactical alterations changed the game in Real Madrid's favour. But senior figures on the United board questioned Mourinho's suitability; some worried that his abrasive style might damage the club's image.

In his long and illustrious managerial career, the Portuguese was never far from controversy and often in dispute with his clubs' owners. Never one to suffer fools, he resigned from Benfica just weeks after his appointment following a bust-up with the club. He left Chelsea after just three years, and lasted two at Inter Milan and three at Madrid. A clear pattern was emerging. If he left under a cloud, he also left a silver lining: he could point to eight league titles in four countries and two Champions League trophies amongst the 19 major honours won.

Despite earlier reservations, the United board, concerned at the team's continuing underperformance, could no longer afford to ignore such a brilliant track record. Once his second spell at Stamford Bridge imploded on 17 December 2015, Mourinho took a sabbatical from football management while also making himself available should the right opportunity come along. Which it did. Six months later, just days after Louis van Gaal's FA Cup victory, he became United's third manager in the three years since Sir Alex Ferguson's departure.

Failure to qualify for the Champions League and van Gaal's unexciting style of possession football had caused the board to lose patience. The Dutchman's rigid philosophy of the primacy of system and structure had inhibited the team's creativity. Sure, things had improved after the calamity of David Moyes' brief tenure, but restoration of United to the high tables of the Premier League and Europe seemed a remote prospect under van Gaal.

At his official unveiling as manager, Mourinho had a dig at his predecessor, saying, 'I was never very good playing with the words or hiding behind words and hiding behind philosophies . . . I prefer to be more aggressive and say we want to win . . . making your fans proud because you give everything and you win.' If Mourinho had a footballing philosophy, in all likelihood it would be 'The winner takes it all'.

Off the pitch, this handsome, urbane, intelligent family man cut an attractive figure; in 2005, the *New Statesman* chose José as their 'Man of the Year'. But when it came to football, Mourinho increasingly cut a darker, more irritable figure. His spats with opposing managers descended into name-calling – Wenger was an 'expert in failure' – or worse: eye-gouging Tito Vilanova in an unseemly brawl during *El Clasico*. The admonishment of Chelsea's club doctor for disobeying his order to leave an injured player on the pitch was both ugly and disrespectful. The angry three-fingered assertion of his Premier League pedigree to jeering crowds might as well have been two.

At the outset, Mourinho's arrival and the marquee signings of Ibrahimović and Pogba excited United's fans: the club meant business. Winning the League Cup and the Europa League in his first season in charge were major achievements – the first time a United manager had won silverware in his first year. Moreover, as Europa League champions, United were given passage to the holy of holies, the Champions League, despite finishing a lowly sixth in the Premier League.

The summer transfer window capture of Romelu Lukaku added firepower to his forward line. Could United now make a genuine challenge for major honours? Mourinho regarded his second-place finish in the 2017/18 Premier League as one of his greatest achievements. In fact, Mourinho's win percentage of 58 at Old Trafford is second only to Ferguson's. But critics saw the 19-point gap to champions Manchester City as evidence of a huge gulf in class between the red and blues sides of the city.

It was Mourinho's misfortune to manage at a time when United's two biggest rivals were enjoying spectacular success. Liverpool's renaissance was flowering under Jürgen Klopp while City were blossoming under Pep Guardiola. Ironically, these opposing coaches both brought distinctive philosophies to their respective teams: Guardiola had refined the tiki-taka he developed at Barcelona, while Liverpool embraced Klopp's *Gegenpressing*, or counter-pressing, to great effect.

Mourinho, once the bright new kid on the block, now seemed to have been overtaken by new thinking. His detractors said his time had passed, that Klopp and Guardiola were the future. In truth, Mourinho eschewed strategy and philosophy in favour of tactics and pragmatism. His counter to City and Liverpool's adventurism was to retreat into a defensive shell and hope to hit on the break. It had worked at Madrid, and with the right players it could work at Old Trafford. But increasingly United fans despaired of negative, defensive displays; being the toughest defence in the league didn't cut it with supporters brought up on a diet of attacking football. It wasn't the United way.

Mourinho, a shrewd judge of a player, could count himself unlucky in the transfer market. Ibrahimović was injured in his second season; the formidable Lukaku was not yet the finished article; Pogba didn't consistently reproduce his Juventus form; Matić was slow to adapt. More than once he tried to recruit Ivan Perišić, a star of Croatia's 2018 World Cup side, but wasn't backed by the board, who also baulked at Mourinho's defensive target Toby Alderweireld; and a move for Gareth Bale fell through as a consequence of Ronaldo's departure from Madrid to Juventus.

Without reinforcements, it was unwise to pick fights with the squad you already possess. Mourinho's treatment of Luke Shaw was brutal; the benching of his best player Paul Pogba raised eyebrows. The photos of a training-ground bust-up between the manager and Pogba that were splashed over the back pages added to the suspicion that the team was united in name only.

As the difficult third season began, the wheels – as many predicted – started to come off. The clock was ticking. After the 3–0 home defeat to Pochettino's stylish Spurs punctured the early season optimism, the alarm bells were deafening. Perhaps wishing to deflect attention from his players' poor performance, Mourinho went on the attack in the post-match press conference. He demanded respect for his achievements and cited the philosopher Hegel saying, 'The truth is in the whole. It's always in the whole that you find the truth.' Truth is, if you're in a hole, it's always best to stop digging.

On 16 December 2018, the 3–1 loss to Liverpool and the manner of defeat – Liverpool had 36 shots at goal to United's six – was the final humiliation for the United board. Mourinho had to go. His dismissal, three years after his exit from Chelsea, would have been hard to take, but the Herculean challenge of reviving a sleeping giant had proved beyond him. But if the plan is to win at all costs, you have to be prepared to pay the price for anything less.

IDEAL HOMES
Footballers' Mansions

In the old days, in the time of the maximum wage, players and managers rubbed shoulders with the common folk and lived either in digs or in a modest home provided by the club. Players might take the bus to work – Bobby Charlton bussed into Oxford Street on World Cup final day to buy himself a tie for the post-match reception – or cycle – Duncan Edwards was once stopped by the police and fined £3 for riding his at night without a lamp.

Come the age of televised football, its increasing popularity and a growing commercialisation of sport, players became stars, and with that came fame and riches. The first real trendsetter was, of course, George Best. His newfound celebrity required the ultimate bachelor pad at a fashionable address (Bramhall) and, it being George, he really went for it. He commissioned the architect Frazer Crane to design an ultra-modern building that took a year to complete and cost £30,000.

It had all the mod cons: underfloor heating, a TV that disappeared into the chimney, remote-controlled curtains, Sicilian marble, Bastiano leather furniture, a sunken bath, huge tinted windows and an island patio with a moat. But living there wasn't easy. Best was constantly besieged by fans, so a ten-feet-high fence had to be built round the perimeter to keep out prying eyes.

He lasted only three years there before being banished back to his Chorlton-cum-Hardy landlady for breaching club rules. He sold the house for £40,000.

In the Premier League era, young players barely in their 20s had money to burn. Gary Neville took ownership of a 10,000-square-foot property in Bolton complete with gym, infinity pool, tennis court and golf course. There was also room for what was jokingly called the Beckham Suite where Becks spent a year as his Spice Girl wife globetrotted with the band.

Neville had even more ambitious plans for his accommodation. In 2012, he gained planning permission to build his futuristic eco-house. Shaped like a flower with six petals, with its earth-covered roofs and subterranean living spaces, the design was mocked by the tabloids as the Tellytubby House. His plans fell through when locals objected to the huge wind turbine required to make the house carbon-neutral, so Neville shelved the project and turned his attention instead to hotel development in Manchester city centre.

Meanwhile, his erstwhile house guest David Beckham was steadily building a property fortune. He and Posh moved into a converted barn complete with gym and pool in the Golden Triangle hotspot of Alderley Edge. The Beckhams' move to a seven-bedroom mansion sitting in 24 acres of leafy Hertfordshire (inevitably nicknamed 'Beckingham Palace') soon raised questions about David's long-term commitment to Manchester. The portfolio was later supplemented by a townhouse in Holland Park worth in excess of £30 million, a country getaway in the Cotswolds, a six-bedroom house in Beverly Hills and an apartment in Miami.

Not everyone was so extravagant. Eric Cantona, never one to follow the herd, enjoyed living in a rented semi in Roundhay Park, Leeds, in his early days in England, saying, 'The house and the district were definitely not plush or exclusive. I prefer, by far, our little English house with its wild piece of garden to those vast Victorian houses among which I'm sure I would soon get fed up.' To begin with, the family had stayed in Leeds while Eric took a room in a Novotel in Worsley Brow, often going to the nearby Bridgewater pub to play dominoes with the regulars.

Not quite so humble as the Frenchman was the Special One, José Mourinho. He owned a beautiful family home in Belgravia, London, but after taking the position of manager in July 2016 he also decided to stay at a hotel. Not at the functional Novotel, of course, but in one of the Riverside suites of the five-star Lowry.

In all, Mourinho stayed there for 895 nights. The suite cost £600 per night (£22.50 breakfast not included) so he will have racked up a bill in excess of half a million pounds. Any disappointment the Lowry might have felt at his sacking a week before Christmas in 2018 and the departure of their best guest will have been softened by the arrival the following day of Ole Gunnar Solskjær along with a Norwegian TV crew.

In March of the following year, once his managerial position was made permanent, Solskjær announced that he and his family would be moving back into his very own Cheshire eco-house, the one he'd started building in 2007 when he was still on United's books as a player. More Scandi in style than Gary Neville's earth-covered dwelling, at least Solskjær had the pleasure of turfing out his tenant – none other than Virgil van Dijk.

STRIKING SIMILARITIES
Southampton 2 Manchester United 3
29 NOVEMBER 2020

Some said he would be entering the twilight of his career – instead, Edinson Cavani literally headed into the twilight zone. Let's face it, playing at St Mary's on a Sunday in November isn't quite the same as Champions League with PSG or the World Cup with Uruguay.

There are some uncanny parallels between the start of the Uruguayan's United debut season and that of Robin van Persie some ten years before.

Cavani joined United on international transfers deadline day on 5 October 2020. Lacking full fitness, he makes his debut as a substitute 17 days later. He is on the winning side in his first start and he is on the scoresheet.

Robin van Persie signed for United in August 2012 and made his debut from the bench. In his second game, and with his first shot of the game, the number 20 scores and the side are victorious. Van Persie was persuaded by coach René Meulensteen to wear the number 20 as it might be the harbinger of United's twentieth league title.

Cavani chose to wear the number 7 shirt. The iconic shirt number had been something of a bogey for South Americans in recent years: Sanchez and Falcao became shadows of their former selves while Ángel Di María faded after a bright start. Cavani, 'El Matador', on the other hand, demanded the shirt.

And so to their respective second away games. Yes, you guessed it, to St Marys. In 2012 United are 2–1 down with three minutes left on the clock when the Dutchman equalises and, in the second minute of injury time he scores the winner and his 100th Premier League goal. Fast forward to 2020 and deep into the second half United trail by 2–1 when their new striker equalises.

It couldn't happen again, could it? Not the deciding goal in the 92nd minute by the new signing? Well, of course it did. Southampton fans must have been thoroughly sick: they'd barely got over their 2017 League Cup final defeat to er, Manchester United. And the score? It will come as no surprise to learn it was 3–2.

It's just a shame that Cavani hadn't asked for the number 21 on arrival and helped United win the 2020/21 title – then he'd have been worth the other three South American number 7s put together. In less than a year he would be sporting it anyway. But that's another story.

SHAW'S MANC REDEMPTION
The Rehabilitation of Luke Shaw

On the face of it, Luke Shaw doesn't have much in common with Andy Dufresne of *The Shawshank Redemption* other than having to suffer years of abuse, numerous setbacks and crawl through s**t to find redemption.

It all started so well. As a teenager, he oozed promise at Southampton, his performances as an attacking left-back earning him a place in the PFA Team of the Year in 2014 and selection to play for England in the 2014 World Cup. At 18, he was the youngest player to take the field in the tournament.

Later that summer, Shaw and Ander Herrera became Louis van Gaal's first signings since he'd taken over the managerial hot seat. As an England international and a marquee signing at mighty Man United, Shaw must have felt he could walk on water. But he was soon awoken by the cold shower poured on him by van Gaal, who was unimpressed by his conditioning and complained that he was overweight and unfit.

Shaw's debut season was hampered by injury, but by the start of the 2015/16 season he was flying again, his marauding runs offering a potent attacking weapon. Then, in the first European tie of the season, as he threatened the PSV Eindhoven goal he was hacked down by a horrendous sliding tackle by the Mexican centre-back Héctor Moreno. It was a horror scene. Shaw was treated with oxygen on the pitch during a nine-minute stoppage before being taken to hospital. He had suffered a double fracture of his right leg and would be out of action for six months.

Shaw's confidence was bound to have been shaken by the manner of the injury; could he still make those raids into the opponents' half without fearing another brutal tackle? His fragile equanimity would soon face a new challenge. He now had to face the strictures of van Gaal's obdurate replacement, José Mourinho. Mourinho, in his antagonistic Captain Hadley mode, believed in tough love and refused to make allowances for the recovering Shaw. Instead, he publicly berated the left-back for sub-standard performances. When Shaw did play well, the faint praise was damning: 'His performance was good. But it was his body and my brain. He was in front of me and I was making every decision for him, when to go inside, when to press the opponent. He has to grow up. He has to mature. He has to understand the game better. He must accelerate the process because at twenty-one years of age, he is old enough to have a better understanding of the game.'

Despite being voted United's Player of the Year in 2018/19, the constant criticisms took effect; Shaw was now being written off as a young player who hadn't fulfilled his potential. He lost his place in the England team; in 2019, the young academy graduate Brandon Williams, who filled in for Shaw during yet another injury absence, was popular with the faithful who liked to see home-grown talent in the senior side. When, in 2020, Solskjær brought in Alex Telles – one of the better Brazilians to sign for United – Shaw seemed in danger of being pushed out to the fringes.

Whether it was a growing maturity, the competition for places, Solskjær's more attacking style of play, or even the tactical lessons drilled into him by Mourinho, in the 2020/21 season Shaw blossomed into a truly world-class left-back. He was fitter, his confidence was back, and his surging runs were once again a feature of United's attacking play. He saw off the competition both at club and country levels, and earned a call-up to Southgate's Euro 2020 squad. He played every minute of England's seven games, providing three assists and, in a final flourish, scored England's goal against the tournament winners Italy in the final.

He had shown resilience and patience to overcome injury, loss of form and his critics. He had endured his own personal trial of Job. But as he celebrated his Wembley goal that July evening he must surely have thought, job done.

WE'LL MAKE IT OUR BUSINESS
Ownership Under the Glazers

On 2 May 2021, two weeks after the announcement and subsequent collapse of the European Super League (ESL) and the disclosure of Manchester United's close involvement in the ill-starred scheme, trouble flared inside and outside Old Trafford. The fixture against Liverpool due to take place that afternoon had to be postponed as angry United fans gathered outside the Lowry Hotel and then about a hundred stormed the ground. Holding up placards with the message '50+1' (where, as in Germany, fan members own a majority of the cub's shares), they let off steam and flares, and vented their anger at the club's owners, the Glazers.

If the spark for their fury had been the proposed ESL, there had been seething resentment amongst a sizeable section of the United support since the Glazers' takeover of the club in 2005 – a takeover hatched at a poolside meeting with Rothschild bankers at Donald Trump's Mar-a-Lago resort. Fans felt that their loyalty was being taken for granted, exploited even, by distant American businessmen based in Florida who saw United as an investment opportunity, eager to develop the brand and sell it to a global audience. The ESL was the latest and most egregious expression of their business plan; it was the superclub's fantasy: guaranteed income streams, global TV reach, no fear of relegation and no irritating small clubs putting their little snouts in the trough.

The 2005 takeover engineered by Malcolm Glazer cost an eye-watering £790 million, funded largely by bank finance and 'payment in kind' (PIK) hedge fund loans commanding a whopping 14.5% interest rate. It was capitalism, red in tooth and claw. Some of the crippling debt-servicing costs were mitigated when, in 2010, the Glazers raised £500 million from a bond issue and, in 2012, when they made some of their shareholding available on the New York Stock Exchange. But research from Swiss Ramble revealed that in the 15 years of their ownership an operating profit had been turned into a £92 million loss after the payment of £817 million in interest and £125 million in dividends, most of it to the Glazer family.

The legacy of the Glazers' ownership is something of a curate's egg. Their balance sheet shows that, in 2020, annual revenue from commercial activities and sponsorship had increased fivefold to £279 million since 2005. Although that figure fell during the COVID lockdown and the share price had dropped every year since 2018, the sale of Chelsea for £4.25 billion was indicative of the goldmine United had become. More than a net £1 billion had been invested in the team in the transfer market and, for the first eight years of their ownership, trophies continued to be won on a regular basis. While Sir Alex Ferguson – who ground no axe with the new owners – was in charge of team affairs and received the funds he needed to buy the likes of Carrick, Berbatov and van Persie, the majority of fans were accepting of the new regime. Some irreconcilables were so opposed to the Glazers that they formed the acronymic FCUM – FC United of Manchester – as a two-fingered protest. FCUM has since become an established club and, pointedly, built its stadium in Moston, near the site of the original Newton Heath ground.

When David Gill stood down as chief executive in 2013, the Glazers promoted commercial director Ed Woodward to take his place. Woodward, formerly an executive at American investment bank J.P. Morgan, soon became a lightning rod for fans' anger. Excellent financial results couldn't compensate for mediocre performances on the pitch and failings in the transfer market. The stadium, once the best in the land, was showing signs of wear and tear, and gave supporters legitimate grounds for complaint. The South Stand was rotting, the roof was leaking, and there was even an infestation of rodents in the offices and on the playing surface. Under the Glazers' watch, there had been no significant ground improvements at Old Trafford and the once-state-of-the-art training facilities at Carrington were surpassed by those of their rivals.

In January 2020, even before the ESL fiasco, disgruntled fans – the 'Men in Black' – staged an ugly protest outside Woodward's home in Knutsford. Then, when the Super League plans were announced in April 2021, with Joel Glazer as vice-chairman and Woodward being identified as 'a liar and a snake' by UEFA's president, the simmering resentment boiled over. Fans felt they had been sold short and that the Glazers had sold out.

Mercifully, cooler heads prevailed; a dialogue began between Joel Glazer and the Manchester United Supporters' Trust (MUST). MUST, which had seen its membership soar after the ESL debacle and had politicians queueing up to hear their concerns, participated in the government fan-led review into football governance. MUST wrote to the United board demanding the appointment of independent directors, that a share scheme 'accessible to all' with full voting rights be put in place, and that season-ticket holders be fully consulted about any significant changes affecting the club and the competitions it plays in.

This time, Joel Glazer did not turn a deaf ear. In June 2021, he took part in a three-hour conference call with fans' groups.

Promises were made about upgrading Old Trafford, and Carrington – the team that designed the new Tottenham Hotspur stadium, Legends International and Populous – were invited to draw up plans for a £200 million revamp of Old Trafford. There would be new signings; there would be a fans' advisory board; and, most importantly, a fan share scheme, one that would become the 'largest fan ownership group in world sport'.

Could there ever be a time when the fans owned a majority of United's shares? MUST would like any expansion of share ownership to at least allow the possibility. Eric Cantona gave his support to MUST's campaign in June 2021, pronouncing that 'Yes, my friends, I have signed for UNITED again' and inviting fans to register their support for the scheme.

Promises, promises. For the MUST membership – keepers of the United flame – the expansion of share ownership remained the most important issue of all, and they see it as their duty to keep the owners' feet to the fire.

Setting up share schemes is no simple matter and eventually, more than a year later, the Glazers offered fans the chance to buy 'B' shares with twice the voting rights of ordinary shares. Promising. Although MUST supported the offer as a first step, other fan voices noted that the deal would limit fans to a one per cent holding with no prospect of wielding any meaningful influence.

But even if the Glazers opened share ownership to all, it would take a lot of small investors to buy 50.1% of a business worth an estimated £4–5 billion. But then, as the Glazers like to boast, they do have a fan base of over a billion followers and, if Michael Knighton was to be believed, two or three of whom have their own billions to invest. One thing is for sure, in the summer of 2022 the ownership and stewardship of the club remained a burning issue.

MAKING A DIFFERENCE
The Charitable Work of United Stars

Modern-day footballers get a bad rap: the exorbitant salaries, the men-behaving-badly moments of madness, the lavish lifestyles and the media hoo-ha can give the impression that they are no better than clowns performing in a celebrity circus. And there's some truth in that: football is very much a part of the 21st century's entertainment industry.

There are, however, many instances of people in the football community who use their status to help promote good causes and who are also prepared to put their hands deep into their own pockets to set an example. And Manchester United stars, past and present, have been at the forefront.

Leading the way in this field, as in so many other aspects of his life, is Sir Alex Ferguson. A UNICEF ambassador, the Scot is a supporter of dozens of charities and causes, and recently gave £405,000 to the NHS after his own life-saving brain surgery in 2019. When *The Times* and *Sunday Times* launched their Christmas 2020 appeal for FareShare, distributing food to the poor and homeless, he teamed up with Marcus Rashford and pledged £2 million.

In a similar vein, in October 2015, Gary Neville and Ryan Giggs, joint developers of the Manchester Exchange Hotel, amazed the homeless squatters occupying the building by allowing them to stay on site over the winter months.

Topping that, though, is the remarkable work of the Macari Centre in Hanley, Stoke-on-Trent. As the COVID crisis hit, the local council closed shelters. After reading a news story about the homeless, Lou Macari took to the streets of Hanley to see the problem for himself. After meeting with rough sleepers, he adapted an old warehouse and organised the installation of pods to provide socially distanced emergency accommodation. Each pod had heating, a bed and a lock on the door, offering not only respite and security but also a physical address that afforded the prospect for residents of escaping destitution and getting their lives back on track. United legend Macari spends much of his time at the centre, dealing hands-on with the problems that come with caring for the vulnerable. 'Because my name's above the door, I want to be here most of the time because I want to do things right,' he says.

Praise is also due to other United heroes including UNICEF ambassador and famous wearer of the iconic number 7 shirt, David Beckham, who journeyed across seven continents to play seven matches in aid of grassroots football, and Rio Ferdinand, who devotes much of his time to charitable work. The Rio Ferdinand Foundation works in the heart of the most disadvantaged communities supporting young people to tackle inequality through sports, media, arts and education. In June 2022, his charity work was recognised with an OBE. He credited his mum, Janice, as his inspiration. He and his wife, Kate, are also patrons of Child Bereavement UK.

But two players of the modern era deserve special mention. Juan Mata – 'no nicer man in football' according to MUST –

is a man of great intelligence, humility and generosity, whose vision on the field is matched by his inspiration away from it. In 2017, the Spaniard co-founded the charity Common Goal to generate social change through the power of football. Its member players pledge at least 1% of their salaries to a fund that is distributed to football projects around the world. He said farewell to United in June 2022 after 285 appearances and 51 goals.

The second is Marcus Rashford. A local boy from Wythenshawe, Rashford knew hard times as a kid. During the 2020 pandemic, his campaign on social media to have the government reverse its decision on the provision of free school meals during holidays won nationwide support. Not once but twice, the government was forced to make U-turns in response to the public outcry generated by Rashford's respectful and ground-breaking crusade. Over a million people signed his petition, and Marcus was featured on *GQ*'s front cover as the winner of their Campaigner of the Year award, given FIFA's prestigious Foundation award, the Football Writers' Association Tribute award and honoured in October 2020 with an MBE. In February 2021, he became the proud recipient of a Gold Blue Peter badge alongside Greta Thunberg.

More than anything else, he made a massive difference to thousands of struggling families and young children when they needed it most. From helping the homeless and hungry, to visiting the Manchester bombing victims and supporting the NHS throughout the pandemic, Rashford is a true hero, on and off the pitch.

WAY TO GO, OLE
United Break the Premier League's
Longest Unbeaten Away Record

At the end of the January transfer window in 2020, United languished in fifth place in the league, having accumulated 34 points, less than half leaders Liverpool's total and, worryingly, six points behind fourth-place Chelsea in the battle for Champions League qualification. United had just lost two games in succession, and boos were ringing out around Old Trafford. The news that the first COVID-19 cases had been diagnosed in the United Kingdom seemed of less interest to United fans than the announcement that Bruno Fernandes had signed from Sporting Lisbon for an initial fee of £47 million. Maybe he could inject some life into yet another lacklustre season.

Roll forward 19 months to the end of August 2021, and after victory at Molineux – Solskjær's 100th game in charge – United succeeded in breaking Arsenal's 17-year-old record for the longest unbeaten sequence away from home (a record United themselves had ended at the famous Battle of the Buffet). Amazingly, Bruno Fernandes had still to taste defeat on the road in the Premier League.

COVID had undoubtedly played a part. Crowds were kept away from grounds for more than a year and the 'Twelfth Man Effect' of home support was nullified. In the 2020/21 season, there were more away wins (153) than home wins (144); in the previous season, home teams won out 172 times to 116.

Nevertheless, it was a remarkable achievement for Solskjær's team. At the start of 2020, many questioned whether the Norwegian was the right man to have at the wheel. His appointment in December 2018 had started well, winning ten of his first dozen matches, but had fallen away badly, leaving United to finish out of the Champions League places. As their indifferent form continued into the new season, the rumblings of discontent grew louder.

Solskjær's youthful appearance was disappearing under the stress of the job; management is a difficult job at any club, but at United the pressure is off the scale. Could he find a way to improve their fortunes?

The away run began with a 2–0 win at Stamford Bridge in February 2020, thereafter United would go on to win a further 17 games and draw ten to break Arsenal's record. In no fewer than 13 of those games United had trailed their opponents, displaying a resilience and fighting spirit that showed the players were prepared to battle for their manager.

Solskjær may have lacked the tactical nous of some of his rivals, but in the course of his hundred games he had restored many of the qualities that typified the United way. He instilled in his squad a renewed belief, a winning mentality and a willingness to compete to the last – in Sir Alex's words, 'to never give in' – as United scored in added time in six of their away fixtures during the run.

The stats are impressive: during 560 days unbeaten, United had scored 51 goals and conceded 19; the goalkeepers, de Gea and Henderson, kept 13 clean sheets between them. In January 2021, after a 1–0 win at Burnley, United displaced Liverpool at the top of the table. The season ended with United comfortably in second place, but defeat in the Europa League final to Villarreal and yet another cup semi-final disappointment meant that doubts about Solskjær remained.

When Mason Greenwood hit the winner to beat Wolves in August 2021 as United extended their unbeaten run, Solskjær recorded his 53rd victory in his century of games. The run lasted until October when they lost to Leicester; 29 games unbeaten away from home established a record in English league history.

Only one manager could lay claim to have had more success in their first hundred games – and it was neither Matt Busby nor Alex Ferguson but Ernest Mangnall – and no United manager had ever gone a whole season without a defeat away from home. For 20 months, on the road his team were magnificent, but, if he were to follow in the footsteps of United's managerial greats, he still had a way to go. Little did he know he was about to run out of road; a bad run of results and a loss of form broke the spell. Within three months of establishing the record, the likeable Norwegian was on his way.

THE RETURN OF THE MAGNIFICENT SEVEN
The August 2021 Transfer Window

As the 2021/22 season got under way Ole Gunnar Solskjær could reflect on a satisfactory transfer window. Despite the persistent interest of Real Madrid, Paul Pogba was staying, and Jesse Lingard was back from his impressive loan spell at West Ham. The squad had been improved by the additions of Raphaël Varane from Real Madrid for £36 million and Jadon Sancho, after a protracted courtship for twice as much, while the £26 million fee for departing Daniel James represented good business. That was it, or so he must have thought; he would have liked a defensive midfield enforcer or two but otherwise a successful window.

On Thursday 26 August, five days before the transfer deadline, alarming rumours were swirling around social media that rivals Manchester City were in talks with Jorge Mendes, the agent who acted for Cristiano Ronaldo. The fact that City's interest in signing Harry Kane had ended and Juve were willing to sell their Portuguese superstar lent credence to the story. One fan's video of setting his Ronaldo vintage replica shirt on fire went viral on social media. This was the United fans' worst nightmare.

Since Ronaldo's departure from Old Trafford to Real Madrid in the summer of 2009 for £80 million, the Portuguese had enjoyed nine seasons at the Bernabéu and three seasons at

Juventus following a €100 million move in 2018. In a dozen years, Cristiano Ronaldo, or CR7 as he liked to be known, had racked up some impressive statistics. Whereas at United, he was mostly seen, in the words of 'Viva Ronaldo', 'running down the wing', he evolved into a central striker who could score off either foot or with his head. In Spain, he scored an incredible 450 goals in 438 games, winning La Liga twice, the Copa del Rey twice, the Champions League on no fewer than four occasions and the *Trofeo Pichichi* three times. In Italy, he scored 101 times in 134 appearances, winning Serie A twice, the Coppa Italia once, and was the *Capocannoniere* (top scorer in Serie A) in the 2020/21 season.

Ronaldo was also the mainstay for the Portuguese national team. During Euro 2020, he won his 179th cap, and his tally of five goals not only won him a share of the golden boot but also saw him draw level with Ali Daei's record of 109 goals in international competition (a record he was to break in September 2021). He had been a key member of the Portuguese Euro 2016 winning team even though his contribution in the final was restricted to animated coaching from the sidelines following an injury early in the match.

For the past decade and more, the media were enthralled by Ronaldo's exploits and his rivalry with the other great player of the age, Lionel Messi. Between them, Ronaldo and Messi won the coveted Ballon d'Or 11 times in the 12 years between 2008 and 2019 – Messi edging the contest with six awards. Off the pitch, Ronaldo developed his CR7 brand. His commercial activities netted him an estimated £600 million between 2010 and 2019 – in the world of sport, the second biggest earner to Floyd Mayweather – and on social media his profile is massive, achieving Instagram's biggest following of 400 million.

United fans never begrudged Ronaldo's success, preferring to remember his thrilling contribution to the Ferguson era and taking an almost parental pride in his later career. But the prospect of him joining the blue side of Manchester was too much to bear. Rio Ferdinand and Bruno Fernandes were amongst the players who hit their phones, urging him to tell his agent that he should return to Old Trafford. But the pivotal role in the negotiations was played by Sir Alex Ferguson, Ronaldo's 'father in sport', who helped persuade the Glazers that re-signing Ronaldo would be good for business and help mend their troubled relationship with the United fans.

The Glazers, known for their preference for buying young players, had surrendered to the seductive idea, peddled by Mendes, that they were buying football's equivalent of the 40-something Tom Brady, star quarterback of the NFL. At 36½, Ronaldo was a year older than Bobby Charlton when he retired from Old Trafford. But modern sports science, strict fitness and dietary regimes – and the want of Bobby's smoking habit – meant that he was still in supreme physical shape.

On Friday 27 August, the news that all United fans wanted to hear was announced. Cristiano Ronaldo was returning. Four days later, on transfer deadline day, it was made official as he put pen to paper.

Edinson Cavani, ever the gentleman, gave up his number 7 shirt when the Premier League waived its rules to allow Ronaldo to reclaim his old number even though the season had already commenced. Following the news of Cavani's sacrifice, in just four hours following the announcement, United's online store surpassed the highest day of sales ever on a single sports merchandise site outside North America; the first hour of sales alone surpassed the best ever full day of global sales for United Direct, the official club merchandise site. And Ronaldo will no doubt have been delighted that his shirt sales were nearly double those of Lionel Messi's new Paris Saint-Germain offering.

The commercial impact was huge but nowhere near as big as the effect on the United faithful. For the first time in eight years, there was a mood of mounting excitement. Tickets for the home game against Newcastle on 11 September were selling for up to £2,500 on the black market. Manchester crackled with anticipation on matchday. At Old Trafford, as kick-off approached, fans sang 'Viva Ronaldo'. At curtain-up, the number 7 admitted to being 'super nervous' on his second debut. Play began. On the stroke of half-time, he scored – as everyone knew he would: it was written in the script. It was pure theatre as he ran to the corner, jumped, pirouetted 180 degrees and landed in his signature power stance. '*Siiuu.*' For a blissful moment, all was well in the world and fans could dream again.

No one, not even the most fervent United fanatic, believed Ronaldo's homecoming was a guarantee of regaining the title and the top-dog status of yesteryear. But after all the disappointments and mediocrity they had had to endure in the previous eight years, the sight of a global superstar, a living United legend, wearing the totemic number 7 was joyous. Ronaldo was back where he belonged: in the Theatre of Dreams.

Alas, the 2021/22 season soon descended into a living nightmare – United's worst ever Premier League season. Some blamed Ronaldo for his lack of tracking back, for being a 36-year-old anachronism in an age of *Gegenpressen*, but the truth was: bigger problems lay elsewhere. Ronaldo's goals alone took United through to the knockout stages of the Champions League and his two sublime hat-tricks against Spurs and Norwich at Old Trafford provided rare occasions when the home fans finally had something to sing about.

FANTASTIC FANS

When the Glazers pitched their initial public offering (IPO) to the New York Stock Exchange in 2014 they claimed that Manchester United had 657 million followers worldwide. By 2021 that figure had risen to over a billion. Within this nebulous grouping, which includes people who have just about *heard of* Manchester United, there exist some truly dedicated supporters – you might call them superfans – fanatics.

Take Ilan Elkaim for example. A Zimbabwean businessman and sometime football commentator for the local broadcasters, he has travelled tens of thousands of miles to watch United play in numerous countries around the world. For the Champions League final in Barcelona, he and his teenage son Zac journeyed from Bulawayo via Johannesburg and Lisbon to Barcelona *in the hope* that they would be able to buy tickets for the game.

If you think that's impressive, how about Phil Holt, a season-ticket holder who had relocated to Australia, who made it back for every home game in the months leading up to Christmas during the 2004/05 season? Phil had watched United play in 44 different countries. Amex told him to stop accumulating air miles as he was playing havoc with their system.

Retired accountant Ying Soo moved to Manchester from Malaysia as a boy in the 1960s and became smitten by United after securing Bobby Charlton's autograph. Given the nickname Mr Miyagi, he became famous for turning tables into a stage to conduct the United fans' singing on matchdays in the pubs near Old Trafford. He told the *Manchester Evening News*: 'My friend suggested getting up on a chair, and when I did people loved it. The Bishop Blaize pub where I used to perform ended up giving me my own slot. When I am up there I feel like a conductor, I absolutely love it.'

He has also been filmed doing the same in Milan, Amsterdam and Madrid. The expressive interpretations and mimes that accompanied his chants made him a YouTube sensation.

In Lyngdal, a small town in southern Norway, Jahn Eric Birkeland has turned his basement into a shrine to his heroes. There he runs a mini-megastore, the Little Old Trafford pub and the Solskjær Red Café where he hosts like-minded United fans. The facilities include a toilet that features the badges of Liverpool, Manchester City and Chelsea in the pan.

A little under 700 miles south-east of Lyngdal is Copenhagen, home to Faroese-born Instagram model Katrina Maria, whom the *Star* dubbed 'Man Utd's sexiest fan'. Although she has plenty to say on the subject of football and offers unstinting support to the Reds (Ronaldo in particular), it's more likely that she has attracted 100,000 followers through her glamorous modelling of United sportswear. Heaven knows how much she must have spent accumulating her own private megastore of caps, shirts (home and change) and vests, in all their variations as well as other United ephemera. She even made the zebra away strip look good.

In July 2018, the world watched and waited anxiously to discover the fate of the Wild Boars youth team trapped in a cave in Thailand. Although one diver perished in the rescue attempt, the 12 boys and their coach emerged unscathed. Their reward was to meet their hero, ex-Red Zlatan Ibrahimović, on the Ellen DeGeneres television show in the US, and then later to be treated to a visit to Old Trafford where they received the red-carpet treatment. A trip to meet José Mourinho and the players at the Carrington training complex was followed by seats in the directors' box to see United beat Everton at Old Trafford. Kitted out in United tracksuits and scarves, the boys were the picture of happiness.

Those fans who come from far and wide often make financial and other sacrifices in return for the pleasure that comes from being part of the United family. But few can have endured the hardships and drawn upon such deep wells of determination as Marin Zdravkov, a middle-aged bachelor who lived with his mother and a cat called Beckham in a small Bulgarian town on the banks of the river Danube. The only thing of meaning in his life was his love for Manchester United. In 1999, he was glued to his TV watching his heroes playing the final of the Champions League.

With 89 minutes on the clock, United were down 1–0 to Bayern Munich. In despair, this fanatical Bulgarian declared that if his team somehow managed to win the match, he would change his name to Manchester United. And, of course, in the next two minutes, his prayers were answered as United scored twice to win the trophy. So began Marin's ten-year odyssey through courts, churches and state authorities, in his quest to change his legal name to Mr Manchester Zdravkov Levidzhov-United.

Bulgarian film director Stefan Valdobrev produced a moving film, *My Mate, Manchester United*, that documents the Bulgarian builder's struggles and eventually takes Marin to Old Trafford, where he meets his idol, Manchester United striker and fellow Bulgarian Dimitar Berbatov.

Manchester United have 262 officially recognised supporters' clubs in 89 countries. Most of their members will never get the chance to make the pilgrimage to M16. For those unable to travel, take comfort in the words of Walt Disney, 'A good story can take you on a fantastic journey,' and for these fantastic fans – long-distance travellers and fellow travellers alike – what better story than Manchester United?

BACK TO THE FUTURE
Raise a Glass to the Class of '22

As 2021/22 drew to a close and fans surveyed the wreckage of a truly dreadful season, a few green shoots emerged from the ruins.

To the horror of United fans and the delight of their rivals, the men's team was in disarray, succumbing twice to Liverpool in the league (9–0 over the two games) and to City (6–1 on aggregate), and humbled by Brighton 4–0 at the end of the season. Interim manager Ralf Rangnick, architect of the *Gegenpressen* tactical system that had inspired a generation of German coaches, found it impossible to apply his principles to the squad he had inherited. In his 29 games in charge, his attempts at finding a winning system came to naught as he only managed to pick up 11 victories, falling well short of Champions League qualification. In his view, the club was in such poor health it needed an 'open heart operation'.

In a season of many lows, one of the worst came in early February as United lost at home in the fourth round of the FA Cup to Championship side Middlesbrough. But there was some welcome good news for fans, a few straws to grasp at. At the beginning of the month, Richard Arnold's appointment as chief executive marked the end of the Woodward era. For all his success in attracting commercial sponsors and partners, the first team's underperformance, his haphazard player-recruitment policy and his close association with the club's owners made Ed Woodward an unpopular figure.

There had also been a shake-up in first-team management. The appointments of John Murtough as football director and Darren Fletcher as technical director in 2021 finally addressed the glaring lack of oversight in football matters. Together with Rangnick, who had signed up for a two-year consultancy role, they – empowered by Arnold – now had responsibility for team affairs. In April they made their first big call, choosing Dutchman Erik ten Hag as first team manager.

The sides riding highest in the Premier League – Manchester City, Liverpool and Chelsea, winners of eight of the nine titles in the years since Ferguson's final triumph – all benefited from excellent structure and planning on and off the pitch. Would it be too much to hope that Arnold could oversee a similar change at United? He recognised the need to shake things up and moved quickly to overhaul the scouting and recruitment departments. Could ten Hag bring some of the Cruyffian-Ajax stardust that had so inspired Guardiola or the pressing style that had spurred Liverpool's rise to the top? A lot to ask of ten Hag, a newcomer to English football. But at least he had enjoyed considerable success with Ajax and his faith in bringing through young talent would appeal to United supporters.

Meanwhile, there were other reasons to be cheerful. Manchester United Women could finally take a bow in front of a crowd at Old Trafford. Having played (and won) on their first appearance at the ground during lockdown in 2021, they lined up a year later to take on Everton with more than 20,000 spectators – the second-highest attendance in the Women's Super League that season – there to see the Red Devils win. The women's team had been disbanded shortly after the Glazers' takeover, deemed to be loss-making and not part of the 'core business'. The owners were blind to the increasing popularity of the women's game. Giving their rivals a head start, United only revived their side in 2018 and could only watch as, yep, Chelsea, Man City, Liverpool plus Arsenal galloped over the horizon. Casey Stoney led the team to promotion in their first season before Mark Skinner took over, the women achieving two creditable fourth-place finishes in the top division. More encouraging still were the efforts of the Under-21 side, winners of the Northern Division of the WSL as well as the Academy Youth Cup in the 2021/22 season.

As the season drew to a close – which couldn't come soon enough for many of the men's senior squad – all eyes turned to the climax of the men's Under-18 epic cup run. United youngsters had won the FA Youth Cup more times than any other side but hadn't won it since 2011 when Pogba, Lingard and co. were in short trousers. On 11 May, 67,000 fans packed Old Trafford to witness the academy boys overcome Nottingham Forest to lift the trophy. The young Argentine sensation, Alejandro Garnacho, presented with the Jimmy Murphy Young Player of the Year Award before kick-off, scored twice as United won 3–1.

The development of young players has been at the root of Manchester United's philosophy – and success – since the establishment of the academy before the war. United fans could look back at that tradition with pride and satisfaction; and now they could look forward, with renewed hope, to see what their new Dutch master might do with the young talent at his disposal. All the same, what would fans have given for a lift in a DeLorean and to be able to ask the driver to set the dial to 22 April 2013 when United last ruled the Premier League or, even better, have the Doc himself take them back to Wembley on 21 May 1977?

RESTORING ENGLISH PRIDE
United's Euro 2022 Lionesses

On 31 July 2022, 56 years and a day since England had last won a major football tournament, football finally came home. Messages of congratulation poured in from the Palace, Downing Street, showbiz, Becks, Posh and a rack of Spice Girls, you name it. David Baddiel, co-writer of 'Three Lions', tweeted, 'It's come home. A sentence I never thought I'd write'.

Back in 1966, two United players helped to overcome German opposition to win the Jules Rimet trophy; in 2022, once again at Wembley, the women went one better when three United stars helped the Lionesses claim the UEFA 2022 European Women's Football Championship.

The United trio played key roles in England's success. Mary Earps, having been previously dropped by former coach Phil Neville, established herself in Sarina Wiegman's squad as England's number one keeper. Mary repaid Wiegman's faith by making saves at crucial times and only conceded two goals in the entire tournament.

As Mary was keeping the door shut at the back, two United strikers struck fear into the hearts of opposing defences. Both Ellen Toone and Alessia Russo were deployed as impact substitutes to devastating effect. Between them the United pair scored six times in as many games. It wasn't just the number of times they hit the net that mattered as, on three occasions, their interventions were significant. Toone's equaliser in the quarter-final against Spain, late in the game, forced the match into extra time and her coolly taken finish against Germany gave the Lionesses the lead in the final. Toone, a childhood United fan who had been a part of the club's youth set-up, showed that she clearly had a big-match temperament.

Alessia Russo's goal against Sweden in the semi-final was spectacular and propelled her and the women's game into the national spotlight, capturing the public's imagination. Having seen her shot blocked from close range, Russo was quickest to react and, facing away from goal, managed to power her back-heeled shot into the net, nutmegging two defenders into the bargain thereby acquiring instant legendary status.

The nation's craving for success on the international stage had been satisfied. That the Lionesses had succeeded where the Lions had failed has seen an explosion of interest in the women's game. At United, the penny – or should that be cent – has finally dropped. Mark Skinner has the funds to supplement the stellar talents of the Euro heroines with new signings and can build a squad that can challenge the top sides in the Women's Super League.

United's women may only play in front of average crowds of 4,000 at the Leigh Centre but the day cannot be far away when they can host bigger crowds at Old Trafford to see home-grown Lionesses of the present and, hopefully, of the future. The attendance of 87,000 for the Euro 22 final shows the clear potential that waits to be untapped.

Comparisons have been made and parallels drawn between 1966 and the Euro 2022 winners. Mea culpa. Gabby Logan nicely caught the mood with her closing remarks as the BBC's coverage of Euro 2022 finally came to an end: 'You think it's all over . . . but it's only just begun.'

STATZONE
POLE POSITION IN THE PREMIERSHIP
Manchester United's Record in the English Premier League, 1992/93–2021/22

In the 29 seasons since its inception, United have won the Premier League 13 times, finishing runners-up on seven occasions. The next best record is held by six-times winners Manchester City, followed by Chelsea who have won the title five times.

Manchester United are the only team to have won the league in three consecutive seasons, twice in fact: 1998/99 to 2000/01 and 2006/07 to 2008/09.

United have accumulated more points and won more games than any other team, averaging more than two points per game.

Played	Won	Drawn	Lost	Points
1152	703	257	192	2364

In addition to most victories and most points won, United have also scored the most goals – 2,185 (against 1,066 conceded).

In the table of most points scored against other Premier League sides, it's maybe no surprise to see who occupies the top spot. As Sir Alex once famously said in his team talk, 'Lads, it's Tottenham.'

	Played	Won	Drawn	Lost	For	Against	Points
Tottenham H	60	38	12	10	104	59	126
Aston Villa	54	37	13	4	99	34	124
Everton	60	37	13	10	109	59	124
Newcastle Utd	54	32	15	7	113	55	110
West Ham Utd	52	32	13	7	102	46	109
Liverpool	60	28	14	18	79	76	99
Southampton	46	28	11	7	98	52	95
Arsenal	60	25	18	17	82	66	93
Man. City	48	24	9	17	71	67	81
Chelsea	58	17	25	18	72	71	76

STATZONE
THE TROPHY CABINET

United have won a total of 42 major domestic and European trophies. Their collection includes a record 20 league titles, three league and FA Cup doubles and the treble.

Division One/Premier League winners (a record 20 times)
Division One: 1907/08, 1910/11, 1951/52, 1955/56, 1956/57, 1964/65, 1966/67
Premier League: 1992/93, 1993/94, 1995/96, 1996/97, 1998/99, 1999/2000, 2000/01, 2002/03, 2006/07, 2007/08, 2008/09, 2010/11, 2012/13

Second Division (two wins)
1935/36 and 1974/75

FA Cup (12 wins)
1908/09, 1947/48, 1962/63, 1976/77, 1982/83, 1984/85, 1989/90, 1993/94, 1995/96, 1998/99, 2003/04 and 2015/16

Football League Cup/EFL Cup (five wins)
1991/92, 2005/06, 2008/09, 2009/10, 2016/17

FA Charity Shield/FA Community Shield (a record 21 times)
1908, 1911, 1952, 1956, 1957, 1965,* 1967,* 1977,* 1983,
1990,* 1993, 1994, 1996, 1997, 2003, 2007, 2008, 2010, 2011,
2013 and 2016
(* shared)

Europe
European Cup/UEFA Champions League winners: 1967/68,
1998/99 and 2007/08
European Cup Winners' Cup: 1990/91
UEFA Europa League: 2016/17
European Super Cup: 1991
Intercontinental Cup: 1999
FIFA Club World Cup: 2008

Doubles
League and FA Cup (three wins): 1993/94, 1995/96 and 1998/99
League and UEFA Champions League (two wins): 1998/99 and
2007/08
League and EFL Cup: 2008/09
EFL Cup and UEFA Europa League: 2016/17

Trebles
League, FA Cup and UEFA Champions League: 1998/99

STATZONE
TOP TEN GOAL SCORERS

United's top ten goal scorers features players from every decade since the First World War except the current one. Wayne Rooney tops the chart, but Sir Bobby scored the most goals from open play.

	Apps	League	FA Cup	L Cup	Europe	Other	Total
1 Wayne Rooney	559	183	22	5	39	4	253
(2004-17)	best season: 34 goals in 2011/12; hat-tricks or better: 8; penalties: 27						
2 Sir Bobby Charlton	756	199	19	7	22	2	249
(1956-73)	best: 29 goals in 1958-69; hat-tricks or better: 7; pens: 9						
3 Denis Law	404	171	34	3	28	1	237
(1962-73)	best: 46 goals in 1963-64; hat-tricks or better: 18; pens: 15						
4 Jack Rowley	424	182	26	0	0	3	211
(1937-55)	best: 30 goals in 1948-49 and 1951-52; hat-tricks or better: 12; pens: 5						
5 Dennis Viollet	293	159	5	1	13	1	179
(1953-62)	best: 32 goals in 1959/60; hat-tricks or better: 9; pens 0						
6 George Best	470	137	21	9	11	1	179
(1963-74)	best: 32 goals in 1967/68; hat-tricks or better: 4; pens: 5						
7 Joe Spence	510	158	10	0	0	0	168
(1919-33)	best: 24 goals in 1927/28; hat-tricks or better: 5; pens: 3						
8 Ryan Giggs	963	114	12	12	29	1	168
(1991-2014)	best: 17 goals in 1993/94; no hat-tricks; pens: 5						
9 Mark Hughes	467	120	17	16	9	1	163
('83-86, '88-95)	best: 24 goals in 1984/85; hat-tricks or better: 4; pens: 0						
10 Paul Scholes	718	107	13	9	26	0	155
(1994-2011, 2012-13)	best season: 20 goals in 2002/03; hat-tricks or better: 2; pens: 3						

Just outside the top ten is Ruud van Nistelrooy, scorer of 150 goals in only 200 appearances, making him the most lethal striker in terms of goal ratio. His ratio of 0.75 is a better strike rate than any in the top ten. Tommy Taylor, a victim of the Munich air disaster, netted 131 goals in 191 appearances, giving him a goal ratio of 0.69. Dennis Viollet had a ratio of 0.61 and Denis Law 0.59.

STATZONE
BIGGEST WINS IN MAJOR COMPETITIONS

Division One

Newton Heath
Formed in 1878 as Newton Heath LYR, Newton Heath entered Football League Division One in 1892.
Home: Newton Heath 10 Wolverhampton Wanderers 1 (15 October 1892)
Scorers: Donaldson (3), Stewart (3), Carson, Farman, Hendry, Hood
Away: Grimsby Town 0 Manchester United 7 (26 December 1899)
Scorers: Bryant (2), Cassidy, (2), Jackson, Parkinson, Grimsby Town o.g.

Manchester United
The club changed its name in April 1902.
Home: Manchester United 8 Queens Park Rangers 1 (19 March 1969)
Scorers: Morgan (3), Best (2), Aston, Kidd, Stiles
Away: Ipswich Town 2 Manchester United 7 (3 September 1963)
Scorers: Law (3), Chisnall, Moir, Sadler, Setters

Premier League

Home: Manchester United 9 Ipswich Town 0 (4 March 1995)

Scorers: Cole (5), Hughes (2), Ince, Keane

Manchester United 9 Southampton 0 (2 February 2021)

Scorers: Martial (2), Cavani, Fernandes, James, McTominay, Rashford, Wan-Bissaka, Bednarek (o.g.)

Away: Nottingham Forest 1 Manchester United 8 (6 February 1999)

Scorers: Solskjær (4), Cole (2), Yorke (2)

FA Cup

Newton Heath

Newton Heath first entered the FA Cup in 1886.

Home (Third Qualifying Round): Newton Heath 7 West Manchester 0 (12 December 1896)

Scorers: Cassidy (2), Gillespie (2), Rothwell (2), Bryant

Away (Third Qualifying Round): South Shore 0 Newton Heath 2 (14 November 1891)

Scorers: Doughty, Farman

Manchester United

Home (Fifth Round): Manchester United 8 Yeovil Town 0 (12 February 1949)

Scorers: Rowley (5), Burke (2), Mitten

Away (Fifth Round): Northampton Town 2 Manchester United 8 (7 February 1970)

Scorers: Best (6), Kidd (2)

League Cup

Manchester United first entered the League Cup in 1960.

Home (Fourth Round): Manchester United 7 Newcastle United 2 (27 October 1976)

Scorers: Hill (3), Coppell, Houston, Nicholl, Pearson
Away (Fourth Round): Arsenal 2 Manchester United 6 (28 November 1990)
Scorers: Sharpe (3), Blackmore, Hughes, Wallace

FA Charity Shield
Manchester United 8 Swindon Town 4 (25 September 1911)
Scorers: Halse (6), Turnbull, Wall

European Cup
Manchester United first entered the European Cup in 1956.
Home (Preliminary Round, Second Leg): Manchester United 10 Anderlecht 0 (26 September 1956)
Scorers: Viollet (4), Taylor (3), Whelan (2), Berry
Away (Preliminary Round, First Leg) Shamrock Rovers 0 Manchester United 6 (25 September 1957)
Scorers: Taylor (2), Whelan (2), Berry, Pegg

UEFA Champions League
Manchester United first played in the Champions League in 1993.

Home (Quarter-final, Second Leg): Manchester United 7 Roma 1 (10 April 2007)
Scorers: Carrick (2), Ronaldo (2), Evra, Rooney, Smith
Away (Phase 1, Match 3) Brøndby 2 Manchester United 6 (21 October 1998)
Scorers: Giggs (2), Cole, Keane, Solskjær, Yorke

European Cup Winners' Cup
Manchester United first entered the competition in 1963.

Home (First Round, First Leg): Manchester United 6 Willem II 2 (15 October 1963)

Scorers: Law (3), Charlton, Chisnall, Setters

Away (Semi-final, First Leg): Legia Warsaw 1 Manchester United 3 (24 April 1991)

Scorers: Bruce, Hughes, McClair

Inter-Cities Fairs Cup/UEFA Cup

Manchester United first entered the Inter-Cities Fairs Cup in 1964.

Home (First Round, Second Leg): Manchester United 6 Djurgårdens 1 (27 October 1964)

Scorers: Law (3), Charlton (2), Best

Away (Second Round, First Leg): Borussia Dortmund 1 Manchester United 6 (11 November 1964)

Scorers: Charlton (3), Best, Herd, Law

Europa League

Manchester United first entered the competition in 2012.

Home (Semi-final, First Leg): Manchester United 6 Roma 2 (29 April 2021)

Scorers: Cavani (2), Bruno Fernandes (2), Greenwood, Pogba

Away (Round of 16): LASK 0 Manchester United 5 (12 March 2020)

Scorers: Greenwood, Ighalo, James, Mata, Pereira

STATZONE
BREAKING THE BANK
United's Transfer Records

In the days since Sir Alex Ferguson's departure the club has acquired a reputation as big, if not always wise, spenders in the transfer market. In the period following the end of the triumphant 2012/13 season and the closing of the Summer 2022 window, United had invested just shy of £1.5 billion on transfers.

Ferguson, like Busby before him, was relatively miserly when it came to buying players; he was proud of the fact that he only parted with a net £5 million per year over his 26-year tenure. But, like Sir Matt, he would quite happily break the transfer record if the right player became available.

It is notoriously difficult to be exact about fees. Often the sums are undisclosed, or fees can grow over time as add-ons are triggered; Wayne Rooney's fee of £20 million rose to £27 million over time. But that shouldn't stop anyone from making their best estimates.

Landmark transfers

The first transfer fee paid by Newton Heath to secure the services of Gilbert Godsmark from Ashford United in January 1900 was £40.

United's first £1,000 fee was for Leslie Hofton from Glossop North End in July 1910.

The first six-figure fee – £115,000 for Denis Law from Torino in August 1962 – was Sir Matt Busby's biggest transfer outlay, his only other six-figure signing being Willie Morgan from Burnley in 1968.

The first million-pound signing – £1,250,000 – was Garry Birtles from Nottingham Forest in October 1980.

The first in excess of £10 million was £10,750,000 for Jaap Stam from PSV Eindhoven in the summer of 1998.

Fergie's biggest transfer – £30,750,000 – was for Dimitar Berbatov from Tottenham Hotspur.

United's biggest signing was Paul Pogba, whose transfer from Juventus in 2016 for £89.5 million was not only a club record but also a world record.

Record breakers

The records fall into three main categories: British, club and world.

Goalkeepers

Harry Gregg signed from Doncaster Rovers in December 1957 for £23,500, a then world record fee for a goalkeeper.

Alex Stepney's transfer from Chelsea in 1967 for £55,000 set a British record for a goalkeeper.

David de Gea: the £18 million fee paid to Atlético Madrid in 2011 set a British record for a goalkeeper.

Full-backs

Noel Cantwell set the British transfer record for a full-back on his move from West Ham United in 1960.

Luke Shaw became the world's most expensive teenager following his transfer from Southampton in 2014 for £27 million.

Centre-backs

Martin Buchan: United paid Aberdeen a club record fee of £125,000 in 1972.

Gordon McQueen became the most expensive transfer between British clubs when he was bought from Leeds United in 1978 for £495,000.

Gary Pallister's £2.3 million transfer from Middlesbrough in 1989 was a British record for a defender.

Jaap Stam set a world record when he joined from PSV Eindhoven for £10.75 million in 1998.

Rio Ferdinand's £29.1 million signing fee set a world record for a defender in 2002 when he arrived from Leeds United.

Harry Maguire became the world's most expensive defender when he joined from Leicester City in 2019 for £80 million.

Midfielders

Bryan Robson: United broke the British record when they signed him from West Bromwich Albion in 1981 for £1.5 million.

Juan Sebastian Verón broke the British record when he signed from Lazio in 2001 for £28.1 million.

Paul Pogba broke the world transfer record when he returned to Old Trafford from Juventus for £89.5 million.

Forwards

Albert Quixall's £45,000 fee broke the British record when he signed from Sheffield Wednesday in September 1958.

Denis Law broke the British transfer record after signing from Torino for £115,000.

Andy Cole signed in January 1995 from Newcastle United for a new British record fee of £6 million plus an estimated £1 million for the part-exchange of Keith Gillespie.

Ruud van Nistelrooy signed for £19 million from PSV Eindhoven in 2001, thereby surpassing the British record previously set by Leeds United's purchase of Rio Ferdinand.

Wayne Rooney became the world's most expensive teenager after signing from Everton for £27 million from Everton.

Anthony Martial: like Shaw and Rooney before him, Martial became the world's most expensive teenager after his move from Monaco in 2015 for £36 million. That's just for starters. It was another €10 million once he played his 25th game (for Manchester United); €10 million if he had been awarded his 25th cap with the French national team before 2019 (he hadn't); and €10 million if he had won the Ballon d'Or (nope). So let's call it £44 million.

Ángel Di María set a British record when he joined from Real Madrid in 2014 for £59.7 million.

And travelling in the other direction . . .

Johnny Morris, part of the 1948 cup-winning side, was sold to Derby County for a world record fee of £24,000.

Ray Wilkins: his transfer to AC Milan in June 1984 was a British record at £1.5 million.

Mark Hughes set a new British record two years later when he was transferred to Barcelona for £2.3 million.

Cristiano Ronaldo smashed the world record when he joined Real Madrid in 2009 for £80 million.

United's top 20 most expensive transfers

With so much smoke and mirrors surrounding transfer dealings, it's difficult to quantify how agent fees, options and add-ons affect the final cost. Various sources give widely differing guesstimates so I have picked one, *United in Focus*, whose valuations seem to sit in the middle of the range, to be my guide.

1. Paul Pogba signed from Juventus in 2016: *£89 million*

2. Antony (Matheus do Santos) signed from Ajax in 2022: *£80.75 million*

3. Harry Maguire signed from Leicester City in 2019: *£80 million*

4. Romelu Lukaku signed from Everton in 2017: *£75 million*

5. Jadon Sancho signed from Borussia Dortmund in 2020: *£72.6 million*

6. (Carlos) **Casemiro** signed from Real Madrid in 2022: *£60 million*

7. Angel di Maria signed from Real Madrid in 2014: *£59.7 million*

8. Aaron Wan-Bissaka signed from Crystal Palace in 2019: *£50 million*

9. Bruno Fernandes signed from Sporting in 2020: *£47 million plus add-ons*

10. Fred (Frederico Rodrigues de Paula Santos) signed from Shakhtar Donetsk in 2018: *£47 million*

11. Lisandro Martinez signed from Ajax in 2022: *£46 million plus add-ons*

12. Juan Mata signed from Chelsea in 2014: *£37 million*

13. Anthony Martial signed from Monaco in 2015: *£36 million plus add-ons*

14. Donny van de Beek signed from Ajax in 2020: *£35 million plus add-ons*

15. Raphael Varane signed from Real Madrid in 2021: *£34.2 million plus add-ons*

16. Victor Lindelof signed from Benfica in 2017: *£31 million*

17. Memphis Depay signed from PSV Eindhoven in 2015: *£31 million*

18. Dimitar Berbatov signed from Tottenham in 2008: *£30.75 million*

19. Rio Ferdinand signed from Leeds in 2002: *£30 million*

20. Eric Bailly signed from Villarreal in 2016: *£30 million*

STATZONE
ONCE IN EVERY LIFETIME
United's Youngest Players

United are renowned for their youth system and for blooding players at an age when they aren't able to vote, drink alcohol or, in some cases, drive a car, join the police or even buy a lottery ticket.

The 20 players listed below made their debut in the first team in a competitive fixture either as a starter or as a substitute. Players who went on to make more than 100 appearances for United are highlighted in italics.

David Gaskell (goalkeeper) 16 years and 19 days on 24 October 1956 v. Manchester City in the Charity Shield
Jeff Whitefoot (full-back) 16 years, 3 months and 14 days on 15 April 1950 v. Portsmouth
Duncan Edwards (half-back) 16 years, 6 months and 3 days on 4 April 1953 v. Cardiff City
Willie Anderson (forward) 16 years, 8 months and 7 days on 22 April 1957 v. Burnley
Angel Gomes (forward) 16 years, 8 months and 20 days on 21 May 2017 v. Crystal Palace
Norman Whiteside (forward/midfield) 16 years, 11 months and 17 days on 24 April 1982 v. Brighton & Hove Albion

Shola Shoretire (forward) 17 years and 19 days on 21 February 2021 v. Newcastle United

Alex Dawson (forward) 17 years, 2 months and 1 day on 22 April 1957 v. Burnley

Ian Moir (forward) 17 years, 3 months and 1 day on 1 October 1960 v. Everton

Ryan Giggs (forward) 17 years, 3 months and 1 day on 2 March 1991 v. Everton

Sammy McIlroy (forward/midfield) 17 years, 3 months and 4 days on 21 September 1971 v. Manchester City

Peter Coyne (forward) 17 years, 3 months and 8 days on 21 February 1976 v. Aston Villa

Paul Bielby (forward) 17 years, 3 months and 17 days on 13 March 1974 v. Manchester City

George Best (forward) 17 years, 3 months and 23 days on 14 September 1963 v. West Bromwich Albion

Mason Greenwood (forward) 17 years, 5 months and 3 days on 6 March 2019 v. Paris Saint-Germain in the Champions League

Jimmy Nicholson (half-back) 17 years, 5 months and 8 days on 24 August 1960 v. Everton

David Sadler (U) 17 years, 6 months and 19 days on 24 August 1963 v. Sheffield Wednesday

Gary Neville (full-back) 17 years, 6 months and 29 days on 16 September 1992 v. Torpedo Moscow in the UEFA Cup

Lee Sharpe (forward) 17 years, 6 months and 29 days on 26 December 1988 v. Nottingham Forest

Federico Macheda (forward) 17 years, 7 months and 14 days on 5 April 2009 v. Aston Villa

Alex Dawson, Peter Coyne and Federico Macheda all scored on debut.

STATZONE
RECORD APPEARANCES

It's astonishing to think that, by the time he had retired from playing, Ryan Giggs had been involved in more than a sixth of all the games ever played by Manchester United. Most of our top ten hail from the great Busby or Ferguson eras, but hats off to Joe Spence, one of the few heroes of the bleak inter-war years.

All ten players in our chart have made more than 500 appearances for United in competitive football (the eleventh, Arthur Albiston, appeared 485 times). Competitive fixtures include league matches, FA and League Cups, UEFA competitions, Super Cup, World Club and Inter-continental Cup and FA Community or Charity Shields.

The list may have had a different composition if the playing careers of three United legends had not been interrupted by war. Jack Rowley (1937–53, 424 appearances) would be number 23 on the all-time list, Allenby Chilton (1939–55, 381 appearances), number 35, and the 'Welsh Wizard', Billy Meredith (1906–21, 335 appearances), number 48.

Player	Dates	League	FA Cup	League Cup	EC/ECL	Other Europe	Other	Total
1 Ryan Giggs	1991-2014	672	74	41	151	5	20	963

Debut aged 17 yrs, 94 d. Honours: 13 Premier League titles; 4 FA Cup; 3 League Cup; 2 Champions League; 9 Community Shield; 3 others

| 2 Sir Bobby Charlton | 1956-73 | 606 | 78 | 24 | 28 | 11 | 11 | 758 |

Debut aged 18 yrs, 361 d. Honours: 3 First Division titles; 1 FA Cup ; 1 European Cup; 4 Charity Shield

| 3 Paul Scholes | 1994-2011; 2012-3 | 499 | 49 | 21 | 130 | 4 | 15 | 718 |

Debut aged 19 yrs, 309 d. Honours: 12 Premier League titles; 3 FA Cup; 2 Champions League; 5 Charity Shield; 2 others

| 4 Bill Foulkes | 1952-70 | 567 | 60 | 3 | 35 | 17 | 6 | 688 |

Debut aged 19 yrs, 343 d. Honours: 4 First Division titles; 1 FA Cup; 1 European Cup; 3 Community Shield

| 5 Gary Neville | 1992-2011 | 400 | 47 | 25 | 115 | 2 | 13 | 602 |

Debut aged 17 yrs, 211 d. Honours: 8 Premier League titles; 3 FA Cup; 2 Champions League; 3 Community Shield

| 6 Wayne Rooney | 2004-17 | 393 | 40 | 20 | 88 | 10 | 8 | 559 |

Debut aged 18 yrs, 340 d. Honours: 5 Premier League titles; 1 FA Cup; 3 League Cup; 1 Champions League; 1 Europa Cup; 4 Community Shield, 1 other

| 7 Alex Stepney | 1966-78 | 433 | 44 | 35 | 15 | 8 | 4 | 539 |

Debut aged 23 years, 364 d. Honours: 1 First Division title; 1 FA Cup; 1 European Cup; 1 Charity Shield

| 8 Tony Dunne | 1960-73 | 414 | 55 | 21 | 23 | 17 | 5 | 535 |

Debut aged 19 yrs, 83 d. Honours: 2 First Division titles; 1 FA Cup; 1 European Cup; 2 Charity Shield

| 9 Denis Irwin | 1990-2002 | 368 | 43 | 31 | 64 | 11 | 12 | 529 |

Debut aged 24 yrs, 291 d. Honours: 7 League titles; 2 FA Cup; 1 League Cup; 1 Champions League; 4 Charity Shield; 1 UEFA Cup Winners' Cup; 2 others

| 10 Joe Spence | 1919-33 | 481 | 29 | 0 | 0 | 0 | 0 | 510 |

Debut aged 21 yrs, 258 days. Honours: Promotion from Second Division 1924-25

HOW MANY UNITEDS?

People sometimes ask how many football teams there are with the United suffix. It's a popular appendage and has been around since the 19th century. But how many in the Premier League? In the Football League? In England? In the United Kingdom? The world?

Fans of teams from Newcastle, Sheffield and Leeds can all too frequently be found complaining on social media posts or in phone-ins that commentators and broadcasters refer to the 20-times-title-winning team from Old Trafford as United and their team by its city name. Do the media – mainstream or social – know something that they don't?

Well, the answer is obvious to the Old Trafford faithful who will happily remind anyone in doubt: 'There's only one United.'

And who am I to argue with them? Not me, nor the billion other fans around the planet who are enraptured by the most romantic, most stylish, most poignant, most exciting story in football.

GGMU

SOURCES AND ACKNOWLEDGEMENTS

There's little point in writing a book without a publisher and much gratitude goes to Peter Burns of Polaris for placing his trust in a first-time author. To my wife Judy who overcame her allergy to football to offer support and helpful suggestions. Thanks to Ilan Elkaim for the feedback he gave me, promptly answering any questions I raised. Sir Alex Ferguson's autobiography and Jim White's *Manchester United: A Biography* were invaluable, and I quarried books by Iain McCartney, Andrew Endlar, Jeff Connor, Daniel Harris, the club's official history and many others. The internet was a rich seam to mine in the form of the Premier League website, the BBC, the Sky archive, the *Guardian*, *The Times*, the *Mirror*, the brilliant 11v11 website, the mufcinfo site, the official manutd.com site, MUTV, FourFourTwo, the Bleacher report, Planet Football and Transfermarkt to name but a few.